Official Get Rich Guide to Information Marketing

Second Edition

Build a Million-Dollar Business within 12 Months

ROBERT SKROB

Foreword and Epilogue by Dan Kennedy

Entrepreneur. Press

Jere L. Calmes, Publisher
Cover Design: Andrew Welyczko
Production and Composition: Eliot House Productions

This publication is designed to provide accurate and authoritative
information in regard to the subject matter covered. It is sold with the
understanding that the publisher is not engaged in rendering legal,
accounting or other professional services. If legal advice or other expert
assistance is required, the services of a competent professional person
should be sought.

Library of Congress Cataloging-in-Publication Data
Skrob, Robert
    Official get rich guide to information marketing / by Robert
Skrob.—2nd ed.
        p.   cm.
        ISBN-13: 978-1-59918-410-4 (alk. paper)
        ISBN-10: 1-59918-410-9
        1. Information services industry—Management. 2. Information
    services—Internet marketing. I. Title.
        HD9999.I492S57 2011
        658.8'72—dc22   2010053202

Printed in the United States of America

15 14 13 12   10 9 8 7 6 5 4 3 2 1

Contents

SECTION I
Prepare to Succeed

Contents

SECTION III

Allowing Others to Launch Your Info-Marketing Business for You

Contents

SECTION IV

Launch Your Info-Business with a Provocative Diagnostic Survey

Contents

SECTION V

Making a Big Splash in Your Industry with a New Event

SECTION VI

Create an Info-Marketing Business to Generate New Customers for Your Service Business

Contents

SECTION VII

Transitioning from Launch Mode into Growing a Successful, Sustainable Business

Important Disclaimer

I DON'T BELIEVE IN "GET RICH QUICK," BUT I DO BELIEVE IT'S ENTIRELY possible to "get rich" if you work hard, provide a lot of value to your customers, and are not afraid to ask for money in return for the value you provide. The importan information and resources in this book will help you create a business that generates a healthy income for you. I make no guarantees about your ability to get results or earn any money with the ideas, strategies, and tactics described in this book. My goal is to highlight how other people have built their businesses, provide you with the steps they followed, and "highlight the path" you can follow.

Each reader will pick up this book with different experiences and skills. Whether you succeed or not depends on how well you persist through adversity and how you acquire the skills you don't have. The income numbers you see in this book and on the accompanying website are for illustrative purposes only. The numbers are only estimates and should not be considered exact, actual, or a promise of potential earnings.

What you are holding is the book I wish were available ten years ago. It contains a distillation of more than 100 interviews with successful info-marketers, more than 250 one-on-one coaching sessions with beginners, and a decade of dedicated study of what works in the info-marketing business. Although I believe the content is accurate, complete, and current, I make no warranty as to its accuracy, completeness, or currency. It is your responsibility to verify any information before relying on it. Don't construe anything in this book as legal advice. I'm not an attorney, and I'm not practicing law. If you need legal advice, please seek the advice of legal counsel. I hope the "lessons learned" and shortcuts outlined in this book will help you launch a successful business generating quick, sustainable wealth for you and your family.

Acknowledgments

THANK YOU TO ALL THE INFO-MARKETERS WHO TOOK TIME FROM their businesses to allow me to interview them for this book. Even though I couldn't include all of you in the book, your stories and experiences helped me craft a useful tool for others to follow.

I appreciate my wife, Kory, daughter, Samantha (15), and son, Robert (12), who have given me the encouragement and time to help more people. I missed a lot of family dinners, and frequently I needed to invest my weekends in writing at my office. Thank you.

Special thanks to my editor, Susan Trainor. She combed through my first manuscripts, some of which were transcripts from dictation, to help me compose the five drafts that resulted in the book you are holding. Through the drafting, editing, and publishing process, Susan read this book more than 12 times to help me communicate better and provide you with the best possible book we could create.

Foreword

Welcome to the Most Profitable Business Ever Devised

by Dan Kennedy
Chairman Emeritus, Information Marketing Association

THE ORIGINAL *DRAGNET* TELEVISION SHOW USED TO OPEN WITH a statement about there being 8 million stories in the city. In the industry that I've played a large role in birthing, defining, and developing, the one we now call "information marketing," there may not yet be 8 million stories. But there certainly are hundreds of thousands. A few dozen of them are in this book, not for want of hundreds or thousands more, but in the interest of putting a book on the bookstore shelf that will fit there. The commonalities of these stories are important and fit into two categories: proof and mechanics.

The first is proof. These stories feature ordinary people from all sorts of backgrounds, walks of life, businesses, and interests who have created extraordinary incomes, lifestyles, wealth, and positive influences on others, from scratch. In most cases they have done so very quickly, and in some cases with limited resources. Otherwise, they have little in common. I know many you will meet in this book. Some are highly educated; some are barely educated. Some are young; some old. Some brilliant; some are anything but. Some are pretty good writers; some can't write a grocery list. Some come from successful businesses; some do not. There is absolutely nothing "special" about them that you lack. Their stories are revealing of a mind-set, not of prerequisite qualifications. I think this is extremely important. In my experience of coaching countless people to million-dollar-a-year incomes and multimillion-dollar wealth by starting and developing these kinds of businesses, it's been my observation that at the start and as they progress, virtually all stumbling blocks are inside their own beliefs about what they can and cannot do, what people will and will not pay, how fast results can occur.

The other is mechanics. Within their stories and examples, you can find—and should diligently look for and list—the same basic steps repeated, the same strategies employed. Their products, their markets served, whom they sell to, and what they choose to sell in what order and at what price all differ. But the *structure* of their businesses is the same. You have in this book a collection of examples accurately representative of hundreds more just like them, all with the same structures. It is here for you to see. Here for you to copy.

The information marketing industry has become quite large but is almost entirely made up of small businesses, from homebased solo operators or tiny teams generating a million to a few million dollars a year to entities doing 10 to 20 times that much, yet still "lean 'n mean" by traditional standards. At different times, 20 to 50 of these "info-entrepreneurs" have been in consulting relationships and private coaching groups with me, and if you combined any year's group as one entity, it would boast more than $200 million of yearly revenue and a multiple of that as equity. Less directly, I've helped launch or have worked with well more than 500 of these businesses, and were they all combined, we'd easily be accounting for more than $1 billion a year. Just as interesting is the incredible reach and influence of these businesses, individually and collectively. Those who work in business and professional niches, again combined, influence several million business owners a year. Also, in large part thanks to the internet, these businesses are global. In Glazer-Kennedy Insider's Circle™, for example, roughly 20 percent of our members (customers) are from places other than the United States and Canada.

No other business offers you the kinds of fascinating and lucrative opportunities that information marketing does. You can pursue things that interest you, travel or not as you please. If you please, you can legitimately make it tax-deductible. Operate globally from your kitchen table, and place yourself in the top 1 percent-income-earners' club in as little time as one year. You can become a celebrity or remain anonymous if you prefer. You can begin humbly or audaciously. One of the people I first studied when I was starting 35 years ago had begun selling a $5.00 booklet (about ridding your garden of gophers) via tiny classified ads in rural newspapers and farm magazines. One of the most recent info-businesses I helped launch started out selling a $40,000.00 coaching program. You can work when you please, where you please, as you please. You can have some employees, lots of employees, or no employees. You can outsource whatever you aren't good at or interested in. You can personally interact with your customers through teleseminars, seminars, or coaching programs, or you can make millions without ever meeting a single one of your customers face to face. I could go on with this long list of flexibility. The point is this: You make the rules. You bend this business to your preferences. You need sacrifice nothing for enormous financial success.

This brings me to one last comment, about the phrase "get rich" in this book's title. The implication is "get rich quick."

There's no virtue in getting rich slowly. There's nothing wrong with doing it quickly. When you make bank deposits, they don't add a bonus for slow nor deduct a penalty for fast. You may have been conditioned and programmed to believe that there is something wrong with getting rich quick or that the very idea is "fool's gold," implausible, possibly even an outright lie. I ask you to ask yourself: Have any of the sources of that viewpoint gotten rich quick? Or at all? Quite frankly, if you spend any time with the people in this book and the thousands they represent, you'll get a very different perspective. As someone who repeatedly, consistently, and quite routinely works with people who accelerate from standing starts to giant incomes in info-marketing, "get rich quick" is my reality. With what you will discover here, it can be yours, too.

So, step into a unique world virtually unknown to the general public, where entrepreneurs are alchemists, where ideas morph into thriving businesses at blinding speed—free of the operational burdens and constraints of all other businesses—where people earn giant incomes while immersed in their own interests and passions.

About the Author

ROBERT SKROB IS PRESIDENT OF THE INFORMATION MARKETING Association, and he has personally coached more than 1,000 info-marketers over the past five years. In addition to his writing, training, and speaking in the info-marketing industry, he has diverse business experience, having personally run info-marketing businesses in more than 37 different industries. Mr. Skrob is a brilliant marketer, a licensed Certified Public Accountant, and the absolute go-to guy for practical, proven strategies to show you how to create a business that generates quick, sustainable wealth for you and your family.

Who Else Wants to Be in the Single Best Business for Creating a Great Lifestyle and Income Others Only Dream About?

You won't find over-promises, untested ideas, idle boasting, weird and impossible examples, or hype. *The Official Get Rich Guide to Information Marketing on the Internet* is the real deal. It includes practical, doable steps, real-life examples, and proven strategies to help you harness the powers of the internet and make your information marketing business explode!

- Master the five steps to internet information marketing success: Salutation, Presentation, Consummation, Perseverance, and Enticement.
- Use the Power of ONE—a proven trick that gets visitors to stay and interact with your site.
- Learn proven ways to capture more than 80 percent of visitors' names and e-mail addresses.
- Use three profit-proven models that inspire sales.
- Learn the seven laws for effective order forms.
- Discover how to drive customers instead of traffic.
- Also, get the inside scoop from today's most successful online information marketers!

Pick up a copy of the *Official Get Rich Guide to Information Marketing on the Internet* at a bookstore, from an online book seller, or by visiting EntrepreneurPress.com today.

There's a Big Difference Between Creating a Top-Selling Information Product and Creating an Information Marketing Business . . .

Too many people confuse social media, internet marketing campaigns, or information product creation with business building. They chase the next online marketing secret, raise their prices, or try a new joint venture tactic but miss out on what it takes to build a business that lasts. It takes a specific set of skills to create a long-term, sustainable business.

The Information Marketing Business Pyramid™ gives you examples, step-by-step resources, and worksheets to help you get your information marketing business launched. But that's only the beginning. It also guides you through the process of turning your new venture into a long-term wealth generator for you and your family. It even reveals how to build an info-business even if you don't know how to create information products or have no idea what type of information product you should create.

Visit InfoMarketingPyramid.com for free videos, a 24-page outline of how the Information Marketing Business Pyramid™ works, and an opportunity to receive additional free resources. This site is available only for a limited time at InfoMarketingPyramid.com. Grab your Information Marketing Business Pyramid™ today.

SECTION I

Prepare to Succeed

Chapter 1

The Business Model that Generates Quick, Sustainable Wealth

WHY DO SOME BUSINESS OWNERS GET RICH WHILE OTHERS toil for decades with little to show for their efforts? Not all businesses are created equal. In some, the owner can work 80 hours a week for 40 years and produce barely enough profit to maintain a household for his family. Other business models allow their owners to work normal workweeks, take vacations, and generate millions of dollars in "take-out-of-the-business" profits that give them the freedom all business owners dream about.

Imagine the difference between a rowboat and a motorboat. You can paddle the rowboat with all your might, and you won't get as far as the guy in the motorboat powering through the water. There are profound differences in the types of businesses that generate quick, sustainable wealth for their owners. You won't become successful or wealthy without work, but success is not a result of working harder than everyone else. It's about building a business with specific attributes that enable you to accumulate wealth.

People all around you are getting rich. Within your neighborhood.

Why are they getting rich? Because they are doing things that generate more money than they spend, allowing them to accumulate wealth.

You aren't holding one of those self-help books that tells you what you imagine will come true. This is the book that gives you the road map of how you can make your dreams come true by doing certain things that generate more money than you spend. If you follow the step-by-step paths outlined within these pages, you will build a life that surpasses what you can imagine today.

In the next few pages, I'll reveal the dependable millionaire-maker business model. Within this book you'll read examples of men and women who have discovered this business model and used it to generate real wealth for themselves and their families.

KEY CONCEPT Wealth isn't produced by thinking, dreaming, or imagining what you want. Money doesn't care what you think about most. Money is attracted to you when you create a business that produces value for paying customers.

Five simple criteria will help you determine if a business has the power to generate wealth or if it will merely dominate your time and provide you with few results. Before you launch a new business, you need to ask yourself these five questions:

1. *Is it formulaic?* Has the business been proven to generate wealth for others in the past? For instance, if you don't see anyone getting rich as a plumbing contractor or by running a sandwich shop, it's a good guess that you won't get wealthy that way either. Instead, look for a consistent pattern of a good percentage of business owners getting rich within the industry; technology, real estate, and publishing are proven winners from the past.

2. *Does it have a large business scope?* Businesses dedicated to one community or one county can get destroyed with one flood or one plant closing. Instead, serve customers nationwide or even internationally to diversify and expand your marketplace.

3. *Are there high margins?* Selling products at higher prices with a low production cost allows you to do much more marketing. I had a client who sold frozen yogurt. With new customers spending only $5.00 to $10.00, it took a lot of them to pay for any advertising. Instead, get into businesses with high margins to make it easier for you to generate a healthy profit.

4. *Is there a low startup investment?* Too many business owners invest their entire life savings into a venture only to discover there is no market for their new products. Instead, keep your investments low, to $10,000.00 or even less. This way, even if you make a mistake, it won't be financially devastating to you. Plus, it will allow you to start multiple businesses over time to generate more wealth as your skills improve.

5. *Are there any professional licenses?* Government-issued licenses are one way competitors control each other. Industry lobbyists conspire with politicians to "protect consumers" by passing new restrictions and threatening to take your license away. These laws do nothing for consumers. They are designed to protect your competitors. Stay away from professions that require a professional license, such as insurance, financial advising, law, or medicine. That license is used to control what you say in your marketing and to restrict your ability to generate wealth.

I stumbled upon this business model myself about ten years ago. I worked in the association industry. Associations are groups of people with a similar interest. You've probably attended association annual meetings, trade shows, or seminars for your industry.

As an association executive, I witnessed a surge in for-profit companies that were doing many of the same things I did. I published newsletters, and they published newsletters. I produced seminars, and the for-profits produced seminars. I created home study courses, and the for-profits created home study courses. I was producing value, but not within a business model that charged a fair price for the value it provided its customers.

I began studying these for-profit operators and discovered they called what they did *information marketing*. They had combined elements from several different industries to create a business model with high margins, flexibility for its owner as well as stability.

For the last ten years, I've used information marketing strategies to build 18 different businesses in as many markets, all with fewer than five full-time employees. And these businesses are as lucrative as they are easy to operate.

But when I explain the business model, it's easy for the inexperienced or the cynical to dismiss it. You may recognize a component or two, but it's how the components work together that gives the info-marketing business its power.

Here is an everyday example. An airplane is made of simple components. Aluminum similar to that of your soda can makes up 80 percent of an airplane by weight. The rest is mainly copper wiring, hydraulic fluid, and computers. Most people take for granted that there is a genius out there who can take so many disparate parts and build a machine that transports hundreds of people across the world in just a few hours.

The components of the information marketing business aren't exciting, either. In fact, they are similar to components in consulting, publishing, event management, and coaching businesses. In each of those businesses, people regularly toil without remarkable results. It's the smart combination of those components that can propel you to wealth and freedom in your life.

Since 2006, I've had the honor of serving as president of the Information Marketing Association. It has given me the opportunity to speak with hundreds of information marketers, coach several dozen, witness what works, and watch several business failures. No one has witnessed more in the info-marketing world than I have.

I have taken the most effective info-marketing business launch methods and outlined them, complete with graphics and illustrations, within the pages of this book. You benefit from having exactly what you need to launch a successful info-marketing business, outlined in an easy-to-learn-and-apply format.

This book isn't just for reading. Think of it as an owner's manual for the most lucrative business in the world. You'll learn how to build it and run it for success and profit.

While most of this book focuses on how you create and run your own information marketing business, let me first explain why this business surpasses all others in opportunity, sustainability, and profit. There are six advantages of an information marketing business:

1. Replaces manual labor by "multiplying yourself" and leveraging what you know.
2. Buyers of your information products will buy more.
3. A small amount of interaction with buyers is possible.
4. Few staff members are necessary.
5. Little investment is needed to get started.
6. Large profit potential exists.

So, let's talk about No. 1 first.

1. Replaces Manual Labor by "Multiplying Yourself" and Leveraging What You Know

How does the information marketing business replace manual labor by "multiplying yourself" and leveraging what you know? ("Leveraging" is just a one-word way to say "makes what you know do the work for you.")

Whether you're working for someone else or you're a professional selling your services by the hour or by the job, you are being paid for what you produce. The moment you stop producing, you stop getting paid. This is true for everyone employed in a job; it's even true for professionals such as attorneys, doctors, CPAs, and businesspeople who have large incomes.

Trying to "multiply yourself" by hiring employees to increase the amount of product you can sell is full of hassles. You have the employee who leaves and takes clients with him. You have training issues. You have liability issues even if the employee does a good job. There are hundreds of ways an employee can get the business owner into trouble. The work and the aggravation never end.

With an information marketing business, you create a product once and you're done. It takes a lot of work to create the product, but once you do, you can sell it many times, often over a period of several years, without having to do any additional work. Creating an information marketing business is a terrific way to "multiply yourself." Few businesses allow you to duplicate yourself in this way. With an information marketing business, you take information you already know and create a product.

You might think you have to be a genius and invent a newfangled device or identify a trend before it happens. You might worry that if you create a product, you won't know how to protect it through the trademark and patent process. You might not have any idea how to find a manufacturing and distribution company to put your product on the market.

With an information marketing business, everything you need to create a new product is already inside *you*. You don't need dozens of experts. You don't need newfangled distribution methods. An information marketing business allows you to take the information, the secrets, the techniques, *the things you already know*, and leverage them. That's the easy way to "multiply yourself."

You may have a hobby and find yourself answering other people's questions about what you do in online chat rooms. If that's true, you can be sure there are plenty of people who want this information. You can package what you know into an information product and make money with your own information marketing business. Or you may have developed great ways to perform services in a particular business. You can leverage that knowledge by creating a product to show others how to do what you do. By creating your product one time, you provide that business solution over and over again instead of performing the service yourself each time. That's how you "multiply yourself" and leverage what you know!

2. Buyers of Your Information Products Will Buy More

People say to me, "I'm already a consultant; if I create an information product that explains my entire process, won't people just do it themselves and stop hiring me to do work for them?" Absolutely not.

People who buy your information products are much more likely to hire you to perform services than other customers you market to. Quite simply, having your own published information product makes you the obvious expert. It shows the customer the complexity of the services and the special ability you have to perform them. The only possible conclusion for the buyer is that he should hire you when he needs additional help with his business or hobby. Publishing your own information product will only increase the services you're currently providing and expand your businesses far beyond what you're doing now.

In addition, the people who buy your information product will buy other information products from you, whether they are products you create yourself or products you license from others. You can partner with other information marketers to sell their products to your customers. Once you find a customer who wants information about a particular subject, that customer will continue to buy information from you on that subject.

Encouraging repeat business helps you further leverage yourself. Once you've gotten a customer, you're going to be able to sell that customer many things in the future for as long as you continue to provide high-quality information at a good price.

3. A Small Amount of Interaction with Buyers Is Possible

One of the best things about the information marketing business is that very few customers insist on coming to your business location to buy your products. This means you can work at home with your computer in a closet or build your information product on your kitchen table. You don't have to worry about customers showing up at your door to buy your new book. You can create products and sell them online from your beach home or as you vacation across the world. As long as you've got a way to create a product, you don't have to be in any particular location for people to buy it.

Not only is this exceptionally convenient, allowing you to do business from anywhere in the world you enjoy living, it also helps you get into this business with very little overhead expense.

4. Few Staff Members Are Necessary

The information marketing business is a terrific business because you don't need a lot of people to run it. Many info-marketers have no employees. They pay independent contractors to help maintain the customer database, ship products, and handle customers' questions. You can operate a business that makes well above $1 million a year with little or no staff and have little operating overhead.

5. Little Investment Is Needed to Get Started

The information marketing business does not require a lot of equipment. It doesn't require fancy offices, furniture, or multiple computers. It doesn't require special licenses (in most cases). And it doesn't require a special education or degrees. You just need to leverage the information you already know. How? By 1) identifying a market of people who are excited about the information you have, 2) creating a product those people want, and 3) offering it to them in a persuasive way.

That's why you can get into the information marketing business with a relatively low startup budget. One word of caution: Many info-marketers do not invest enough in their marketing and end up with a very slow start. Investing money in marketing when you are launching your business increases revenue more quickly. You can take a "stair-step" approach by investing a small amount in your first campaign and reinvesting your sales revenues into the next campaign. You can increase your marketing investments as you continue to have success in selling your product. That way you can start with a very modest investment, but by continuing to reinvest profits into making new sales and getting new customers, you can build your business.

Just remember: You don't have to go to school for 12 years, you don't have to pass any exams, you don't have to buy special equipment, and you don't have to have huge facilities. But you must be willing to put *some* money on the table to find potential customers and to market your product to them. If you try to do this business without any investment at all, you're certain to fail. Even the smallest franchise has an initial investment of $10,000.00 to $15,000.00, and there are continuing fees.

You should not be fooled into thinking you can start an information marketing business with no investment. Some think the moment they create a product and put a sales page on a website that people are suddenly going to flood that site and buy their products. That is a myth. Don't believe it.

But don't be discouraged! This is an easy business. This is a business with a lot of profitability, but you will not create a business that generates more than $1 million a year by investing nothing. You must be willing to test a marketing strategy to find new customers (known in the business as a front-end marketing funnel) and test it until it produces positive results. When you get positive results, you must invest in expanding that marketing campaign and growing your customer base.

6. Large Profit Potential Exists

Many info-marketers are making million-dollar incomes through their information marketing businesses. Each one started out like you, with no products and no customers, and they gave it a shot. Those new info-marketers researched potential customers, found out what those customers wanted the most, offered it to them in a compelling way, and then continued to sell their products until they were making a lot of money. Some info-marketers have $50 million to $100 million businesses. Some info-marketers are making in the high single-digit millions and have five to ten staff members. Other info-marketers are making half a million dollars with one or two staffers. This is a business that is completely scalable, that is, you can make it as small or as large as you want.

As you read through the components of successful information marketing businesses, you'll recognize many of them. I've heard many people tell me "I already know about publishing newsletters" or "I already put on seminars; information marketing is nothing new." Allow me to warn you now before you discount the business model because of the simplicity of its parts. Remember my airplane and soda can example: Just because an airplane is made out of the same aluminum as soda cans doesn't discount the machine's ability to get you where you want to go. Even though some of the components of the information marketing business may appear familiar, the way the components work together provides greater leverage, a better lifestyle, and more profit than any other business model.

But don't think an information business doesn't require work. It does. Just as you see entrepreneurs working hard in the mall, in a retail store, or in a new restaurant they've created, you should plan on working hard on your information marketing business. The good news is if you build an information marketing business and put in the necessary work, you can replace your manual labor by "multiplying yourself" and leveraging what you know to create new products. Your customers are going to buy more from you in the future. You can run your business with little interaction with your customers. You can be successful using a very small staff. It takes a small investment, but the payoff can be huge—if you stick with it and continue to develop your business.

Chapter 2

Information Marketing and How To Generate So Much Money

WHAT EXACTLY IS INFORMATION MARKETING? Is IT OFFERING coaching programs? Is info-marketing producing seminars? What about home study courses? Selling e-books? How about members-only websites? Is selling digital PDF and audio files by digital downloads information marketing?

The answer is information marketing is all those things. I'll go into more detail about specific products in Chapter 8, but the short answer is info-marketing is all those products and more.

Allow me to give you a standard definition: *Information marketing* is responsive to and fueled by the ever-increasing pressure on people's time. Businesspeople and consumers alike need information provided to them in convenient forms. Methods and strategies that might have been taught to them a mere ten years ago now need to be done for them. The *information industry* encompasses products like traditional books, audio programs, videos, or DVDs that you might buy in a store, from a catalog, or online; magazines, newsletters, e-books, membership websites, teleseminars and webinars, telecoaching programs, and seminars and conferences; and combinations thereof. Much of this business is comprised of lone wolf, small, quiet operators, many with homebased businesses, most with zero to no more than a few employees, most working only part-time hours, and most netting seven-figure profits.

But that, of course, doesn't give you a satisfactory picture of what information marketing is. For me, information marketing is providing solutions to problems in a convenient and useful format.

When I create an information product, I spend a lot of time studying a market, examining the problems its members face, and designing my offering as the solution to that problem. Whether

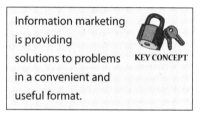

Information marketing is providing solutions to problems in a convenient and useful format.

KEY CONCEPT

I deliver that solution as a coaching program, a seminar, a home study course, or a digital download depends on the best way to deliver my particular solution, what the members of the market prefer, and which format gives me the best possible chance of making a nice profit.

Below are 29 different examples of information marketing businesses so you can see the diversity of the products offered and the markets served. In addition, this listing will also illustrate the similarities of these apparently diverse businesses.

1. Chiropractors can help accident victims recover and get back to work more quickly, but not if the chiropractor doesn't know how to get the patient into his office. Ben Altadonna has created an entire practice management process that helps chiropractors get great patients, get paid, and build strong practices.

2. Schools today emphasize vocabulary and skills without teaching kids how to learn. Speed reader Howard Berg has created a program that teaches any student how to study quickly and get great grades.

3. While a dentist may be terrific at repairing teeth, she needs a staff around her to run her office effectively. Suzanne Black provides a coaching program for dentists and their staffs to enable them to run their dental practices as successful businesses.

4. How you keep in contact with your customers and nurture relationships with new customers has turned into a business offering home study courses, seminars, and coaching programs for Ali Brown, the E-zine Queen. Ali has grown this business to offer marketing strategies and personal development for thousands of entrepreneurs.

5. Investors looking to make high returns quickly become frustrated with the fluctuations of the stock market but may be intimidated by more "exotic" investment alternatives. Brett Fogle has created a home study course teaching how to invest in options, and his seminars are well attended.

6. Companies needing to increase their sales often hire experienced trainers to provide better sales management systems and training. Colleen Francis offers a variety of home study courses for salespeople who want to improve their own skills.

7. Executives perfect their work for years, and then when they are asked to give a speech, many freeze up. Many of these anxious public speakers seek personal executive speech coaching from Patricia Fripp so they can deliver knockout presentations.

8. Salespeople get discouraged after suffering rejection over and over again; that's why Ari Galper has created home

study products and a coaching program teaching his proprietary sales process that defuses rejection and helps salespeople close more sales.

9. One of the most competitive businesses in America is personal injury legal services. Advertising is expensive, and it's difficult to get good cases. Ben Glass has created a coaching program and seminars that teach attorneys how to create advertising that yields the best cases for their practices.

10. Gym owners have all the new clients they want in January, but the rest of the year can be a challenge. Sean Greeley provides a monthly coaching program that helps gym owners to create effective marketing to keep new customers walking in the door.

11. Families with aging relatives often face difficult legal challenges when "Grandma starts slipping." Bill Hammond has created a coaching program that helps estate law attorneys reach out to these families to help them with complicated legal situations.

12. Property and casualty insurance agents face tremendous competition when marketing for clients and managing their businesses profitably. Michael Jans has created a membership site called the Quantum Club that provides insurance agents resources in 12 practice areas to help them take home more of their commissions as profits.

13. Many people want to become a gunsmith or a locksmith but don't know how to get started. Gene Kelly provides a catalog of home study courses as well as a certification program to equip anyone interested in this new career.

14. While investing in real estate can generate a lot of money, few people want to become a landlord. Ron LeGrand has created home study courses and seminars to teach

anyone how to buy and sell real estate to generate cash profits without having to be a landlord.

15. Charities who have signed photos and memorabilia from celebrities or athletes for their fundraising auctions generate more money than those who don't. That's why Jordan McAuley has created *The Celebrity Black Book*. It provides the names and addresses for thousands of celebrities these charities can contact. Jordan also has created an online directory available by subscription that is always updated with current information.

16. While many professional speakers worry about not having enough speaking gigs, there are hundreds of potential clients searching for great speakers. James Malinchak has created seminars, a home study course, and a coaching program to teach speakers how to get more gigs and make more money from their businesses by creating add-on products and services.

17. Beauty salon owners have no idea how to generate new customers. That's why Greg Milner has created his coaching program to provide them with that training.

18. Recognizing that coaching programs need personal development training to improve member retention, Lee Milteer has created an add-on coaching program called Millionaire Smarts. Lee provides personal development training and allows a coach to focus his attention on the areas of his expertise.

19. While dentists go to school for years to learn the anatomy of the mouth, no one teaches dentists how to get patients into the chair and to pay their bills. That's where Ed O'Keefe has stepped in with a monthly membership costing $495.00 that provides dentists with ready-to-send marketing campaigns they can use to keep their appointment schedules booked with patients.

20. Even though you may be a black belt in martial arts, it's still difficult to get families to enroll their children in classes at your studio. Stephen Oliver provides home study courses as well as a franchise program that does all this work for the studio owner.

21. With more computers in the home and digital photography all but replacing film photography, scrapbooking fans want to learn how to create great-looking pages using the new technology. Rozanne Paxman has responded with a monthly program delivering several scrapbook templates a month as well as access to a forum where her customers can teach each other how to create scrapbooks their families will cherish for generations.

22. While it's always been a challenge recruiting and hiring good employees, the current legal environment makes it downright dangerous for employers today. Don Phin has created a membership program that helps employers deal with difficult employment matters in a way that improves employee retention, recruits great team members, and avoids liability.

23. While computer repair services may know how to fix your computer, they don't know how to get customers to call them or how to properly charge for their services. Robin Robins has created a home study course and a coaching program, and she offers seminars by speaking at industry events around the country.

24. Homeowners often delay the sale of their home because they don't make it ready for new buyers to see themselves living in the home. Karen Schaefer has helped to build an entire home staging industry, complete with education, certification, and public awareness campaigns.

25. Salespeople always want to sell more products with less rejection, so Art Sobczak has created home study courses

and is a paid trainer at corporate sales training events around the country.

26. With all the competition out there, it's expensive for used car dealers to create great advertising that generates good customers. Jimmy Vee and Travis Miller have stepped in with their home study course and marketing coaching program, as well as their system of creating ready-to-use advertising for their clients.

27. Too many retailers look out their front windows watching the traffic go by with too few customers stopping in, so Claude Whitacre has created his Unfair Advantage Retail Advertising System, which he sells by appearing at retail industry seminars.

28. Recognizing that few restaurant owners want to learn marketing themselves, Ron Wilkinson has created a system that teaches an employee of the restaurant how to implement a marketing system and generate new customers.

29. Few people understand how to use a life insurance policy as a way of controlling all their banking needs, so Pamela Yellen has created marketing tools that she licenses to insurance agents across the country. This allows her licensees to differentiate themselves and sell more insurance because they are boosting the value of the insurance with additional training on how to use it.

While the differences in these businesses are clearly evident, it's easy to miss the similarities. In all cases these information marketers assist their customers with a problem. That problem could be how to do digital scrapbooking, how to earn more money, how to better manage employees, or any of the other examples above. But in the end, information marketing is about providing creative solutions to customers' problems.

Please note that these are only 29 examples out of the more than 1,000 members of the Information Marketing Association. Many of these 29 niches have multiple information marketers serving customers. I included only one per market to demonstrate the diversity of the information marketing business. But you could easily take this list and multiply it by 50 to get the true picture of the diversity of the information marketing business.

Chapter 3

A Detailed Outline of the Business You Are Building

IN ELEMENTARY SCHOOL MY TEACHER TAUGHT ME ABOUT perspective by asking my classmates and me to look at a picture of an elephant. She asked us to imagine a blindfolded child who had never seen an elephant before, walking up to the elephant, feeling its trunk, and describing what he felt. Then another blindfolded child walking up to a leg and describing for her friends what she felt. And then a third blindfolded child approaching the elephant's tail to describe what he felt there. Each would have a completely different report of what an elephant is based on what he felt. And every child would be correct, except that the children had an incomplete experience based on their limited perspectives. No one of them had a complete picture of the elephant.

It is the same with the information marketing business. Many different people create products that teach their experiences within the industry; however, each person's experience is usually from a limited perspective. Thus, it's easy for readers to become confused.

In this chapter I'm going to draw a picture of the complete "elephant" for you, so to speak. I'll outline what this business looks like so you can see all the moving parts you are working to build.

In Figure 3-1, I diagram the beginning of your **Information Marketing Business Pyramid**™. The pyramid is the most stable

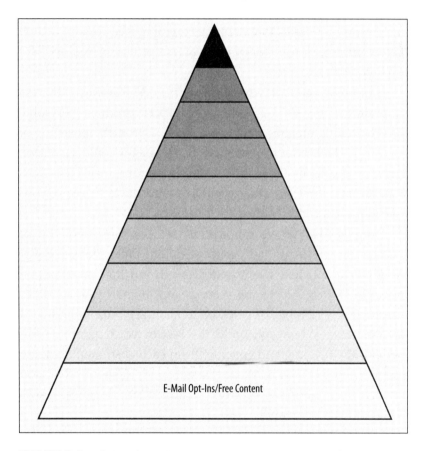

E-Mail Opt-Ins/Free Content

FIGURE 3-1. At the base of your Information Marketing Business Pyramid™ is your free content, given away to attract customers to you and designed to move them to take the next step up the pyramid.

way to build a structure. The Great Pyramid of Giza in Egypt was constructed around 2584–2561 B.C., and it's still standing today, more than 4,500 years later. If you build your info-marketing business following the pyramid structure, you'll create a stable, sustainable business.

At the base of your **Information Marketing Business Pyramid**™, you have the free content you offer to attract new customers to you. Your free content could be articles you publish, videos you make available on your website, or an e-mail auto responder series that provides ongoing free content. You'll have your largest number of users at this level. It's free, so there is a low barrier to entry.

Your next step of your **Information Marketing Business Pyramid**™ in Figure 3-2 is an introductory product. For some info-marketing businesses, this is a $199.00 product consisting of six CDs and a binder of materials. For others, it could be a book that's available in bookstores. This book provides customers with an easy first step to try out your products to see if your information is right for them.

Here is also where e-books fit in. You've seen a lot of online marketers marketing e-books on their websites. For them, it's an efficient way to offer an introductory product that moves customers up to the second step of their pyramids. To maximize the number of e-books you can sell, you must invest in marketing. When you build the rest of your pyramid, you increase the revenue you generate from each customer, allowing you to invest more in marketing to get a new customer than you could with an e-book as your only product. Your business grows faster and is more stable.

Once your customers experience your product, you offer them the opportunity to receive ongoing information through a monthly continuity program. These continuity programs are monthly subscription programs where you provide interviews,

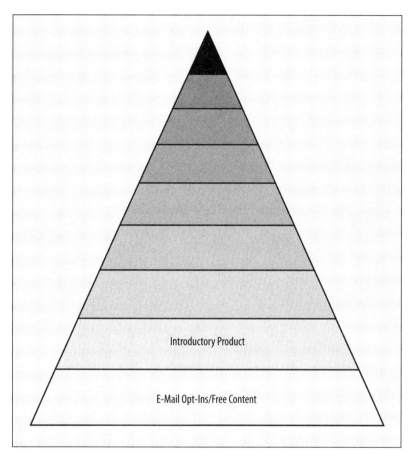

FIGURE 3-2. All of your new customer marketing systems should promote a single product to make it easy for new customers to make an initial purchase.

newsletters, and/or access to a membership site where your customers can get more of the information they loved in your introductory product. The pricing for these programs can be from $9.95 a month for a membership site to $199.00 a month for a program that includes newsletters, group coaching calls, and expert interviews on CD. I provide more information on continuity programs in Chapter 4. For now, I just want to show you where they fit in to your business in Figure 3-3.

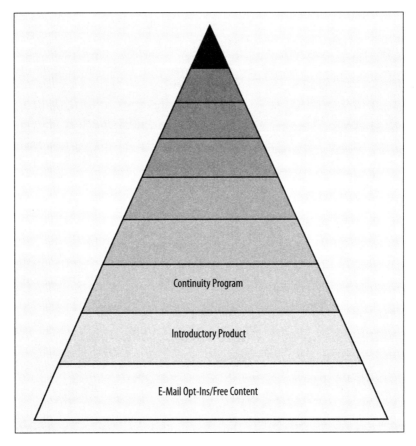

FIGURE 3-3. After making an initial purchase, customers are more likely to want updates and on-going resources. Invite new customers to take a step up with an ongoing continuity program.

You can invite your customers to participate in your continuity program immediately after they make their first purchase. There is no need to wait any length of time after the sale. A lot of info-marketers invite new customers to experience their continuity program through a free trial offer. These offers can be as short as a week or two weeks to as long as two months.

The next step in your **Information Marketing Business Pyramid**™ is high-priced specialty products shown in Figure

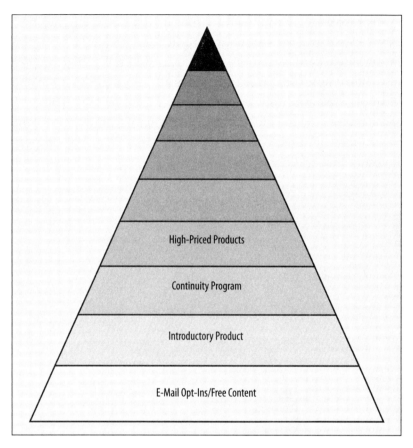

FIGURE 3-4. Once customers experience your introductory product they are a lot more likely to want your advanced products. These additional purchases have a large impact on your customer value and boost the amount of marketing you can do.

3-4. It's impossible to build one product that provides all the information any of your customers could want or need about a particular topic. Instead, you provide a high-quality introductory product that outlines your strategies and provides useful examples to follow. Then for different areas of expertise, you provide additional products that provide additional details about that particular aspect. You will be able to sell these specialty products for much higher prices, from $495.00 to $1,995.00 or more.

For instance, if you have an information marketing business directed to parrot owners, your introductory product has chapters on feeding, cages, and teaching the parrot to talk. Then you can also offer a specialty product that has advanced information and examples focused only on teaching a parrot to talk. This way the customers who enjoyed your introductory product but who want more information on a particular area of parrot care can invest in that additional resource.

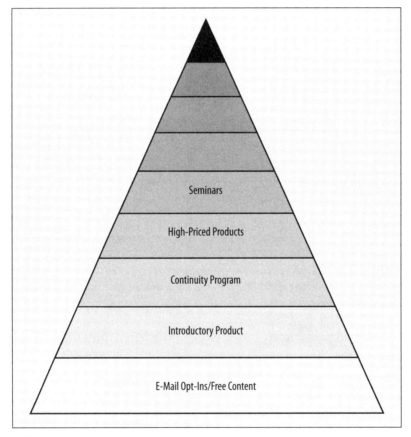

FIGURE 3-5. Every large info-marketing business includes seminars. There's nothing as powerful as being face to face with your members. They love the experience and when done properly, can be a large profit center for your business.

The next area of your **Information Marketing Business Pyramid**™ is seminars, shown in Figure 3-5. Many info-marketers choose not to offer seminars, and that's fine. But for those who do offer them, it can be a lucrative part of their business. Customers who enjoy your products and invest in your continuity program are interested in coming to hear directly from you on your strategies and tactics. This is especially true if you have new updates and information to share.

Info-Marketing seminars are usually priced between $750.00 and $1,995.00 per person or more. The seminar also provides you a great opportunity to introduce your members to the other programs you have to offer within your **Information Marketing Business Pyramid**™.

Notice how your **Information Marketing Business Pyramid**™ has relatively large numbers of customers at the bottom, and then as your price levels increase, you have fewer and fewer customers. That's a normal part of your pyramid. With a large base of low-priced customers, you'll have a certain percentage that will want to increase from one level to the next. You must build additional levels to give your customers that opportunity. That's why if you try to run a business by only selling e-books, you'll never reach a high level of success. That's because you won't be increasing your average customer value by offering additional products and services.

The next section of your **Information Marketing Business Pyramid**™ is a coaching program. I talk a lot about moving your customers up your pyramid into group coaching and seminars in Chapter 10, but for now, recognize this is an important level of your pyramid. Group coaching gives your customers the opportunity to receive personal help implementing your teaching in their own lives. Even though your products can provide complete, step-by-step, paint-by-numbers instructions to implement, many customers will prefer personal attention.

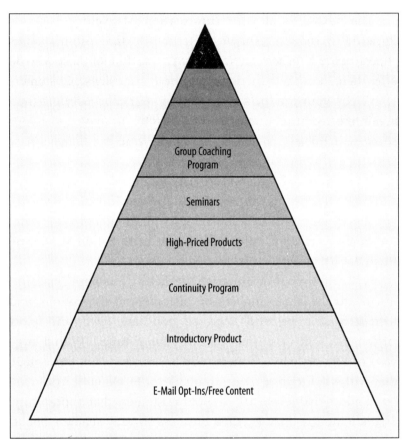

FIGURE 3-6. Once customers have experienced your products and events many will be excited about the opportunity to participate in a coaching program to help them implement what they learned.

Your coaching program provides them a way to receive that personal attention. See Figure 3-6.

I'll introduce a couple of advanced topics to you here, but I don't want you to get too caught up in them right now. You will have plenty of time to learn about them later. Right now I want you to see the complete picture. In Figure 3-7, you'll notice the last two boxes are filled in with Implementation Services and Personal Coaching.

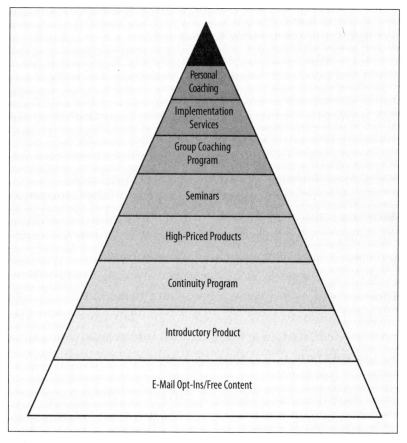

FIGURE 3-7. After reviewing all of your products, some customers will choose to have your team and you implement on their behalf. This investment generates faster results for the customer and a larger lifetime customer value for you.

Despite all the teaching you provide, some customers prefer to have you do the work for them. Instead of learning how to set up their websites, they want someone to do it for them. Rather than learning how to write a perfect marketing campaign, they want someone to do it for them. Because they don't have time to publish a monthly newsletter, they want someone to publish it for them. Once a customer has purchased your products and believes in your strategies, she will often choose to invest in having you implement those strategies for her. This provides a terrific revenue opportunity for you.

At the top of the **Information Marketing Business Pyramid**™, you'll find personal coaching. Some customers will invest in all your products and still want to sit down with you for one-on-one, personal assistance. And the best part for you is they will be willing to pay you for that privilege. You may choose whether or not you want to offer those personal coaching services, but within your info-business, you'll have that opportunity.

I want to point out again that at the base of the **Information Marketing Business Pyramid**™, you have large numbers of customers paying little to nothing. Then as you move up the pyramid, your customer value increases as you deliver more products and services at higher prices. It's easy to say, "Wow, I just wanted to sell some e-books and make money; I'm not prepared to do all this." Don't get intimidated too early. This book is dedicated to explaining the **Information Marketing Business Pyramid**™ and showing you how to get your business launched quickly.

This pyramid is here so you can see the entire "elephant." I'm helping you avoid being blindfolded, standing under the elephant where the poop comes out, without any idea what's going on. I've found that part of the elephant more than once. Allow me to walk you through the process of creating your information marketing business in the easiest way possible so you can generate quick and sustainable wealth.

Chapter 4

Three Most Important Factors in the Success of Your Info-Marketing Business

---

THREE PRIMARY DRIVERS SEPARATE SUCCESSFUL, MATURE information marketing businesses from those that never reach their full potentials. And while this book primarily covers how to start and launch your information marketing business, I thought it was important to give you upfront the three key factors you're going to need as part of your business launch to have a long-term, sustainable business. At some point you're going to be done with your launch process, and you're going to be looking to build a more mature, long-lasting business. So you need to keep these three factors in the forefront of your mind as you begin your business: *Marketing Research*, *Continuity Income*, and *Marketing Systems to Generate New Customers*.

Marketing Research

The single most common reason information marketing businesses fail is inadequate market research. Over and over again when I talk to an info-marketer who has faced some sort of setback with his business, it can be attributed to inadequate research. Many of us get caught up in creating just the right marketing strategy, writing the perfect sales letter, or building the perfect product, but in fact, very few of those things can have as much impact on your business as thorough market research.

In Chapter 6, I outline how to do your research on your market, but many info-marketers assume they already know their markets. They take the position that they've been in the industry long enough, they understand it, and so they don't need to do additional research. What I've found is that as someone who is considering doing information marketing, you are very unique among your peers and your marketplace. Your peers may see things quite differently than you do, and the things you consider important they may *not*.

KEY CONCEPT Too many new info-marketers assume they know everything about their market. Researching your market and interviewing potential customers is the shortcut to launching a profitable business quickly.

I made this same mistake myself before launching my first info-marketing business. I was by far the best membership salesperson I knew in creating sales letters and marketing campaigns to generate new members, keep them longer, and get them engaged in the association.

I set out to create a particular info-product because I thought I knew the industry. I created a big kit that provided the examples, membership strategies, and all the information I thought I would have wanted someone to offer me when I started out in membership marketing.

I soon discovered that a big kit was not what my market wanted; instead, it wanted seminars. And because I hadn't done adequate research, I wasted time and money creating the wrong product for my market niche.

Research is crucially important to helping you create the right product and the right marketing message the first time. It is the shortcut to success.

Continuity Income

Continuity income is revenue you receive from your members on an ongoing basis. You may have seen offers where you can join for $29.00 a month to receive a newsletter every month, or for $99.00 participate in a membership website and receive a newsletter, or for $299.00 receive coaching. Monthly continuity programs can be very lucrative to you as an information marketer.

Too many other businesses are deal oriented. For example, consider being a Realtor®: If you're not closing on home sales, then you're not making any money. It doesn't matter if you did 2 or 20 closings last month; until you close a home this month, you aren't making any money.

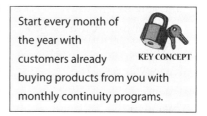

Start every month of the year with customers already buying products from you with monthly continuity programs.

KEY CONCEPT

An information marketer who relies on large seminars for income can be in a similar situation. Even though those seminars can be very profitable, chances are you're doing only one or two or perhaps four a year. That leaves periods of several months when you're not generating that income.

Thus, continuity income can be crucial for your business. As you generate new customers, you're able to increase the numbers you have participating in your continuity income.

Just think about this: If only 5 percent of your new customers participate in your continuity program, then every month your monthly continuity income continues to grow.

The power of these programs is in providing monthly cash flow for your business. So when you have a big promotion or a seminar and make a large amount of money, you can pull it out in profit because your monthly continuity income is paying your monthly bills.

You start each month billing customers' credit cards so you can provide the newsletters, products, or services you've committed to those subscribers. It's a great way to start in business every month—with revenue already in the bank.

Marketing Systems to Generate New Customers

The real secret to the information marketing business is to build a marketing process, a funnel if you will, that generates new customers over and over again. This process generates leads, and those leads go into a sales system that helps potential customers learn about you and how you can solve their problems before inviting them to make a purchase.

Once they've made a purchase, the sales system invites them to make other purchases based on their interests. That helps increase the value of every customer. And in addition to their purchases, you invite these new customers to participate in your monthly continuity programs so you can grow your monthly income as well.

Too many info-marketers try to use the same systems they used to launch their information marketing businesses to run their businesses. If they used a teleseminar to launch their business, then they repeat that process over and over again, convincing themselves that it's the only way that works for them.

The processes outlined within this book are great tools to help you get your business launched quickly. They are simplified to make it easy for you to use them the first time with the fewest steps possible.

But once you have your business launched, you will want to use additional strategies to run a successful business. This allows you to generate customers from many sources. This new customer acquisition system provides steady growth for your business. You got into information marketing to build a better life, and the way you build that lifestyle is to create a successful marketing system that continually generates new customers.

The second part of a successful marketing system is monitoring. As you create your marketing system, you need to constantly measure the number of new leads you're able to generate from each of your lead generation sources.

>
> **KEY CONCEPT**
>
> Every new business needs new customers to grow. Information marketers unlock the "business owner" lifestyle by creating an automated process to generate new customers every month from a variety of sources.

Then you should measure how long those new customers participate in your monthly continuity program.

You'll want to track those percentages and measure them over time so you can always judge the health of your information marketing business based on the new customers you are able to generate. New customer generation is one of the most difficult parts of any business and often can be the most expensive as well. This is why so many new info-marketers move on to other areas of their businesses once they get their businesses going. They become focused on product creation or putting on a new seminar, for example.

However, as an information marketer, it's crucial that you set up ongoing systems and processes to help you generate new customers. You need to have a marketing funnel that helps put new customers into your business on a continual basis. With these three keys—*Market Research, Continuity Income,* and *Marketing Systems to Generate New Customers*—you can build an information marketing business that unlocks all your lifestyle goals.

Chapter 5

What About Creating an Internet Business and Getting Rich Selling E-Books?

I GET A LOT OF QUESTIONS FROM PEOPLE ASKING, "HOW DO I create one of those businesses where I just sell e-books and make a million dollars? Or one of those businesses where I'm able to sell expensive products to customers who just go and download them so I can set it and forget it? How do I set up a business like an ATM machine that keeps putting money in my checking account?"

Well, unfortunately, those businesses rarely exist, and even when they do, most of them were rather haphazard in the way they were created and involved more luck than skill.

I also receive a lot of criticism from people who review my products and say, "The info-marketing business is all about MP3 audio files and online video; Robert's book was too much about off-line marketing." The truth is this book is about the business of info-marketing. Online video and digital downloads are one way to deliver products, but they are not a business.

There are plenty of people selling you the next new set-it-and-forget-it type of business. But remember, the people who are selling these systems rarely have those types of businesses themselves. The fact that they are providing this information by standing in a seminar selling their products demonstrates they are not doing the hands-off business they say they are. While current information marketing strategies benefit from the internet-marketing tools pioneered through the process of trying to create businesses that are completely internet-based, hands-off, set-it-and-forget-it types of businesses, "set it and forget it" doesn't really exist today.

Certainly there are portions of your business you'll be able to automate and then forget for a long time. For instance, I have marketing processes and websites I created three years ago that still generate new customers for me every month. But one of the harsh realities is they don't generate as many customers as they did three years ago, and if I hadn't created other processes to generate new customers, that company would have gone out of business a long time ago. But the process I created three years ago still works, just not as well as it did and also not enough to sustain the business on its own.

Even in a set-it-and-forget-it situation, you still are going to have to innovate; you still need to replace, update, correct, improve, monitor, and build new processes as you go. The concept of creating a great business and then going on vacation for five years while that business chugs along putting money in your checking account is a myth created by people selling how-to courses.

This book focuses on how to create a real business that will meet your lifestyle goals. It includes a lot of internet components; there are digital downloads and even online video. However, my emphasis is to teach you the business principles first, and then you'll see how the online components fit together. This will help you avoid the hype and a lot of wasted time chasing the next internet marketing fad.

Let me give you an overview of the internet marketing components you will be using within the information marketing world. And while I do this, I'll dispel many of the myths you hear about "amazing" marketing breakthroughs.

KEY CONCEPT Internet marketing provides a lot of great tools information marketers can use to create, sell, and deliver products. However, internet marketing tools do not create a business. Instead, your focus has to be on creating a business first and then using internet marketing tools to allow you to grow more quickly.

Online Order Forms

A few years ago, customers had to fax an order form with credit card information or mail a check, but today they can use their home computers to go to your website and buy something online. Those online order forms have made it tremendously easier for customers to buy. In fact, when I offer the option of online ordering, I see that 50 percent of my sales are coming through the internet. Customers today prefer to use an online order form rather than filling out a paper form or sending a check. So, that's a tool born from the concept of internet-only marketing that certainly will help your business. Software such as InfusionSoft (**InfoMarketingCRM.com**) will allow you to create secure online forms so your customers can place their orders.

Digital Delivery

Even in my businesses that are focused on delivering paper products, paper courses, and monthly printed newsletters, I still deliver many products digitally.

For instance, within the Information Marketing Association, all members receive a copy of the Best Practices in Information Marketing monthly teleseminar on audio CD in the mail.

But I also post the MP3 file on the members' only website **MyInfoMarketingForum.com** along with the transcript of the recording for quick reference. My customers have the CD if they want the convenience of listening to it in the car, but they also have access to the audio download as well as the printed transcript online.

While I'll get into products in more detail in Chapter 8, know that digital delivery is a great way to deliver your products, and it's a useful addition to an existing information marketing business.

Membership Sites

Membership sites have been around since the advent of the internet. I created my first internet membership site back in 1997 for the geologist industry. It had a password-protected area for members only as well as pages that anyone could access.

Membership websites can be an important part of an info-business. Plus, they can be a useful forum for members to exchange ideas. However, you may have seen marketers promoting how to create membership sites where everybody interacts and communicates, with members contributing all the content so you don't have to do any of the work. Those membership sites are very rare, making up less than 1 percent of the sites that are created.

Most membership sites are a great tool to help facilitate a membership program that also provides printed content and monthly teleseminars, and they also serve as forums for delivering content for coaching programs.

The membership site that stands alone, generates new customers by itself, and generates content by itself because all the participants are communicating with each other on message boards and uploading samples? That site is a very rare beast.

Still, the membership site is a very useful add-on and is helpful for an information marketer, even though the promise of a set-it-and-forget-it business isn't a reality for most people.

No Storefront

One of the best elements of the internet marketing phenomenon has been the elimination of the storefront. It used to be if you were getting into a retail business where you were selling something, you had to have a store. You had to sign a lease on some retail space on a high-traffic street so you were in a convenient location for your customers to come in and buy. Today, customers have no expectation that they're going to come to your store; most are perfectly happy with buying online and having you ship a product. The "no expensive storefront" is a great innovation of the internet marketing business.

Why is it that it's impossible for the promises of a set-it-and-forget-it internet business to become a reality? Well, let's take a moment and review the reasons why those types of businesses rarely exist for any length of time.

First of all, in the information marketing business, the customers who love you are going to want to invest in more products and services from you. If you have a business that is simply selling a particular product over a website, you're not maximizing the marketing investment you made in generating new customers by selling them additional products and services. You need a way of providing those customers additional products, additional programs, and additional systems so they are able to solve additional problems in their lives and you are able to make more money from your business. Any business that doesn't have that element is not generating as much profit as it should be. Sooner or later, anyone who creates one of those online-only businesses ends up creating additional products and services to sell to their existing customers. It's better to go ahead and set up those systems from the beginning rather than having to do it on the fly later on.

Next, why do so many people who teach online marketing hold seminars? If it is so effective simply to create a website and sell product on the internet, why would marketers go through the trouble of hosting a seminar where they have to prepare a presentation, wake up early, and stand on stage in front of people to teach? Isn't that a lot of manual labor for someone who has a set-it-and-forget-it business? Standing in front of people and giving a presentation is an old technology, probably around since the beginning of time. And yet you see all these internet marketers who are promising automated systems using seminars to deliver their content.

Well, the reason they're doing it that way is because customers often prefer seminars to digital downloads. And the internet marketer can make a lot more money by having those seminars. For you, it's better to go ahead and get into business with the expectation that you're going to be interacting with your people because eventually you are—if you want to generate the real money you want and unlock the lifestyle you desire.

Finally, there's the issue of human interaction. I know one of the elements that really attracted me to the information marketing business was limited interaction. And it actually is a benefit, as mentioned in Chapter 1, but my picture of limited human interaction was that I never had to interact with customers *at all*. They would consult my frequently asked questions if they needed something; otherwise, they'd go to the site, buy, receive the product, and I would never have to interact with them.

Well, the fact is many of the people who buy your products will want additional help and support from you or your team. While many customers go to the website to buy, many others browse the website and then pick up the phone to place their orders with live operators. If I didn't have someone there ready to take their orders, I would lose those sales.

While we all might prefer to have a business that's completely automated, completely hands off, and chugs away generating profits and depositing money into our bank accounts, the sad reality is those businesses just don't exist. And if they do exist, they're so rare that you just might have better success playing the lottery.

Many people will promise you can create those businesses, but a whole lot fewer people are actually delivering on that promise. What they can deliver, though, are great tools and strategies to help you generate new customers for your information marketing business so you can have more of them buying additional products, attending your seminars, and participating in your coaching programs. Those are the real ways you're going to generate more profit through your information marketing business.

What I reveal in this book are the time-tested strategies real business owners use to run their businesses. These aren't pretend strategies or the way things "should work." You are reading what *has* worked for hundreds of people before you and will allow you to achieve your goals and dreams through your information marketing business.

Chapter 6

Identifying a Market That Will Support You in Style

I HAVE GONE THROUGH A SERIES OF TERRIFYING REVELATIONS IN my life. Fresh out of college, I thought I knew everything. No one could teach me anything because my education gave me everything I needed to know. After all, I'd gotten great grades in graduate school while obtaining a master's degree in accounting. Obviously, I knew everything I needed to know.

I soon discovered, however, that I knew nothing. I started making mistakes that all my coworkers knew were obvious because they had been working in the field for a few years. What a terrifying year or two that was. No matter how much I tried to learn more, how many magazines I read, and how many books I studied, I realized it was a small fraction of everything there was to know. I felt so stupid, like I had nothing to offer anyone and that I was destined for a low-level job forever.

That's when it occurred to me.

During conversations with my clients and coworkers, I figured out everyone else was an idiot, too. Even the professionals—the attorneys and the doctors—yep, they were guessing, too. What a quandary: not only was I an idiot, but everyone else around me was one, too!

Even though I was an idiot, with a grasp of only a narrow bit of knowledge, my study had given me far more knowledge than anyone else around me, and they knew it. I've discovered that only a small number of people ever have this revelation. They are stuck in the stage where they realize they know nothing. Most people are constantly intimidated by everyone around them because they are searching for the person with all the knowledge.

Now, I'm not saying that everyone is stupid. What I am saying is although most people have an area of great expertise, outside their expertise they have a lot to learn, and most of them know it.

For instance, the brain surgeon. That surgeon can open a skull, conduct surgery while the patient is still awake, and then sew up the patient better than when the surgery started. That surgeon has a lot of expertise in brain surgery, more than I could ever learn. However, chances are that surgeon knows very little about billing and collecting fees from insurance companies for his services, knows little about getting new patients to fly from around the world to pay cash for his services, and knows little about investing his money to grow a savings account for his children's college education or his own retirement. This creates a terrific opportunity for anyone with this expertise to create and offer products.

KEY CONCEPT It's not important for you to become the foremost expert in all topics; instead, become an expert in one topic that's useful to your target market. They'll become your customers even though they may know more than you in other areas of expertise.

You don't have to be the world's foremost expert on all topics to be able to create and sell an information product. You simply need to know information that others want. And the best part is you don't even need to know it *before* you begin. Instead, you can figure out what people want, then go out and find the information. You can begin this business right where you are, whether you have 30 years of experience or you are just starting out.

The Best Business Positioning

When my daughter, Samantha, was 7 years old, I took her fishing. She was so excited as we went to Wal-Mart to buy a fishing rod, hooks, bobbers, sinkers, worms, and a special fishing hat. My dad always took me fishing, and now it was my turn to be the dad. After we arrived at the lake, I got Samantha's rod set up, and I lugged the chairs, a cooler, and fishing rods to a shady spot at the water's edge.

That's when the casting lessons began. Even with a kid's rod, it takes some practice to be able to cast a line into the water more than a foot or so from shore. But finally everything was set, and I could sit back in my chair and enjoy the day.

Less than two minutes later, Samantha asked, "Daddy, when are we gonna catch a fish?"

"We have to wait until a fish comes by and bites your bait," I explained.

"But when is the fish coming by?" she asked.

She put down her rod and started to walk around. She was bored with fishing; she was ready for catching. I stuck it out for another 20 minutes, and then we packed it up for the day.

The next week I read in the newspaper that a local charity was hosting a fishing derby for children. They had stocked a small netted area of a lake with fish and were inviting kids to come and catch some.

I took Samantha and discovered the hungriest fish I'd ever seen. The volunteers running the charity had put fishing nets under a dock to create an underwater fish corral. Then they stocked that area with small brim. They must have let those fish get really hungry. Within seconds of dropping her line in the water, Samantha could reel in a fish. She had a blast, catching five fish that morning.

She told me, "That was a lot more fun than last time."

I agreed. It's always more fun when you are throwing your bait into a pond with hungry fish.

And this is the most important consideration when launching

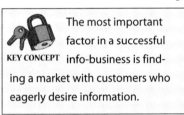
KEY CONCEPT The most important factor in a successful info-business is finding a market with customers who eagerly desire information.

your information marketing business. You've got to find the market that is excitedly expecting what you have to offer, or you have to offer what your target market is already excitedly expecting. Without this, it'll be a lot like my daughter's first fishing trip: poor results and frustrating.

The Key Is Identifying a Hungry Market

You must find a market of individuals who are aggravated, who need help, and who want to escape from everyday problems. Using my fishing example, it's a lot easier to catch hungry fish that are in a netted area under a dock than it is to go to a random shady spot at a lake and drop in your line.

Ed O'Keefe with Dentist Profits went from being a college student majoring in nursing to a motivational speaker to a book writer, and he has used the skills he picked up along the way to create an extremely profitable information marketing business that provides automatic implementation marketing for dentists.

Two years out of college, Ed was "dead broke" and tired of traveling from place to place trying to make a living speaking to people at schools, businesses, and athletic groups. "Quite honestly, it was no fun fighting for gig after gig," Ed remembers.

Attending a Dan Kennedy Customer Appreciation Event helped put Ed on a new road to success. He bought Dan's Magnetic Marketing toolkit and put it to work. His first info-product was the Ultimate Mental Toughness Training for Volleyball Players and Coaches, and he was able to tailor that product for a number of niches. Several years later, Ed was making "some money, but not much," so he started looking for another opportunity. This time he put some of his college skills to work and hit the library.

Ed believes it is important for anyone in the info business to "choose the market before you choose the product." How do you do that? In a word: RESEARCH.

Ed began his research with the Yellow Pages. He went through the entire book, noting the number of ads for each profession and niche industry. From this, he was able to gauge which industries were investing the most into marketing.

"Some friends of mine thought I was absolutely nuts. They were like—'What are you doing?' And I said, 'I'm getting rich,'" Ed says, smiling and shaking his head. "I knew I needed a change. I remember seeing one guy selling software for 99 bucks a month, and it hit me right in the face. I did the math. There I was schlepping my $47.00 book and audiotapes to coaches who didn't have any money. That software guy wasn't any more intelligent than you or me or anyone else. He was just doing something right!"

Ed was determined to find his own "right thing," so he researched 47 different industries and professions. He called trade publications and requested media kits. He found out how many people were involved in each niche. He looked at the media already reaching each niche. As Ed says, "Everyone says to go find a target market and research it, but not too many people go into as much detail as I did. But it's so beneficial."

With his research done, Ed was ready to choose his market. Now Ed does direct-mail lead-generation campaigns for dentists.

Dentists can sign up for Ed's system, select the types of patients they want, and then Ed takes care of all the marketing. The dentists are notified when the postcards go in the mail, and the next thing they know, they have new patients calling the office. Ed's customers don't have to learn anything. All they have to do is ask Ed to take care of the service, and he handles everything.

KEY CONCEPT Conduct the necessary research to completely understand your customer so you can imagine yourself in his skin, going about his day, and coming across your sales message.

As you plan your information marketing venture, be sure you start with the market first. Find out what the market desperately wants before you create a product and a marketing campaign to sell it. Too many info-marketers create the product first and then try to find individuals to sell it to. It is a lot easier to identify potential buyers first, allow them to tell you what they want, and then simply offer it back to them in a compelling and exciting way.

Here are the factors I consider when analyzing a new market for an information marketing product.

Market Size

You can make big money in small markets. I have two info-marketing businesses where the target markets have fewer than 100 businesses. Each of those generates more than $250,000.00 a year; however, it's unlikely those businesses will ever double that.

The larger your market is, the larger your opportunity. Consider one of the largest info-product markets, weight loss. There are billions of dollars sold in the weight loss niche alone. And it's not as if the information is changing; it's still eat less and exercise more.

One of the challenges in a large market is it requires a large marketing investment. In weight loss, you'd have to invest millions of dollars to begin to get your new product noticed.

As you consider markets, don't be afraid of smaller markets. If I were launching a new info-product targeting dentists, I'd consider directing my marketing toward dentists in business for five years or less. This is a much smaller market than the broader dentist market, so it would be easier to buy a list from a list broker and less expensive to reach. And there's no reason why I couldn't expand my business to include more dentists as I began to grow.

Market Reachability

Getting to fish in a pond where the fish have been corralled by a net is the perfect fishing environment. It was easy for my daughter to catch fish at the charity tournament because they were already gathered in a small area right under her spot on the dock.

When you study a market, ask yourself these questions: Has anyone already "corralled" your potential buyers? Is there an association, trade magazine, industry vendors, another info-marketer, or a list you could purchase from a list broker that gives you immediate access to the market without doing all the expensive corralling yourself?

If another marketer has a list of your potential customers as well as a relationship in which that marketer is maintaining contact with those customers, that can be a great shortcut for you as you launch your business.

One of the launch methods outlined in Section III of this book focuses on working with individuals already established within the market to help you launch your own business.

Market Trends

Is your target market growing or shrinking? A couple of years ago, I had a thriving business that served mortgage brokers. When the foreclosure crisis hit, the lending companies left the market. Before the crisis happened, something like that was impossible to contemplate. How could more than 100 top lenders stop writing mortgages? They'd have to fire thousands of internal employees underwriting and closing loans, mortgage brokers wouldn't have any way of providing mortgages to borrowers, and the entire industry would collapse.

That's exactly what happened. More than 200,000 people who were mortgage brokers in 1998 are doing something else now. That's 200,000 people who aren't buying products to teach them how to sell mortgages. My info-business serving the mortgage niche is gone.

In this case, it was a normal business cycle. The same thing happened in 1989 because of the savings and loan crisis. If you go through history, you'll see it happens every 15 to 25 years. I hadn't seen it before, so I had no idea I should look for that cycle.

Every industry has trends to watch. Medical spending in our country is higher than in any country in the world. And with baby boomers getting older, the industry is poised for further growth. That means more doctors, more nurses, more equipment manufacturers, more retirement communities, and more nursing homes. This is a growth trend that's hard for profit-minded info-marketers to ignore.

How do the current economic trends impact your target niche? How are generational differences among baby boomers, Gen Xers, and Gen Yers changing the demographics of your market's target customers?

Transaction Size

I recently had a client who sold consulting services worth $500,000.00 to $5 million. Imagine in one deal selling $5 million to a customer! This client was willing to invest a lot of money in my consulting services to generate new clients, all because of the average customer's transaction size.

My worst experience in consulting was trying to help a friend of mine with marketing for his frozen yogurt shop. It takes a lot of customers buying frozen yogurt to generate enough profit to pay for a $1,500.00 newspaper ad because of the average customer's transaction size.

In business niches, I prefer selling to markets where there is a large transaction size. For instance, cosmetic surgeons sell services worth $10,000.00 to $50,000.00; real estate agents sell homes that produce a commission of $5,000.00 to $15,000.00; home builders can easily generate $10,000.00 on a new home. Whenever a business has a large transaction size, those owners are usually willing to invest more money in resources that will help them generate more customers.

If you don't care about selling to businesses but instead are interested in selling information products to a hobbyist niche, this is still an important consideration. How much do hobbyists invest to do the hobby? If it's something like needlepoint, the new hobbyist can get started for a few hundred dollars. If the hobbyist is a golfer or a private pilot, the investment is much higher. As the investment for a hobby increases, so goes the hobbyist's willingness to invest in information to do that hobby better.

Market Villains

In my mortgage brokerage info-business, my customers' villains were bankers and the rip-off artists who were giving the mortgage industry a bad name. If you offered a product to a mortgage broker that gave her an edge on the rip-off artists or enabled her to outsell a banker, you had yourself a new customer.

While all customers of information products aspire to get better, they are often more motivated by their anger to outperform someone they see as a villain. Every industry has villains. Nurses battle doctors for the right to help patients in more ways while doctors want to prevent nurses from eliminating the need for patients to see them. Auto mechanics don't like auto manufacturers that force their customers to go to their dealerships for service work. Chiropractors want respect as legitimate health-care providers from doctors and insurance companies. Any salesperson gets mad at the home office for rejecting important client entertainment investments on his expense account, and the accounting team at the home office resents salespeople who make larger salaries and spend the company's money on elaborate meals.

A current of frustration runs through any niche. Don't think this doesn't apply to you if you are marketing to hobbyists. For a golfer, reducing his score by a few strokes makes the difference in whether or not he beats his buddies the next time on the course. For a quilter or a painter, her villains could be the other people in the art fair competition.

People are always thinking about their villains. If you enter a market with a new information product aimed at helping your market overcome their villains, you'll be fishing off a dock in a pond of fish hungry for your bait.

Best Markets for Information Products

While there are info-marketers successfully operating within every imaginable niche, there are some niches where info-marketers flourish. Within these markets there is a strong demand for the newest and best information products. Plus, there are mailing lists of customers available as well as other info-marketers you can do joint ventures with to launch your new product.

Business and Entrepreneurship

One of the best markets for information products is business owners or individuals who want to get into their own business.

The reason: You can deliver a lot of value with your information to these markets.

If you are able to teach a business owner how to improve her marketing to generate a new customer each week, that could mean tens of thousands of dollars in new business for her. That piece of information has a lot of value to the business owner. Similarly, if you are able to teach a government employee how to buy a home as an investment and then sell that home in two months for a $20,000.00 profit, you've given him a tool to completely change his economic future. That's what makes business information products so profitable; the information has such a large potential economic value to your customers that they are willing to pay higher prices for it.

Some of the most consistently successful topic areas include:

- Marketing systems for businesses
- How to obtain additional customers
- Getting more productivity from employees
- Saving money in your business
- Methods of selling at higher prices than your competitors
- Unique selling strategies that convert more prospects into customers
- Investing in real estate
- Starting a business
- Investing in franchise and business opportunities
- Communication skills, public speaking
- Tax reduction, tax strategy
- A successful person's plan for business success
- Business biographies

Self-Improvement

The psychology/self-help sections of bookstores have exploded in size over the past two decades. Successful individuals are always looking for that additional "slight edge" they can use to expand their productivity and achieve greater success in their lives.

In addition, Americans' desire for the next new system, diet, and exercise program is endless. These products have a large demand because of the positive impacts they have on your customers' lives. Customers are willing to buy information, strategies, and techniques within each of these categories:

- Dieting
- Exercise
- Better sex
- Goal-setting
- Time management and personal organization
- Sales skills
- Special personal development "philosophies"
- A hugely successful individual's own "plan" for success
- Self-esteem and self-confidence
- Relationships

Hobby-Oriented

Few people in the world are more aggressive customers than golfers. If you can teach a golfer how to lower his score from 80 strokes to 78, there's almost no amount he wouldn't pay. Not only that, how about the best golf courses to play, trip itineraries of golf courses in different parts of the world, or biographies of famous golfers? The fact is people are extremely interested in consuming information about their hobbies and interests.

Walk into a pet store. You'll always find a huge rack of magazines and books relating to animals. If you've never been, you'll be amazed at how many bird books there are. Can you imagine people getting in their cars, driving to a store, and buying bird books? If not, you need to do more research because it's happening every day.

Look at the classified ads of any golfing, pet, or auto magazine. Chances are you'll find ads selling every sort of information about how to do that hobby better or differently. If you have a hobby or an interest that occupies your time, you have the makings of a terrific information marketing business.

Business Opportunity

Many business opportunities are little more than information products. The business startup manuals sold by *Entrepreneur* magazine are some of the best examples of this genre. The people at Entrepreneur publish dozens of startup manuals, each for a different, very specific business: muffin shops, carpet cleaning, balloon vending, etc. They also offer a generic manual that covers basics common to all businesses.

The entire *Entrepreneur* magazine business was started by Chase Revel, with little one-inch display ads headlined: HOW MUCH DOES JOE MAKE? See if you can find a used copy of the out-of-print book *Secrets of a Successful Mail Order Guru: Chase Revel* by Ron Tepper. This book is well worth studying, and it includes the details of how Revel started and built his business, and will give you terrific insights into the business opportunity market.

Many information product marketers specialize in reaching out to the business opportunity market. You can find current copies of most of the magazines exclusively serving this market on the newsstand or at your public library. They include:

Black Enterprise
Home Business
Business Opportunities Guide
Business Opportunities Handbook
Entrepreneur
Franchise and Business Opportunities
Franchise Handbook

Franchise Times
Franchise World
Income Opportunities
Money Making Opportunities
Opportunity World
Small Business Opportunities
Working Mother

One of the best features of this market is its stability. Many advertisers have been running the same or very similar ads for the same offer for 5, 10, 20, or even 30 years. Once you develop an offer that works, you can live on it for many years.

How to Find Out What Customers Want

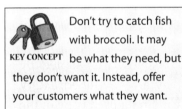

Don't try to catch fish with broccoli. It may **KEY CONCEPT** be what they need, but they don't want it. Instead, offer your customers what they want.

There's an easy way to find out what customers want. Ask! And keep asking. Here are five easy market research steps to identify your markets and figure out the problems they want you to solve.

Easy Market Research Step 1

Do extensive research to uncover the daily frustrations of your market. What everyday things aggravate them the most? What really drives them crazy? For businesspeople, quite often it's employee problems. Lack of new customers. Problems satisfying customers. Problems finding good suppliers. Worries about future trends or changes in the industry. Large companies luring business with low prices. Small companies stealing customers with false promises. Find out what frustrates your potential customers the most. For golfers and other hobbyists, they want the pride of doing their hobby better.

Easy Market Research Step 2

Make sure you have accurate information about the market. How large is it? How many customers are there? Are there regional distributions? How many potential customers do you have in each state? How easy is it to contact this market? Are magazines already being sold to the market? Are there multiple magazines for a particular market? Are there specialties or subniches, groups of people within the market that are interested in more specific programs and ideas? You need the answers to these questions before you can create a product that will sell. In addition, you might find out this market isn't worth creating a product for!

Easy Market Research Step 3

Consider who else has tried to sell something to this market. Have other information marketers offered products to this market in the last two or three years? What products were they? Did they succeed? Are they still in business? Are established competitors aggressively selling to this market already? (While nobody likes a lot of competition, it can be a good sign that this market wants information products and services.) Don't ignore vendors that are not marketing information products. For example, are there equipment manufacturers? Vendors with services? How are they promoting themselves in the market? Which ones are the successful vendors in the industry, and who are the contact people? Are there ways to work with those individuals?

Easy Market Research Step 4

Review any printed magazines or publications within the market. It's worth subscribing to these publications so you can read the same things your customers are reading. Also, contact these publications to ask for their media kits. This will give you advertising rates. And when you ask for these kits, many magazines will send you an issue or two for free so you can review them in consideration of placing your ad. However you get your hands on them, review these publications carefully because they provide insights into what providers in this market believe their customers want.

Easy Market Research Step 5

Look through websites. Research competitors. Research individuals within the market. Uncover the big companies within your market. Find out what trends are happening. Are there mergers and acquisitions? Have new products and services created a buzz? Are large economic factors impacting the market in a significant way? Or if you're researching a hobby niche, what new ideas, technology, and information are affecting this niche?

You need to carefully consider and extensively research your market before you jump into doing business as an info-marketer. This is not something you can short-circuit. Even if you already believe you're an expert in the market, you must go through these steps, conduct this research, find out more information. You'll be glad you did. It can save you hours of time and thousands of wasted marketing dollars. You don't want to market a product people don't want or aren't ready for. You don't want to repeat the mistakes others have made. Find out what has worked and what hasn't. Then you'll be ready to create your product.

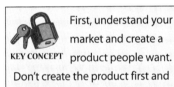

First, understand your market and create a

KEY CONCEPT product people want. Don't create the product first and then try to find customers to buy it.

Too many info-marketers create what they believe is the "world's best information product" based on what they wish had been available to them when they were starting out. Often, they then struggle to find a market to sell their product to. This is backward. Your success depends on understanding the needs of your potential customers and then offering them the product they want.

Chapter 7

How Two Info-Marketers Connected with a New Target Market

BRETT KITCHEN DESCRIBES HIS BUSINESS LIFE BEFORE INFOR-
mation marketing as "worse than working at Walmart."
How he broke out of this job, researched a completely
new business niche, and launched an info-marketing business
is a good illustration of the market research process I outlined
within Chapter 6.

"I was an insurance broker," Brett says. "I sold commercial
property casualty insurance, workers' compensation coverage,
and business liability, that sort of thing. The only thing I liked
about the insurance business is that it got me into the information
business," he half jokes.

"Basically, in the insurance business, you get treated like
a Walmart employee. You have to have your cell phone on 24
hours a day, seven days a week," he says. "Actually it's worse
than being a Walmart employee—at least they get to go home!
When you're in the insurance business, you're the first person
that clients call when a disaster happens. You get calls like 'My
son just killed somebody' or 'My building just burned down; am

I covered?' If you or one of your staff members makes a mistake, and the event is not covered, then you're personally liable. I really got tired of that emotional roller coaster."

He gained additional motivation to make a change in his career when his agency's owners gave him a lose-lose decision to make. "All four of the partners were in it for themselves and really trying to get everything they could out of us," Brett says. "So they restructured the business, basically taking away about 30 percent of the brokers' income, or we could quit. In the insurance business, you don't just quit. If you do, you have to start over from scratch because you walk away from your residuals and have a non-compete with all your customers."

Along with a business partner, Ethan Kap, Brett made the tough decision to quit the insurance business and work on building an information business. "Partnering with Ethan helped in two ways: It was better for both of us if we could share the expenses of starting a company, and we tend to have a lot of synergy, so we get a lot more done together than we do on our own," Brett says.

Brett's best friend had started a furniture and mattress company during the time that Brett was transitioning away from the insurance industry. "My friend ended up going out of business because he didn't know how to get customers," Brett recalls. "That was a red flag to us, and we thought there might be a need in that industry we could address. So, we did our research, read the trade magazines, went to a couple of events, and discovered that the furniture business was an industry in turmoil. That's why we chose it for our information marketing business."

Brett and Ethan carefully considered many aspects of the furniture business before settling on this niche. For one thing, neither of them had experience with the industry, so they needed to have other solid reasons to approach this group. "One of the things we considered was whether or not an industry was currently spending a lot of money on getting customers," Brett says. "Furniture retailers spend a great deal of money on advertising, and we knew we had information that could make their ads perform better and even reduce their advertising costs."

To help build some familiarity with furniture retailers, Brett and Evan subscribed to the trade magazines and attended trade shows. "By reading their trade magazines and going to their events, we learned our potential customers' lingo and began to understand their concerns. That was very beneficial to us," Brett explains.

Brett's and Ethan's time at the trade shows was spent chatting with retailers, uncovering their biggest problems. "There's nothing like being there in person," Brett says. "Through casual conversations, we were able to uncover the furniture retailers' biggest concern. Without question, it was a decline in traffic. Their advertising wasn't working as well as it should. That is right up our alley, so we knew we had a good match."

After researching their niche, Brett and Ethan created a lead-generation direct mail piece that told the story of Brett's friend and his failed furniture business. "The headline was something like 'How my friend Morgan Garrett was left bankrupt, bloody, and sweaty, standing with broken pieces of his company because he didn't follow these three marketing guidelines.' Morgan had actually cut out the inner coils of a mattress and was standing on the sidewalk trying to get traffic into his store," Brett says. "It was July, it was 110 degrees, and he was sweaty and bloody from cutting his hands on those mattress coils. Shortly thereafter, he ended up going out of business. It was a compelling story, and we started generating leads for our box of information on how to improve advertising to bring in more business."

A not-so-successful lead generator was advertising in a large trade journal. Brett explains why his ad didn't work: "Basically, we didn't know the market as well as we should have. We ran an ad with my photograph in it. I looked like I was only 21, and most of the people in the industry are 50-plus. There I am, looking like their grandson, with the title 'Home Furnishings Marketing Guru' under my name. It was totally unbelievable, so we wasted $2,700.00 on an ad that generated almost no response, and it didn't start us out on the right foot."

What they did next runs counter to what most info-marketers advise. They took their photos out of their advertising. "We just looked too young," Brett explains, "so our photos weren't giving us the credibility we needed."

To build their status within the industry, Brett and Ethan exhibited at industry trade shows and got to know people in the business. "I spent at least 70 percent of my day just meeting people," Brett recalls. "I ended up meeting the editor for *Furniture World* magazine, and I offered to write articles for him. It changed our credibility instantly when we started appearing in magazines."

Brett recommends befriending editors in the industry, beginning with local or regional publications. "After you get published in one magazine, the next time you approach an editor, you can say 'Hey, we write articles for XYZ.' That really changes an editor's perspective on working with you."

Another way to get in the door of a publication is through advertising. "If you're going to write in magazines, your best chance at getting in is to spend money with them first," Brett says. "We have found over and over again that if you start advertising with them and then you start asking to write for them, they're much more receptive. You don't necessarily need to continue to advertise with them every single month in order to become a longstanding writer for them. But they want to see your commitment to them, so you should spend a few bucks on ads, start a relationship that way, begin writing for them, and then later you can back off from advertising." Brett warns that the one thing editors do not want in an article is a sales pitch. "You want to send an article that's loaded with content," he says.

Brett says their demographic is 40- to 65-year-old Caucasian men who have conservative values and are extremely skeptical. "They're not a run-out-and-buy-a-product-because-you-want-to-fit-in-with-the-crowd group. In fact, they're just the opposite. When they see our list of testimonials, they'll sit there and call them before they do anything else. They'll look them up on the internet; they'll ask their friends; they'll call all our customers," Brett says, shaking his head. "It's kind of irritating, but that's who they are, so what we have found works absolutely the best for us is teleseminars."

The duo also used small regional seminars to sell their program. "Our first conferences were $50.00 refundable preview seminars where we brought people in from a local radius and sold them into the coaching program. Each time we spoke, we generated a 20-percent closing ratio, so we would get five, six or seven new members that way."

Chapter 8

Information Marketing Is as Easy as Selling Paper and Ink

WHEN MY SON, ROBERT WILLIAM, WAS 7 YEARS OLD, HE proved that sometimes it is easy to create a lot of value for your customers.

I couldn't go anywhere with Robert William unless he had his fans. These were not electric fans. Robert manufactured his fans by pleating construction paper in small folds back and forth. The only motor for this type of fan is your hand as you wave it back and forth in front of your face. Any time we went to a restaurant, a baseball game, or even the grocery, I had to wait while my son ran to his room to manufacture and stuff his pockets with fans for the trip. Only then were we ready to go.

Robert's fan marketing program involved him approaching strangers, showing them the fans, and asking them, "Would you like to buy a fan?" There were three or four color choices. Most folks were pretty gracious, and for a while the fans sold well at 25 cents each.

Well, he tested the price elasticity for construction paper fans and began charging $1.00 each, donating 25 cents of the proceeds to the Hurricane Katrina Fund. Sales increased, and he made three times the money for each fan he sold. For months we were going to the Red Cross office once a week with every fourth dollar to make his donation.

His sister was furious because he was basically manufacturing money by folding up some construction paper and asking people to buy it.

That's not a lot different from what we do in the information marketing business. By taking inexpensive blank paper and blank CDs and packing them full of useful information, you deliver a lot of value to your customers and generate money for yourself.

There are many ways to package information for an info-marketing business. The key word here is *information*. You are not selling the packaging; you are selling the value of the content (the information) within your product. For example, if you package your information in a book, you need to promote your book as an information product. After all, the book itself is not valuable. It's just paper, ink, and a binding. It's the same if you offer your information as a speaker or as a coach. The value to your customer is in the information you provide, so remember that your product is the information itself, not the way you're going to deliver it.

When you are creating a product, your goal is to create something that provides excellent value for the buyer, yet can be sold for 10 to 20 times what it costs you to produce. Information products are almost the only type of product that allows you to sell at 10 to 20 times your cost.

You don't need to have writing or speaking talent to create your own information products. Plenty of individuals have

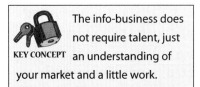 The info-business does not require talent, just an understanding of your market and a little work.

created audio series stuttering all the way through them. Or they have written manuals by struggling through one page a day. Your buyers are not interested in perfect English; they are interested in buying the information you are imparting. It's critical that you understand you *can* create successful information products.

It's also worth mentioning that most kinds of information products can be put together without investing a fortune. Many paper-and-ink products can be produced on an ordinary office photocopy machine or, in small quantities, at the local storefront print and copy shop. I know quite a few people in this business, each earning hundreds of thousands of dollars a year, who make up most of their products as they need them to fill orders.

This section of the book will jump-start your thinking about what you know that can be converted into information products and what kinds of products might best fit your knowledge and markets.

Here is a quick partial list of various information products. You might start with one. You might develop a product line that includes all of them.

41 Types of Information Products

Paper and Ink

1. Reports—one to eight pages, addressing specialized topics
2. Tip sheets—one page, very specialized, very how-to, no fluff
3. Manuals—usually published in loose-leaf notebook or spiral-bound format
4. Books
5. Boxed sets of books

6. Home study courses—may include printed product with other types (e.g., audio, video)
7. Tests and quizzes—self-scoring or computer-scoring
8. Seminar or speech transcripts
9. Newsletters
10. Back issues of newsletters or reports
11. Other continuity products, such as "Book a Month"
12. Sets of cards (e.g., reminder cards, recipe cards)
13. Forms (e.g., time management systems, step-by-step processes)
14. Posters
15. Multi-author publications (several authors contribute to one product; each gets to sell it)

Audio and Video

16. Audiotapes—live recorded speeches, seminars, consultations
17. Audiotapes—how-to instructions, usually studio recorded
18. Audiotapes—interviews, conversations, roundtable discussions
19. Audiotapes—collections of radio broadcasts
20. Audiotapes—interactive, with a workbook
21. Audiotapes—subliminal, self-hypnosis, etc.
22. Videotapes—live-recorded speeches, seminars, consultations
23. Videotapes—how-to instructions
24. Videotapes—interviews, conversations, roundtable discussions
25. Videotapes—interactive, with a workbook

Internet Products

26. E-book—book delivered electronically over the internet
27. Download—customer downloads manuals and audio over the internet after purchase

28. Online videos—entire products are now often delivered through online videos either made using screen shots of PowerPoint presentations or through live-action videos of a live seminar or someone teaching in front of a camera

29. Membership site—customers are allowed to access information on password-protected website

30. Structured lessons—customers are led through a series of lessons; may include examinations

Miscellaneous

31. Trainer kits—multimedia, for use in conducting classes, workshops, etc.

32. Memberships

33. Devices (e.g., stress card)

34. Plaques

35. Computer software

36. "Packages"—of a variety of related information products, offered at a special price

37. Continuity programs involving multiple-information products, multiple media

38. Services—tied to memberships or purchases or used as premiums

39. Customized—to different markets, different clients/users

40. Private-labeled—for other marketers, users

41. Licensed—for republication

The more specifically tailored your products are for your target market, the better. By focusing on smaller niches, more individuals within those subniches will react "That's for me." If after marketing to the same small group for a time, you determine that you need to expand your market, you can do that, but you'll already have a base of customers supporting your new marketing efforts through their purchases and testimonials.

My son also applied this technique. When we went to Florida State University games, he wrote "FSU" on each of his fans. In addition, he tried to bring red, yellow, and black fans to those games. He's not shy; he even brought the appropriate color fans for the visitor's team. That way he had products appropriate for any team a fan was rooting for.

Publish on Demand

You do not need to create large inventories of product before you sell them. As long as you ship promptly, you don't need to manufacture the product until after you receive an order. In many cases info-marketers promote a particular book, manual, or workbook. When they receive an order, they send somebody to the copy machine to produce it. They may have a few blank binders or a few blank tape holders, but when they receive the order, that's when they actually produce the materials, the books, or the audio CDs.

Publishing on demand is especially important when you're starting out. You should not take your initial investment and use it to purchase inventory. You need that money to invest in marketing. Instead, get ready to ship your product, but then manufacture and deliver the product after you've received the order. That's especially important if your marketing campaign happens to be unsuccessful. You don't want to have 632 copies of your book lying around unsold! You should publish only as much as you need, when you need it.

Automatic Implementation Products

There has been an evolution during the last several years in how customers want to receive information products. While books, manuals, and audio CDs still sell very well, one of the secrets of the info-marketing business is to provide as much as possible of the system already implemented for the customer.

A number of years ago, info-products were detailed manuals that taught a process of how somebody should do something. Then that started to change. People wanted more workbooks to lead them step-by-step through a process. Then people started asking for ready-to-go samples and fill-in-the blank examples of the things they needed to do. Most recently people have decided they want everything done for them—and they're willing to pay a premium for it. Now info-marketers are able to create products that are completely turnkey for their customers, literally "done for them."

Let me give you an example of the evolution related to client newsletters. It is well documented that everyday businesses that publish a monthly newsletter, print it, and mail it to their customers experience tremendous increases in customer value over businesses that don't publish newsletters. This monthly communication increases the frequency that customers come back to the business to make purchases, it increases the amount of money they spend with each visit, and it increases the referrals a business receives, an extremely cost-efficient means of acquiring new customers. This rule applies to all businesses, from service businesses like plumbers, carpet cleaners, and auto repair to retail stores to restaurants and even to medical services such as physicians, dentists, and chiropractors. All experience a significant increase in new customers as well as repeat purchases from existing customers when they publish a client newsletter.

Teaching business leaders that newsletters are important is nothing new. Info-marketers have been teaching this for many decades. However, the ways info-marketers teach this strategy have changed, and it's illustrative of the transition many info-marketers are making to help their customers.

- *Popular Product in 1975.* Info-marketers created guides on publishing customer newsletters for businesses. These products detailed the benefits of customer newsletters; provided information on where to obtain or how to write articles; and gave tips for the printing, mailing, and distribution.

- *Popular Product in 1985.* Even though the results of businesses that published newsletters were remarkably good, many business owners never found the time to go through the monthly process of creating one. They just couldn't seem to get the first one out. Or if they did get one out, often there wouldn't be a second issue. A significant innovation for info-marketers was the workbook. Info-marketers created a couple of dozen fill-in-the-blank newsletter templates. This way, the business owner could adapt one to his needs and then publish his own newsletter to his customers. The increase in ease of implementation helped a lot of business owners get better results.

- *Popular Product in 1995.* For many business owners, the templates were not enough. Info-marketers began providing actual newsletters each month, ready to mail. All the business owner needed to do was drop in her own name, print it, and mail it out to her customers. This was a huge innovation because business owners no longer had to go through the creation process at all. In fact, the task became something any administrative person within the office could implement.

- *Popular Product in 2010.* Now customers don't even want to touch the monthly newsletter. In response, info-marketers are creating monthly programs in which the customer gives the info-marketer the customer list and the info-marketer creates content, prints customized newsletters with the business owner's information, and mails them out for the business owner. The business owner never has to think about the newsletter. If someone is ambitious and wants to significantly customize a newsletter, this can be done in just a few minutes a month.

While this example was about client newsletters, this trend has occurred throughout the info-marketing business.

There is a trend away from giving individuals information for them to implement new processes and marketing programs within their businesses to creating monthly products that do all the work for the customer. This is good for the info-marketer because these products create customers who pay every month for a service rather than customers who pay every few years for new manuals and audio programs.

Here is an example of an "automatically implemented" service you may be familiar with. While the weight-loss company Weight Watchers gives you a points system and a log book to track the amount of food you eat with each meal, NutriSystem

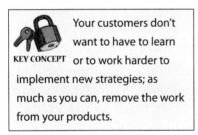

KEY CONCEPT Your customers don't want to have to learn or to work harder to implement new strategies; as much as you can, remove the work from your products.

delivers prepackaged food to your door; all you have to do is eat. NutriSystem is implementing the weight-loss program for the customer by creating menu options, creating meals, and delivering them in ready-to-heat-up packages.

I'm not saying one of these companies is better than the other. Some customers will be attracted to the flexibility of the Weight Watchers program while others will love the structure that NutriSystem offers. As an info-marketer, it is important that you determine which system is in demand from your customers.

Examples of automatically implemented products that info-marketers often sell include monthly newsletters created, published, and shipped for customers; and online staff training systems so managers can let an online computer program train, test, and evaluate their employees.

Specialize, Specialize, Specialize!

When you create your product, the information should appear as specialized as possible. It's critical for your potential customer to look at your product and say "Oh, that's for me. I need that!" You must understand your market and then design your product to be exactly what your customers want. Basically tell them: "Here are the four things you asked for. Here are the four things we delivered." Then they'll say "That's for me" and buy your product.

Don't Fall in Love with a Product

One of the things that trips up beginning information marketers the most is that they fall in love with a product and then want to perfect it. There is no perfect product, and no amount of time you can spend on a product will make it perfect. The definition of perfect is always changing. There's no reason to delay your marketing implementation so you can create the perfect product. Today's perfect product will probably be less than perfect 30 days from now. So, there's no reason to wait, slow up, change, edit, or try to make it perfect. You must make it *done*.

You Must Deliver to Make Money

The most important product, the only product you can sell in the information marketing business, is one you can deliver. Even if it's not the perfect product, even if it's just Phase 1, you must execute it and deliver it.

Once you're selling your product, you can incorporate your customers' feedback and add their ideas to your product to improve it. Too many beginning info-marketers spend months or years trying to create the "perfect" product when in reality the only perfect product is one you can begin selling immediately.

Chapter 9

Essential Ingredients of a Successful Information Marketing Business

FTER YOU'VE DONE YOUR RESEARCH OF YOUR MARKET AND you've decided what products or programs you want to create for it, the next step is to go ahead and begin creating your information marketing business. But what are the raw materials? What are the key elements you need to go into your business? What you need for your information marketing business falls into two categories: 1) the raw materials and 2) the skills.

The Raw Materials

You need three raw materials for your information marketing business: 1) your story, 2) your examples, and 3) proof that what you're teaching works.

Your story is simply how you came to be in the information marketing business. Chapter 2 provides 29 examples of info-marketers' stories. Some of those entrepreneurs are part of an industry and chose to create a product because they are familiar with their industry's needs. Others are industry outsiders who have a skill and have applied it within an industry where that skill had not been applied before. But each of them has a unique story of why they got into the information marketing business and why they are providing the information they do.

Your story is extremely important to your customers. While it might make sense to think that all your customers are really looking for is the solution to their problems and that they don't care where that solution comes from, the fact is your story distinguishes you from everyone else selling the same or similar information. Some people will be attracted to your story when they're not attracted to anyone else's. If you try to hide your story behind a big corporate veil, you are going to miss out on a lot of new customer opportunities.

I have already told you my story of having been in the association industry and seeing how similar associations and their membership programs, meetings, membership directories, and home study courses are to those in the for-profit world. That's why I made the transition to creating my for-profit information marketing businesses rather than the associations I had been building. That's my story, and that's why I'm qualified to teach; I've been in the information marketing business my entire career.

Why are you qualified to teach what you're teaching? What is your background, what is your story? Refining that story is going to give you tremendous help in marketing your information marketing business.

Next are the examples that demonstrate before and after pictures of how your products will solve your customers' problems. You've seen it many times in the diet industry: pictures of people when they're fat and then photos of them when they're skinny. Those photos prove the solution being offered actually works. You need to demonstrate a similar transformation within your marketing. When you're first starting out, your only example may be your own example, so you will tell your story to demonstrate that your solution works. But as you grow, you will want to include additional examples of individuals who have successfully implemented your solutions to prove to your students your program works.

Let me refer you to Chapter 2 again, where I gave those 29 examples of different information marketing businesses. In part, I was trying to explain how the information marketing business works and to illustrate the variety of niches available, but I also wanted to give you several examples of individuals who have created their own businesses to show that you can do it, too. I demonstrated that information marketing is a great way to generate income and to create a business for yourself.

When you create marketing and products for your market, you need an inventory of several examples of individuals who have had success implementing the solutions you teach.

Finally, the last raw material you need is proof. You need to have as much proof that your system works as possible; proof in the form of testimonials, proof in the form of tests, proof in the form of before and after pictures of businesses or individuals that show the amount of revenue they gained or the things they created or the products they produced. You need clear proof demonstrating that what you have to sell really delivers the solutions you say it delivers. Proof is one of the keys you'll need to really maximize the sales you generate within your information marketing business.

The Skills

You need two main skills to be successful in the information marketing business, and the good news is they are both easy to learn. I had neither of these skills before I started working in the information marketing world, even though I had been successful in the association world for many years. While making the transition, I had to acquire those two skills to build my information marketing business. Over time, and with the help of a lot of great resources, I was able to perfect those skills, and you will, too.

The first key skill for your information marketing business is to learn how to do direct response marketing. This is quite different from brand building or other types of marketing. With direct response marketing, you're creating a marketing message and then measuring the number of people who respond to each marketing message. This way you are evaluating each message by its return on investment. You're tracking how much money you invest in buying an ad or publishing a sales letter and then comparing that figure to the amount of revenue generated in new customer sales as a result of that marketing effort.

Creating advertising that provides a good return on investment is critical in the information marketing world. It involves writing effective sales copy, creating ads, and writing attention-grabbing headlines. All these are things you can learn how to do or outsource to someone else. But even if you outsource them to professional copywriters, you'll still want to have the skill of direct response marketing so you can evaluate how well your copywriters are producing the advertising you have paid them to produce.

The second skill you need is familiarity with the available technology. I recently co-authored with Bob Regnerus *The Official Get Rich Guide to Information Marketing on the Internet*, also published by Entrepreneur Press. It discusses everything you need to know to create an information marketing website to sell your products and services online. Within that book, there is no discussion of how to write computer code to build the actual websites. It's not important for you to know how to program a website or how to program a series of e-mail messages that go out automatically after someone visits your website.

It is important for you to know that all those things exist and how the best marketers use them to generate new customers and to encourage existing customers to buy more. You don't necessarily need to know how to program them yourself; you can find inexpensive webmasters for that. But you should know how they work so you can create marketing programs that leverage those technologies.

In that book, *The Official Get Rich Guide to Information Marketing on the Internet*, Bob Regnerus and I show you how to delegate all those activities to a web expert. That's how I run my own business. I don't build any sites or post updates. I provide the information to my web guy, and he does all the work. He does all the programming and makes it all happen.

But because I'm familiar with the technology, I know how to get all those things created in an efficient way. One of the essential skills in the information marketing business is becoming familiar with the technology that's available so you can maximize that technology to generate more customers for yourself and your business.

Before we end this chapter, let's talk about what's *not* necessary. First and foremost are super powers. And I say that with all seriousness. You've gone through eight chapters of this book, and I know I've outlined a lot of information already. What I don't want is for you to become overwhelmed with how much information I've provided you.

Up to this point, I've given you a general description of the information marketing business. Beginning in Chapter 13, I'll provide you with several "recipes" to follow to launch your own business. Think of it as if you were cooking a meal. First, I'd teach you about the ingredients, such as chicken or beef, and what the differences are. I would also teach you about spices and the different kinds of pots and utensils to use. You'd need a basic familiarity with terminology and understand the general process of cooking. This way, when you saw an actual recipe, you would know how to follow it.

That's exactly what I've done in the first section of this book: It gives you a familiarity with the terminology and the overall goals of the information marketing business so when you see the recipes that follow, you'll immediately know how to implement them.

Don't become overwhelmed, don't become anxious or worried that there's too much here. Stick with me for the next few sections, and you'll see how everything comes together. Above all, remember: You don't need super powers to be successful in the information marketing business. Lord knows I don't have any super powers, and yet I've been able to build many successful businesses over the years.

Chapter 10

Where All the Money Is in the Info-Marketing Business

IN THE COMING SECTIONS, YOU'RE GOING TO READ ABOUT SEVERAL recipes that provide step-by-step directions on how to create your own information marketing business, complete with illustrations to show you how the business works. When you read those, I want you to see what the real profit generators are within the information marketing business. The recipes I will share are perfect for helping you get your business from zero to launch with initial success. But these recipes aren't going to take you all the way through the long-term building of your business.

In Chapter 3, I showed you the **Information Marketing Business Pyramid**™. The pyramid illustrates the types of programs you'll transition into once you have your business launched. Too many people who read a book or see a system like this about how to launch an information marketing business try to use the same strategies over and over again to run their businesses. They end up falling behind and are never really able to get the lifestyle they thought they were getting when they started their information marketing businesses.

Some sections within the **Information Marketing Business Pyramid**™ are intended to generate the majority of your business's profits. Other sections are designed to generate a steady flow of new customers into those profit generators.

I want to emphasize that nothing happens unless you are providing great value to your customers. You'll be able to build a long-term business only if you are providing great products and services.

Let me review the key profit generators for an information marketing business so as you create your business, you can keep these in the forefront of your mind and work to build them into your business as you grow it. That way your profitability can continue to grow along with your business's revenue.

New Customer Upsell

One of the key sources of profit in your business is through product upsells to your new customers. Someone who has purchased a solution to a problem is by far the best prospect for selling an additional solution to that problem. You might think that because you have already solved the problem, your new customer won't want anything more. Think of it like this. It's kind of like building a new pool so your family will have a place for recreation in the back yard. After weeks or months of work being done behind your house, the pool is finally ready. You're done, right? Not exactly. Now you need outdoor chairs so you can sit on the patio around the pool. You also need floats, you need supplies, and you need accessories to go with the pool. Even though you just solved the problem of providing summer recreation for your family, you still need to acquire additional products and services to go along with that solution.

Very often it's the same situation within information marketing. After your new customers have invested in a product to solve a particular problem, you will have opportunities to create additional products that provide even more resources, tools, and examples so your solution can be applied to their problem more quickly. So in creating and building your business, you will want to have an automatic system that invites every new customer to invest in additional relevant information and resources.

Once you create your system, you'll need to test it to improve your results. Some information marketers find it's best to immediately invite new customers to invest in additional products. In this case, someone comes to a web form, buys a product, and the very next page invites her to buy an additional product. Other info-marketers have found it works better if you wait for three weeks to invite the customer to buy another product. You'll want to test both options to see what works for you and your business.

KEY CONCEPT New customers are difficult to get. One of the key benefits of operating an info-marketing business is many of your new customers are willing and interested in investing in additional products and services from you. This is a key profit generator for your business.

I know what you're thinking. You're going to go through all this work to create a product, and now I'm telling you the very next thing you need to do to leverage the new customers you just acquired is to go create additional, advanced products to sell to them. But don't worry; once you've created the first product, it's going to be so much easier to create additional ones. If you want to find the real money in information marketing, you need to offer your new customers the opportunity to invest in other products. That way your average customer value will be much higher, and your business will be more profitable. Use systemized upsells to move customers from the bottom of the **Information Marketing Business Pyramid**™, where prices are low, to the top of the pyramid, where you have better margins and are able to provide more value by helping your customers to generate better results.

Group Coaching

Over the past ten years, coaching has become a national phenomenon. Everyone from Fortune 500 executives to the person growing Bonsai trees has a coach to help them do it faster and get better results. Because of that desire for faster and better, coaching has become very lucrative for everyone, including information marketers. One of the challenges of coaching, though, is that the traditional model is one coach and one client. The coach interacts with the client directly, and that does not provide a lot of leverage for you as an information marketer. It's really more of a consulting relationship than it is a coaching program.

Over the last few years, info-marketers have created several innovations within group coaching programs. Group coaching programs allow you to deliver coaching to a lot of people at one time. Instead of having a 30-minute, private one-on-one call with a coaching client every month, you offer a group coaching call that lasts for two hours. All your coaching clients can join the call and ask their questions, so they benefit not only from getting the answers to their questions, but they also get to listen to everyone else's questions, getting advice and input from the other callers as well.

Information marketers used to believe that you could have only 18 to 20 members of a group coaching program participating at one time. The thought was that you had to have smaller numbers to give more people an opportunity to participate. Well, we found that isn't necessarily true. Some info-marketers are

Customers are willing to make large investments in coaching that **KEY CONCEPT** provides them with quick answers to their immediate questions. Group coaching programs allow you to offer coaching to many people at one time so you can make more money by helping many customers.

selling coaching programs with 100 members in them. The members come to three meetings a year, and they work together in small groups. So, instead of these info-marketers being limited to having only 10 or 20 people in coaching, they are able to sell 100 memberships.

A very common price for a coaching program seven years ago was $10,000.00. If you can sell 100 people into a $10,000.00 coaching program, obviously you will generate a greater profit than if you're selling 20 people into the same $10,000.00 group coaching program. Group coaching programs are a very lucrative part of the information marketing business, and you're going to want some element of group coaching within your business so it will be profitable long term and you will have money to reinvest in marketing to generate new customers.

In Chapter 6 you learned about Ed O'Keefe with Dentist Profits and how he came to choose dentistry as the market he wanted to serve. See Figure 10-1 for a couple of the group coaching programs Ed offers to dentists so you can see the types of benefits info-marketers often offer to get and keep their coaching program members.

Seminars

Another primary profit generator for the information marketing business is seminars. Even in today's connected, social media, technology world, customers still want to get together. They want to come to meetings, see you face to face, and learn from and interact with you in person.

Even in a big group environment, where there's one you and 500 or 5,000 registrants, going to a seminar is still very appealing to your customers. In the information marketing business, it's not unusual to offer seminars with a $1,000.00, $1,500.00, or even $5,000.00 registration fee, so you can see that offering those

Ed O'Keefe's Inner Circle

Member Benefits

FOR THOSE INTERESTED IN DOING WHAT THEY DO FASTER, EASIER, AND MORE PROFITABLY!

'Silver' Inner Circle Membership at $450 per month.

Participation in Silver includes:

- Ed O'Keefe's Monthly Insider Marketing Newsletter
- Access to the "Members Wealth Portal" virtual masterminding on our exclusive Web-based forum with access to audio/video training modules
- Access to downloadable, customizable, successful ads being run by other dentists all across the country. Get what's working and get it now!
- Monthly Exclusive "Ed O'Keefe Interviews . . ." CDs
- Weekly Insider Marketing Tips via fax
- Three live coaching calls with Ed every month
- One special Closed Door Meeting with Ed and the other Silver Members per year
- 2 H3 Marketing Critiques

'Gold' Inner Circle Membership for $850 per month.

Participation in Gold includes every benefit offered in Silver, plus:

- Customized Consultations with Ed; Gold members get two customized consultations each year where Ed will record his answers at your fingertips
- Two private emergency access calls per year to get immediate answers from Ed
- Our Monthly "Magical Smiles & Motivational Mentor" Patient Newsletter, free for one year
- 5 pre-arranged private phone consultations per year
- 3 Closed Door Meetings per year with Ed and the rest of the Gold Members
- 6 H3 Marketing Critiques
- Free Tuition to the Ultimate Dental Practice Profit Explosion Super Conference
- Exclusive access to all celebrities brought in to our live seminars

FIGURE 10-1. Ed O'Keefe's Dentistry Offer

Ed has more than 700 members in his Silver level. This ongoing monthly revenue allows Ed to do a lot of marketing to encourage new dentists to join his programs, with plenty of profit left over.

programs can generate a lot of cash for you and your business. Not only that, at the seminar you have an opportunity to offer additional resources and products to your customers.

Think about it. If they come to a seminar and learn about a new strategy they really like, what's the likelihood they're going to be able to run home and apply that strategy within their own lives? Probably pretty small, but if you offer them a product that gives them a step-by-step resource to help walk them through the process of implementing that strategy, their chances of getting a good result will increase substantially. That's why seminars are so important, and offering additional products and services at your seminars can be a valuable revenue generator for you and a results generator for your clients.

KEY CONCEPT Even in today's super-busy, technology-driven world, customers still want to attend seminars so they can separate themselves from their everyday pressures to focus their attention on learning new solutions to their everyday challenges.

And finally, those seminars are a great place to launch a group coaching program. There you have a large group of your best customers sitting in front of you, ready for you to offer them your coaching program. In fact, this is one of the models I will walk you through in Section V. If that sounds intriguing to you, keep reading, and you'll get a lot more information on how to use seminars to help you launch your coaching program.

So those are the three key profit drivers within your information marketing business: product upsells to new customers, group coaching, and seminars. Keep in the forefront of your mind that you're going to use those profit generators as you grow your business because they will help you become more successful more quickly.

Chapter 11

Determining What to Charge for Info-Marketing Products and Services

ONE OF THE BIGGEST MISTAKES BEGINNING INFO-MARKETERS make is creating products that provide inadequate markups from cost to retail. Info-marketing businesses depend on large gross profits from sales to succeed. The rule of thumb is that your markup should be at least eight to ten times from your cost to retail. That means that a product that costs you $1.00 should sell for at least $8.00 to $10.00. Any markup less than this will not be economically feasible, in most cases. And this is a conservative figure. What we *prefer* to see is a markup that's twice that high, that is, 15 to 20 times. Ideally, an item that costs you $1.00 will sell for $15.00 to $20.00.

Defining Cost

I told you about my son's paper fan business in Chapter 8. Robert used to walk up to people and speak too softly or take no too easily. However, selling construction paper fans isn't as easy as you might expect. Yes, of course, you have to follow all the principles of getting attention and using persuasion, but there is a lot of competition out there as well as some sales resistance. It is a big task to sell a fan, and you cannot take it lightly.

It's the same for info-marketers. A lot of research and work go into pricing your product properly; you can't shortcut this step.

Before you can use the above markup objective to figure out what an item's selling price should be, you have to accurately calculate what the item actually costs you—which is not quite as simple as you might think. An item's cost is a total of:

1. The manufactured or wholesale cost of the item
2. The inbound freight you pay to get the item or the component parts that make the item shipped to you
3. Some factor for any miscellaneous costs you incur in getting the item made or delivered, such as auto expense in driving to the supplier's place of business, long-distance telephone communication with vendors, etc.
4. Packaging for the item to prepare it for safe shipment from you to the customer
5. Shipping cost to deliver the item to the customer

There may also be other factors particular to a given product or business that need to be added into the total cost. You have to carefully analyze your product and every step of your business process to identify each of these factors.

Determining the Selling Price

Once you've established an accurate cost, you should multiply it

1. by 8
2. by 10
3. by 15
4. by 20

Then consider each of those possible prices. How does the price compare to competitive or similar products already being marketed to your prospective customer? How does the price compare to the value the customer will receive from the product? Can the customer see that the price is a good value?

Many times, the impracticality of the price will rule out the product. Don't ignore this warning signal. If an eight-times markup creates a price that is too high to be saleable, the product is simply not suitable for your first information product.

Sometimes, a product may warrant a price that is even higher than cost times 20. When this occurs, you've got a number of great options. You can sell the product for the higher price and enjoy a superior markup; you can afford more expensive advertising and marketing; or you can market

> **KEY CONCEPT**
>
> No one can guess the perfect sales price before offering a product to a market, but more info-marketers go broke from underpricing their products than they do from overpricing. High prices allow you to do more marketing, and price is one of the last concerns on your customer's mind.

your product at the 20-times price and offer the consumer a superior value.

Study what other information marketers are doing within other industries. In the end, the only advice for making pricing decisions is to pick a price and test it.

In one of my monthly continuity programs, I tested two different prices. The first was $39.95 a month, and the other was $49.95 a month. Every other visitor who visited my website saw one of the two prices. This way I could study whether price made a difference in sales and also how long a member stayed in continuity at each price. For my market I found that slightly fewer people purchased at the higher price, but both groups stayed in continuity the same length of time. But even though slightly fewer people bought at the $49.95 level, I made a lot more money because of the additional $10.00 per month per customer.

When you are launching your business, you'll have to use your best guess as to pricing, making sure your prices are high enough to give you large enough margins to enable you to fund a large investment in marketing. As you grow your business, you'll have opportunities to test different prices to make sure you are generating as much profit as possible from your new business.

Chapter 12

The Best Way to Launch Your New Info-Marketing Business

F OR YEARS I'VE HEARD THE QUESTION "CAN YOU CREATE A step-by-step outline of how to create an information marketing business?"

My answer always had to be "No." Different people bring different experiences, needs, and expectations to the business. For instance, investing $50,000.00 to $100,000.00 to create a million-dollar-a-year business is an easy decision for some. After all, it's a better return on investment than you'd get from a Subway franchise, where the best you can hope for is $50,000.00 a year from each store you own. Other new info-marketers can't conceive of investing that amount of money into a new business. All they have to invest is $5,000.00 or even $500.00 in their new ventures.

Since 2006, I've hosted a monthly coaching call for members of the Information Marketing Association. Every month IMA members call in for advice and help growing their existing businesses or launching new ones. With the goal of answering this step-by-step guide question, I read through the transcripts and listened to those Jump Start Coaching Calls, more than 53 hours of recorded audio.

I analyzed the recommendations I gave members during those calls and discovered a collection of dependable launch models I've been recommending for years. While I can't provide one step-by-step process, I have been outlining five different launch models through those calls. I've documented those five models to provide you with the easiest and most effective info-marketing launch models. And within this book, I provide the step-by-step processes to follow once you choose the best launch model for you. I provide you with a decision tree to choose the best model for you and your business. However, I recommend that you read all the launch models as part of your research.

Each model creates the same business. Whichever launch method you choose, you are still building the same **Information Marketing Business Pyramid**™. It's just that each launch method takes a different path to the same destination.

Figure 12-1 is a quick guide to help you decide which launch model is best for you.

Use this chart as a guide only. Life is complicated, and there are many variables. While I've attempted to provide you with some key factors to consider, you should trust this chart about as much as you trust those relationship surveys in the women's magazines. Consider this chart as one of the factors but not as the only factor in choosing the best launch model for you.

Now that you have an idea of which launch method is best for you, allow me to explain each of them in Sections II through VI. In addition to the detailed step-by-step instructions, I have included several profiles so you can see how each business works. Think of it this way: If I were going to explain how to use a hammer, I'd have to describe the shape of the hammer, where to hold it, how to hold the nail, and where to hit the nail with the hammer. But you still wouldn't know exactly how it works until

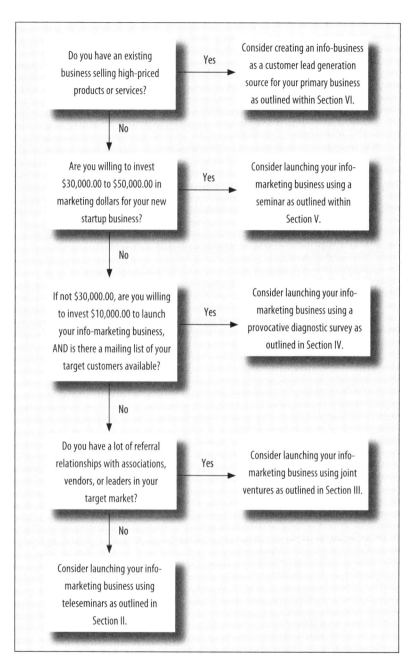

FIGURE 12-1. Which Info-Marketing Launch Model Is Best for You?

I actually demonstrated it by striking a nail. When you see an example, then it's easy to see how something works.

That's the purpose of the info-marketer profiles, to show you how a business works rather than merely explaining it. As you read the profiles, note the similarities and differences, carefully documenting what works for each business.

Many of the profiles include exhibits. To stretch my hammer analogy even further, these exhibits are like my showing you a house so you can see what you are able to build with a hammer and nails. The exhibits are important visual examples of the types of documents and items you are going to be creating as you implement your info-marketing business launch.

After I show you the launch models, in Section VII I'll explain some business issues that apply to all models and a bit of "what's next" to transition from business-launch mode to business-building mode. Until then, enjoy learning the best ways to launch the most lucrative and fun business there is.

The Cheap and Easy Way to Launch Your Info-Marketing Business

Chapter 13

An Easy Way to Get Paid to Create Your First Information Product

A N EASY QUICK-START FORMULA FOR LAUNCHING A NEW INFO-business is to have a teleseminar series. Let me take you through the steps.

First, you need to select a topic that is of particular interest to your niche or market. Then you can break that topic down into four or five topics by asking yourself a simple question. For example, if it's marketing for plumbers, ask yourself, "What are the five things plumbers need to know to market their businesses better?" Then create from your answers five really good titles that describe what you think plumbers must have when they're launching and marketing their businesses. Possible topics could be about creating service contracts that sell, effective ways to answer the phone, money-making Yellow Pages ads, how to talk to customers while in their homes, and how to get referrals from satisfied customers. Developing the content for these calls isn't as difficult as you might think. You simply outline four to five bullet points that address each topic and explain what the call will be about.

The next step is to select a date ten weeks in the future. Circle that date on your calendar because you're going to have your teleseminar about Topic No. 1 on that date. You'll cover Topic No. 2 the next week, and so on, for a total of five weekly calls.

Now you're ready to create a marketing piece. Continuing with our example, the headline might be "Everything a Plumber Needs to Get More Customers Each Month, A Five-Part Teleseminar Series." In the body of your marketing piece, you will list the five topics, with four or five bullet points for each one. You will also explain that you are going to record the calls on CDs so your customers will be able to review the content at any time. When your customers send payment, you simply send them the telephone number and access code for the calls.

Finally, you need to decide on a price. I usually tell my clients to charge $100.00 for a five-week teleseminar series. That amount for five different calls is very inexpensive, so price won't be an object when you are promoting and selling your first teleseminar series.

You have your topics, you have your marketing piece, and now you're ready to begin marketing your teleseminar series. You don't have to use a marketing service, and you don't have to worry about setting up any fancy businesses or doing any additional paperwork. You have a page, maybe two pages, of what you're going to do. You're conducting calls on these dates. When people register, you'll send them the access information to the calls as well as a copy of the CD after each call is recorded. You could probably sell your series for $495.00, but for now, let's sell it for just $100.00.

Now, using all the resources in your industry, the contacts you've met, the different industry events you've been to, the speakers you've heard, and the industry's association, begin promoting your teleseminars. You can send your marketing piece to the association and say, "I'll give you half of the $100.00

registration fee, or we can increase the fee to $495.00 and I'll give you everything except $100.00 per registration if you sell it." You can also promote your teleseminar through speaking at industry events or purchase a list and send out e-mail or postal mail marketing.

The point is to use the ten weeks between now and your first teleseminar to promote the series in different ways in your target market. Even after the series has begun, you can continue to promote the series by sending follow-up marketing that says, "Hey, we have two calls already recorded, and we'll send you those immediately. The rest of the series will be delivered via teleseminars during the next three weeks."

Using teleseminars allows you to launch your business now, get paid immediately, and have your product created in the next ten weeks. That may seem overwhelming to you, but let me tell you why I recommend doing it this way. It's time for a true story.

It was July, and I was on vacation, a few months after a big Dan Kennedy information marketing event. I decided I was ready. I was going to launch my own info-business. I decided I was going to get up and be at the office every morning by 6 o'clock and work for two hours on my information marketing business. The first five weeks I spent creating products. I wrote an outline of the products I wanted to offer, I created an order form, and after a while, I created several of the items for the kit I was going to sell.

After about six or eight weeks, a regular work project would come up, and then on maybe two of those mornings a week, I was working on a client's project instead of on my new business. After all, this was paid work, so I should go ahead and do it, right? It wasn't very long after that, maybe 12 weeks, and I wasn't working on my info-product at all. I had made a lot of progress in August and September, but when January came, I wasn't any further along than I had been in September.

Then I met a guy who had been at the same Kennedy seminar that had inspired me to start working on my info-business. It was in May, a year after the seminar, and I still hadn't made any more progress since the big push I had made during the previous August and September. But this guy had already made $100,000.00 with his new information marketing business! And I thought, wait a minute. He and I went to the same seminar. He and I learned about this business at the same time. He's made $100,000.00 already. He's got a business with customers he can sell other things to and a product so he can sell another $100,000.00 in the next 12 months. And I still have nothing.

Here is what I did. I set aside three days in the middle of

the last week of May to create my sales material. I wrote a 32-page sales letter and my lead generation advertising. By July, my ads were generating leads, and I was making sales. Yes, I still had to create a product, but I can tell you, when you have actual customers asking for the product and checks

KEY CONCEPT — Teleseminars allow you to get paid to create a new product. Within a few short weeks, your new product is complete, and you'll gain a lot of insights into your market from the questions your participants ask during your teleseminars.

arriving in the mail, it is immeasurably easier to get the product done!

That is why developing a teleseminar series in ten weeks is a great way to create an information marketing business. You set a date ten weeks out. You develop five topics with five bullet points for each one. You write an attention-grabbing headline and put a statement at the bottom of the page saying you will send out the CDs of all the calls at the end of the series. Then you ask for $100.00.

Even if you sell only five of them, that $500.00 will force you to prepare for those calls every week for five weeks. And when you're done with those calls, not only will you have something to send to the people who bought your teleseminar series, but you also will have a complete information product. And you can sell that product for several years to earn money over and over again on something you did once. You will have learned much from those calls about what people want, and the marketing you do over the next ten weeks is going to tell you a lot that you don't know already.

If you follow this quick-start formula for creating a teleseminar series, you will have information, you will have a business, and you will have customers. Maybe it will be five, maybe it will be 50. It doesn't matter. Using teleseminars to launch your business is a great way to generate customers and create an info-product quickly.

Chapter 14

Marketing Strategies to Sell Registrations to Your Teleseminar Series

A CONFERENCE CALL SERIES IS EASIER TO SELL THAN A PRINTED product home study course, an audio program, a membership site, or even an in-person seminar for three reasons: 1) the content feels more current and timely, 2) audience members expect, or are hopeful of, the opportunity to interact with you, and 3) there is a firm buying deadline.

Whenever you are promoting your teleseminar series, you want to emphasize the fact that you are offering new and current, never-before-available content, because that's one of the greatest benefits of participating in a teleseminar series. The information is so timely, so relevant, that there hasn't been time to put it into a package or a home study course. This is one of the secrets to positioning your teleseminar series for success.

Now, of course, you and I know that you are in the very act of putting this together as a home study course that will be relevant for many years to come. That's the entire point of you even having the teleseminar. But at this juncture, you're not going to mention the home study course; limit yourself to selling registrations to your teleseminar series.

As you promote your teleseminar series, emphasize how new, relevant, and exciting the content is to encourage as many people as possible to register immediately so they won't miss out on getting these new and timely updates.

In addition to providing timely information, teleseminars can be an interactive way of delivering educational content to your audience. With a home study course, you're creating it once and then shipping the same product, sometimes for many years. With a home study course, there's no easy way for a buyer of the product to interact with the producer or the author. It's the same with seminars; with so many people in the seminar room, very often the presenter isn't able to provide an opportunity for participants to interact and get answers to their particular questions.

Teleseminars can be a very intimate way to deliver information because although it might be you and several other listeners on the line, each listener does have the ability to ask questions and make comments during the call.

However you decide to balance your call between information delivery and questions and answers, you certainly want to emphasize within all your marketing materials that you're going to have open Q&A opportunities for your listeners so they know they will be able to get the help they want.

I recommend having the Q&A at the end of each call. That way you can provide the lesson, walk through all the handouts, do all your teaching, and then open up the call to questions and answers after you've spoken for an hour or so. Then for your home study product, you can have the audio editor making your CDs simply edit off the Q&A period, and that way you have all your great teaching as part of your product.

If you want to repackage some or all the Q&A and provide that to your members, there's no harm in that. But if you want a straight home study course that sounds like it was purposely built as a home study course, then you can simply do your Q&A at the end of your call and still provide the opportunity for folks to get their questions answered during your teleseminar series.

Teleseminars are easier to sell because they provide timely information and a way for customers to interact. They also have a firm buying deadline. There's a natural deadline because your teleseminar series starts on a certain day. On that day, the customer either buys the series or begins missing out. That natural deadline gets more people to buy. Very often when you're thinking about buying a home study course, there's no real incentive to getting it now instead of waiting for later. Most of the time if you wait for later, you pretty much never buy it. Having a certain date when your teleseminar is going to launch provides a firm deadline when someone either needs to register or miss out. So that's one nice benefit of having a teleseminar: You're going to increase your sales just because there's a deadline.

Now as I mentioned in the previous chapter, it is perfectly fine for you to continue to sell your teleseminar series after you've begun delivering the series. Certainly, you want to emphasize the deadline during the sales process, but then even after the deadline, you can follow up with those who didn't buy and say, "We missed you on our last two calls. Here is what we covered. We'll send you those calls on CD, and you can still benefit by participating in the next few calls." That's a great way to convert customers who are on the fence and need just a little more nudging to buy.

 KEY CONCEPT Teleseminars are easier to sell than home study products because there is a firm buying deadline (the start of your teleseminar series), your buyer has the opportunity to interact with you, and the content appears more current and timely.

As you promote your teleseminar series, you can use any marketing vehicle you know of to get the message out. I'm going to list a few easy marketing strategies in case you're just starting out and don't have a lot of resources or if you don't have copywriting experience or a team of people to sell the program for you. These aren't the only ways you can promote your teleseminar, but these ideas will help get you started.

The one-page handout described in the previous chapter is a great place to start. It has a big headline of what your teleseminar series is going to provide your listeners, the title of each of your modules, three to five bullets about each module, a price, and a way to sign up. With those simple elements, you have the handout you need. It is also good to include some information about yourself, a little biography, some information about why you're qualified and particularly knowledgeable about the topic. With that, you have all you need to begin promoting your teleseminars, and it will fit onto just one or two pages.

When you're promoting your teleseminar series, include a note in your registration materials that you will provide the recordings of the teleseminars on CD for all registrants so if they are not able to dial into the program live, they can listen to the program on audio CD. I have found this greatly boosts the number of registrants because they don't have to dial into every call to receive the content and they're not as disappointed if they miss a call.

In the times I've seen other people *not* promise the recordings, they've always ended up having to provide the recordings anyway because they had so many disappointed subscribers who, for whatever reason, missed a call and were frustrated that they weren't able to get the information. If you're going to end up having to provide the recording in the end anyway, you might as well sell it upfront and promote it as a benefit of registering.

In terms of a website, I would create a very simple website to start, really limited to the information you're including in your one-page handout. If you want to post a video or an audio file, all the better, but again, I want to keep this very simple so you can start making money quickly without having to do a lot of additional work, such as learning website programming or finding a webmaster.

In terms of getting your message out there, one of the most effective things I've seen is sending e-mails to colleagues and competitors in the industry. You can tell the story that you've been getting a lot of questions about how you do things, and you've finally agreed to create a teleseminar series to answer the five most common questions you've been receiving.

You also can work with your industry's association or trade journals to promote your teleseminars. I know if a member of one of my associations comes to me to help promote a teleseminar series, I am happy to do it. If you've been a member for a while and you tell them you've been getting these questions and want to offer a discount to association members to participate in the teleseminar series, you'll find them pretty cooperative. Now the trade journals are primarily interested in trying to sell you advertising, but if they see you as a small business and probably not a prospect for advertising in the future, then they may very well send your information to their subscribers, publish it in the journal, or send a special e-mail. You won't know until you ask.

Another strategy is to invite vendors in the industry to promote the calls to their customers. It might even be worth naming one or two of these vendors as sponsors in trade for them helping you promote your series. Think about who else is already selling to the individuals within your industry and find out if you can work with them to promote your program to their customers. You can consider naming them as sponsors and/or giving them access to the teleseminars' participants after the series ends. But very often, they might be perfectly happy to promote your teleseminar series simply because it gives them an excuse to be helpful to customers within their market. Again, you might offer a discount for customers of a particular company so that company will be more eager to promote your teleseminar series.

You should also leverage any additional relationships you have within the market to encourage others to promote your program. This group includes everyone you're talking to, whether they're from an association or they're vendors or even competitors. They don't need to know the teleseminar series is part of a new business venture you're creating. They only see that you're creating a series of teleseminars about a particular topic, and so you might find them very cooperative, even though they might be less cooperative were they to realize you are going into business for the long term.

Keep in mind you can have a successful teleseminar series even if you have only two or four registrants. Of course, you'd rather have 40 or 400 paid registrants, but even if you have only four, you still are getting paid to create the teleseminar, which ultimately becomes your product. You were going to create a product anyway. Now you actually are getting paid to do it, and you have people to listen to it and ask you questions so you will know how to improve the modules as you go. So certainly, I want you to have 40, 400, 4,000 registrations for your event, but even if you have only four, consider it a success because it gets your business started.

And then finally, this exercise of promoting your teleseminar series is a great tool for building your list of potential customers. As you're interacting with people and you're sending e-mails, save the e-mail addresses. If you don't have a customer relationship management system, often called a *CRM*, to manage all your names and addresses, then at least keep them in a spreadsheet or a Word file so you can put them into a database after the call and after you're making some revenue. But for now, capture all those names and addresses because they'll be a valuable resource as you launch your home study product. Every name is going to be valuable to you, even if they don't register for your teleseminar or promote your teleseminar series, because when you make your home study course available, they might become your customers then.

Chapter 15

Producing Terrific Calls that Also Create a Great Information Product

OW THAT YOU'VE SOLD YOUR TELESEMINAR SERIES TO paying customers and your date is approaching, you actually have to plan and deliver the calls you promised. I purposely didn't tell you about that before! It's always good to sell a teleseminar series with a date certain, but not get into a lot of the details of planning the actual content until the seminar is upon you. That way you are able to focus on selling the teleseminar series before you transition into the product creation side of your new business.

Here are some tips and insights to get your teleseminar series done quickly and easily so that it takes as little work as possible.

First, the beauty of having a weekly teleseminar series is that you can create the teleseminars as you go. You don't have to create all five programs on one afternoon and then try to record the audio. Instead, you can create one teleseminar each week. It's a great way to create content because it spreads it out over time and into bite-sized pieces so the entire project doesn't overwhelm you.

The first step for creating your teleseminar is to write an outline of what you plan to teach. You can start with the title of your first call and the three to five bullet points you used for marketing it. I usually plan for an hourlong call, but it's fine if it goes 45 minutes or 70 minutes. One audio CD holds an hour and 17 minutes' worth of audio. Just keep in mind that if your module is less than an hour and 17 minutes, then you can fit it onto one CD. If you plan to distribute your series digitally or as a digital download, then you don't have to worry about the length. Either way, I highly recommend offering the audio because, as I covered in the previous chapter, it greatly increases the number of buyers because they're not as concerned about missing calls.

After each call, you're going to have a question-and-answer period. The nice thing about the Q&A is it gives you immediate feedback on your teaching. If you've got quite a few people with questions, then you know you need to provide more details within your teaching, perhaps in one of your next modules. Questions also give you some insights into what your listeners understood and what they may have missed in the information you taught.

Once you've built the outline, you should add promotions throughout the call. At the beginning of the call, you want to resell your listeners on participating in the call. I understand they're already there, but what you want to do is promote what you're going to say during the call. Think of it as being similar to the nightly news. At the beginning of the program, they give you a nugget of a news story, but then they quickly get into what's coming up later in the broadcast. "We're going to tell you this story, we're going to tell you that story, and then we're going to show you this. And then we've got the weather." And they might even throw in a little tease about what the weather is.

You want to do the same thing within your teleseminar. At the beginning of the call, you're going to say, "Welcome to the program. These are the things you're going to learn about during the next hour . . ." You can even go through your bullet points or some of your outline, but either way, talk about what's coming up next.

To keep your listeners on the line throughout the call, you need to insert "teasers" about what you plan to cover later in the call. These teasers keep people interested in the program. They perk up and think, "Oh, I want to hear that."

Similarly, toward the end of the call, you want to promote what you're going to talk about the next week. For example, "The next program is titled XYZ, and this is what we're going to talk about." Now I purposely used the word *program* instead of teleseminar because if you're going to turn your teleseminar series into a product, you may want to use the terminology *program* or *module* rather than the term teleseminar so it sounds as if you're recording a program for a home study course rather than for the audience on the call. It's up to you, but I usually prefer to keep it more generic because that way I can use the audio for many years.

> **KEY CONCEPT**
>
> With a teleseminar series, your product creation work is spaced out by creating just one module a week. Use that week to prepare your notes and your handouts for participants. Include promotions for future modules to keep everyone excited about what's coming up.

Consider creating handouts for your call. You've created an outline for yourself. Some version of that outline is appropriate for the participants in your program. Provide them notes with important key terms and the main things they need to know. You can give them worksheets or exercises that help them implement what you are teaching. If you're teaching them how to do something, consider giving your participants a step-by-step list of things to do, or ask them to answer a couple of questions that will help them implement what you're teaching. You can also provide examples in your handouts that will help your listeners better understand the concepts you are teaching.

If you begin to feel a little overwhelmed, perhaps needing some additional answers or additional content to flesh out one of your outlines, feel free to bring in one or more guest experts. An expert can be someone you interview for the entire program, or you can bring her on for only 15 minutes.

For example, if the call starts at the top of the hour, you can invite the expert to call in at 20 minutes after the hour. That way you can begin the call, present a portion of your content, interview the expert, and then continue the rest of the program. You aren't obligated to have the expert with you for the entire hour; simply have him deliver the content you want provided, give him recognition for participating in your program, and then let the expert go so you can finish the topic.

One thing I want to emphasize is this: As much as possible, include your own stories. Really put yourself into this program. If you have suffered challenges, if you have suffered setbacks, if you have a lot of experience implementing what you're teaching, include those personal stories. I can't stress this enough. Really put yourself and your story into your program.

People magazine has a circulation of 3.75 million subscribers while *Newsweek* has a circulation of about 1.9 million. That tells you what the American populace values. They value stories about people and people's lives. So be sure to include those in your program. Whenever you're teaching something, tell a story that illustrates your point. A case example involving you or your client or even someone you've observed is going to be a lot more effective than trying to simply teach the lesson.

Following these guidelines will help you create a terrific program that's going to help you build your business while you satisfy and excite your teleseminar's registrants.

Chapter 16

Using a Teleseminar Series to Launch Your Coaching Program

I'T'S BEEN SEVERAL YEARS AGO NOW, BUT I FINALLY UNDERSTOOD this concept when I heard Bill Glazer say it during one of his info mastermind meetings: "Whenever we sell a new customer in information marketing, we always want to figure out a way to make that sale a stream of sales rather than a one-time event."

In most businesses, you simply are trying to make a sale. You want to get a customer. She buys something, you give it to her, and she leaves. In information marketing, we want each new customer sale to set up additional sales to that same customer. See Figure 16-1.

So here is what you want to think about when planning your teleseminar series: How can you get the individuals who have registered for your series to buy the next product you're going to offer?

One of the easiest things to offer as a brand-new information marketing business is a coaching program because it doesn't require a lot of preparation. If you're selling a product or a home

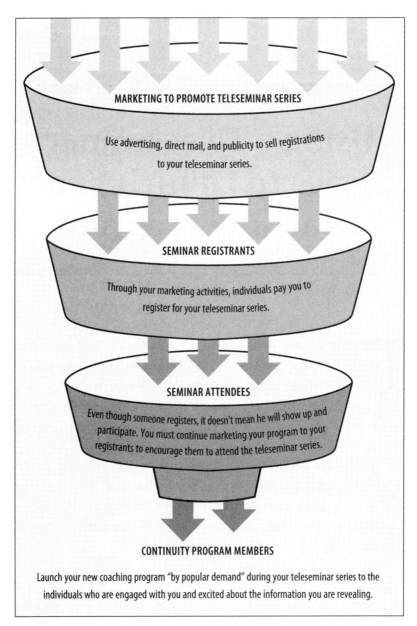

FIGURE 16-1. Marketing to Promote a Teleseminar Series

This figure illustrates the marketing process for launching a coaching program through teleseminars. You have fewer numbers as you move from the top to the bottom of the funnel.

study course, you actually have to create it. A coaching program is something you create as you are coaching students, so you don't have to do any work creating the program in advance. In your teleseminar series, in addition to the great content you provide, you also want to provide your registrants with an opportunity to participate in your coaching program.

For a five-week teleseminar series, in week two, after you have given the content portion of the call and before you open it up to Q&A, say "Over the last several weeks, I've had quite a few people send me e-mails and ask 'Can I get personal coaching? Is there any way to get more help? Is there any way to talk to you for an hour about what I'm looking to do and get your advice and input?' As a result of all those requests, I'm going to create a coaching program."

> Individuals who invest in your teleseminar series are great prospects for a coaching program. Invite your teleseminar attendees to participate in your new coaching program to receive personal assistance with implementing what they are learning.
>
> **KEY CONCEPT**

Then you can go through the benefits of what you're going to deliver within the coaching program. You can choose to name a price, or you can direct your listeners to send you an e-mail or visit a website for more information. Then you can schedule a telephone appointment to sell them the program.

After you promote your coaching program, say "Thank you. That's our program for today, and now we're going to go ahead and open this up to questions and answers." Then you go right into Q&A.

In week three of your teleseminar series, instead of waiting all the way 'til the end, you go ahead and talk about the coaching program at the 45-minute mark. So in between the content, you say, "Well, you know what? I still need to tell you about this, this, and this, and I will in just a moment. But first, I want to let you know that I've had quite a few folks ask me for more personal attention in getting things implemented more quickly, and I'm responding by creating a brand-new coaching program to help you. This is a great way for you to get these things implemented more quickly, and it will help you get breakthroughs and achieve success faster." And you go ahead and talk a little about the coaching program, and then you get back into the content.

Then in weeks four and five, I would go ahead and make the suggestion about the coaching program at the 30-minute mark. Rather than doing it toward the end, go ahead and talk about it in the middle to let folks know you have a program. I wouldn't spend a lot of time promoting your coaching because you've got to make sure you deliver the content your listeners paid to receive, but it's fine to let them know about the additional help and resources you have available should they want to get your personal input, advice, and help in getting the principles you teach implemented more quickly.

Once you are done with your teleseminar series, this becomes the Introductory Product block of your **Information Marketing Business Pyramid**™ (Figure 16-2). This launch exercise becomes an important long-range part of your info-marketing business. Plus, when you structure the calls so they offer your group coaching program, this introductory product helps you build the Group Coaching Program block of your pyramid at the same time.

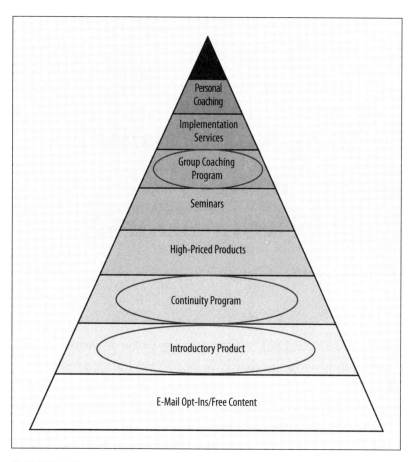

FIGURE 16-2. After you complete your first teleseminar series you have members in your coaching program and you have an introductory product created.

Chapter 17

Why Not Webinars Instead of Teleseminars?

ERSONALLY, I ENJOY WEBINARS AND I BELIEVE WEBINARS ARE A better learning experience than a teleseminar presentation, but there are a few reasons why I'm recommending that you use a teleseminar series as your first option for building your information marketing business.

First of all, a teleseminar series is easier to produce. Rather than having to create a PowerPoint presentation and then figuring out the technology to broadcast it from your desktop and working through all those details, it's really just a matter of creating an outline and getting on the phone and talking. So the logistics are much easier.

Second, it's easier to record the call because the teleseminar service can take care of it. With a webinar, very often you have to hook it up with your own computer or have someone else in your office record it. That's fraught with peril, including such problems as walking off and forgetting the screensaver is on. When that happens, there's ten minutes of you and your webinar, and then the rest of it is the audio of you talking while the screensaver displays photos of the family vacation! Having the teleseminar service record the call, while not perfect, can be much more dependable.

Finally, it's easier to create a product out of a teleseminar than it is a webinar. With a webinar, you either have to create video DVDs or offer the video online so customers can see the slides, or if you transition a webinar into audio only, your listeners will hear you describing things they can't see. For someone starting out, it's easier to begin with a teleseminar because the preparation is easier, the technology of delivering the call is easier, the recording is easier, and the transition into a product is easier.

I have had several coaching clients start out with a webinar, and their first few sessions were challenging. In addition to

> Webinars are a great tool, but if you are just starting out, you will **KEY CONCEPT** have several logistical challenges to overcome. It's better to start with teleseminars and move on to webinars once you've become more experienced.

creating the content and delivering it with all the teasers and coaching program promotions, they had to deal with several logistical details.

Webinars are just a little more complicated, so here is what I recommend: Let's crawl before we walk, then walk before we run, and then we can run. Let's start with teleseminars. It will give you a great experience. It is a great way to create a product. Once you have that process down, you can examine whether or not you want to transition to webinars.

Chapter 18

The Shortcut to Turn Your Teleseminar Series into a Product

I COVER PRODUCT PACKAGING IN A LOT MORE DETAIL IN CHAPTER 52, but here let me brief you on the particulars of taking the materials from a teleseminar series and preparing them as a home study course.

One of the first things you'll need to do as you plan your teleseminar series is to choose a teleseminar company to host your calls. You have many to choose from, and pretty much all of them offer similar services. In fact, there's even FreeConferenceCall.com, where you can have your call hosted for free. That's a perfectly fine option; you just need to make sure you become familiar with the resource and how it works because you won't have the use of an operator unless you upgrade to the paid service.

I use VoiceText.com to handle my teleseminars. While VoiceText.com is not the cheapest teleseminar service, I have had very good success with it. I use a paid service because I want to have an operator assist me during the calls. The operator is useful because he can listen to each call as it's happening and make needed adjustments. For example, if a guest speaker or a caller has a noisy line or is so quiet he is hard to hear, the operator can correct the problem so it doesn't interrupt the flow of the call. Or if someone drops off the call, the operator can call her back so you don't lose the opportunity to get the call completed. Having a call operator is like having a partner while you are doing the call, and it makes the whole process a lot easier.

The teleseminar company will record the call if you ask for this service when you make the reservation. When you request the audio file, you can ask for two versions; one that has the entire session and another that has the question and answer portion deleted. That way you won't have to get a separate audio editor to make those changes later.

Once you've completed your teleseminar series, you have the recordings as well as the handouts and examples you provided to your registrants. Now you are ready to create your product.

Put your handouts into a binder with tabs for each module. Then have the teleseminar audio burned onto CDs using a professional service or your own computer. Package the CDs in a separate box or, even better, use a clear plastic holder that snaps into the binder. That way when you ship the product, everything is in the binder to make it easy for your customer to go through the lessons and then put it on a bookshelf to return to later.

That's how you turn your teleseminar series into a product. You simply take the recordings of the calls, add them to the handouts and the examples you provided to the participants of your calls, and package them together as a home study course. That's all there is to it.

Chapter 19

Best Way to Launch Your Info-Marketing Business: Teleseminar Series

---

T HERE ARE MANY BENEFITS OF LAUNCHING YOUR INFORMATION marketing business by offering a teleseminar series.

First, you quickly discover if your product idea is a real opportunity or something you want to kill quickly. If you offer your teleseminar series to people who already know you, your contacts and relationships within your market, and they don't immediately jump on the opportunity to sign up, then you should think, "Wait a minute; maybe this isn't such a great idea after all. Maybe there isn't as much pent-up demand for this content as I thought there might be." And so offering a teleseminar is a way of researching your market. It's a great tool that can help you fine-tune your product.

Another reason I like teleseminars is because they're immediate. You can begin marketing your teleseminar today. Before you go to bed tonight, you can send an e-mail with your five teleseminar topics and three-to-five bullets for each of those topics, tell everybody it's 99 bucks, and see what they say. If you hear nothing but crickets, well, maybe it's not such an in-demand thing as you thought. If you get a lot of response and people want it, then fabulous.

The third reason why I like teleseminars so much is because they motivate you to take action. When I created my first product, it took me a full year to get started. Most of that year was spent getting ready to create the product, not really doing anything, just getting prepared. I spent a lot of time thinking about it and not doing it. And then when I actually did it, it took only a few weeks of concerted effort. I just had to find the discipline to work instead of procrastinate. Fixing a certain date when you're going to deliver your teleseminar series allows you to focus first on marketing, and then once the date has come to provide your first teleseminar, it forces you to prepare and deliver your product.

That brings me to my fourth reason: faster product development. With a teleseminar series, the product development is nicely spaced out over several weeks. You work on only one module at a time, so it's not too much to do at one time. Yet you get your product done more quickly. From what I've seen, the folks who create a teleseminar series first get a home study product created sooner than the people who try to do it without a teleseminar series. It just a faster way of getting your business launched.

If you refer back to the **Information Marketing Business Pyramid**™ introduced in Chapter 3, you will see that at the end of your teleseminar series, you'll have an Introductory Product completed you can sell and you'll have your Group Coaching Program launched. This puts you in terrific position to move from the launch phase of your business to the growth phase.

While teleseminars have several benefits, there are also some limitations. One of the downsides is you are offering your teleseminar series for a lower price point than you would normally offer a home study course. While your potential customers see the content as new and fresh and perhaps really want it, most of the time these products go for $100.00 or maybe $199.00, but rarely more than that. If you took the same information and put it into a fancy home study package, you might get as much as $995.00 for it in some markets.

Books share this downside. The book you're holding sells for $24.95, even though the content, if broken out, would be worth thousands of dollars because it has never existed before now. But there is a perceived ceiling of what books are worth. Customers

 KEY CONCEPT Although you aren't able to sell your teleseminar series for higher prices, it is a great way to get your product created and to gain important insights from your target market.

aren't going to walk into the bookstore and pay $3,000.00 for a book. There is a price ceiling, no matter how valuable your content is, because of the media. Just as with a book, with a teleseminar you will be limited by the amount you can charge.

Another downside to teleseminars is that they are not the best vehicle for selling a coaching program. Certainly, you can sell coaching through your teleseminar series, as I discussed in a previous chapter, but it's not as effective as some of the other launch methods I will outline later in this book. By far the best program to launch a successful coaching program is to host your own in-person seminar. Having that live interaction gives you a relationship that will sell more people into your coaching program.

To summarize: When you choose the teleseminar series to launch your business, you get faster market research, you get faster product development, and you force yourself to get started. However, you're giving up some pricing by offering your product as a teleseminar rather than as a home study product or a seminar. Plus, it's tougher to sell as many teleseminar listeners into your coaching program than if you used one of the other launch methods.

Even so, I recommend the teleseminar series launch because it will get you started making money quickly, you will learn a lot, and you will be able to move on quickly to the next phase of your information marketing life.

You should have everything you need to get your info-marketing business launched from this book. But I often find some people benefit from seeing additional examples and details. That's why I created the **Information Marketing Business Pyramid**™ to give you more examples, more step-by-step resources, and worksheets to help you get your information marketing business launched through teleseminars.

Within the **Information Marketing Business Pyramid**™, I provide you with several more resources for turning your teleseminar into a product: worksheets to help you create great teleseminar titles and bullets that make people really want to register, more sample marketing pieces from actual teleseminars, as well as examples of teleseminar series that you can look at and learn from. That expanded content couldn't fit within this book. If you like what you've read here, you should check out the **Information Marketing Business Pyramid**™. There's more information at **InfoMarketingPyramid.com**.

Allowing Others to Launch Your Info-Marketing Business for You

Chapter 20

How One Info-Marketer Launched His Business Using Joint Ventures

L ARRY CONN TOOK WHAT HE LEARNED IN COLLEGE ABOUT advertising and marketing, applied it to his carpet maintenance and water restoration business . . . and failed.

Larry discovered that the Yellow Pages' publisher's goal is to make the Yellow Pages an unbiased resource for consumers. "What they mean by that is, in a perfect world, all ads will perform equally well," Larry says. "I have a totally different interest—I want my ads to outperform my competition!"

At first, Larry listened to the ad reps and used what they recommended. The results? Ads that blended in . . . and ads that produced "blended in" results.

"When I began studying direct response advertising and what should be included in direct response ads, I began venturing out and trying other things," Larry says, "and these new ideas dramatically improved the response to my ads."

The transition into selling information was a natural next step for Larry, who had always wanted to be an information marketer. "I saw the value in being able to turn a piece of paper into, say, $10.00 instead of just its normal value. I had thought about doing that since I was 30 years old."

Larry's fortunes took a turn for the better when he saw an ad by Joe Polish in a carpet cleaning publication. Larry sent away for Joe's free report and began his search for why this idea wouldn't work either. "I read his letter over and over and over. I really wanted to find the flaw in the letter," Larry says, "but what was really overwhelming was the number of testimonials that Joe had. I just kept reading those testimonials over and over and over."

Joe's system cost $500.00. "I thought nothing could be worth $500.00," Larry laughs, "but it had a 100-percent money-back guarantee. I figured I would buy it, and then once I saw that it wasn't what I thought it was, I would mail it right back."

He didn't mail it right back.

"When I read Joe's materials, I knew it was the information I had been seeking for the last ten years," Larry says. "I couldn't return it, and I have been on a better path with better mentors ever since."

Larry used Joe's materials to help build his carpet cleaning business and regularly participated in Joe's conference calls. One of those calls changed Larry's life.

Larry recalls, "One day, Joe says, 'I want to do something special for you. I'm going to call you back after the call. I'm going to give you an hour of consultation for free.' And so, he calls me up and says, 'Larry, you know more about Yellow Pages advertising than anyone I've ever met, and you should be creating a product for that media.' I knew the minute he said it that it was really the divine guidance I needed to get on the right topic."

Joe interviewed Larry for his Genius Network Interview Series, "which was a great, great launch pad," Larry says. "It was kind of a spark to the beginning of my business, but at the time

I had no product, and so doing the interview didn't generate me any sales because I had no product to sell!"

Larry knew he had to create a product, or any publicity he received from doing interviews would be a waste of time. "I asked myself what I wished I had known when I first had to sit down and write ads. I thought about the complete novice advertiser and created a 'fill-in-the-blank, by-the-numbers' way of doing print advertising."

Of course, creating that first product wasn't without its challenges. "I was a single parent at the time, and so any of the time I wasn't at work, I was raising my daughter," Larry explains. "I really had to take advantage of a gap in my commitments. There was a time when my daughter was going to be gone for a couple of weeks with her babysitter, and I had a little window where I could sit down and write. At the time, I had never created a single page on a computer. I did not know how to type. And I didn't have the money to pay someone else to do it for me."

Larry didn't let any of that stop him: "I had to just sit down and say, 'You know what? Today's the day. I don't know how to type. I don't know the program Word, but today's the day I'm going to start learning.'"

Larry sat down and started writing, "just biting it off one chunk at a time," as he puts it. Hunt-and-peck letters formed words, words became paragraphs, and paragraphs turned into pages. Two weeks later, Larry had his first system—and it had 20 chapters! "I had set a deadline that it had to be done by the time my daughter got back because I wasn't going to have any more time. And sure enough, by the time she got back, I had developed some typing skills and knew how to do things in Word, at least enough to get it down on the page," Larry smiles.

In addition to those 20 chapters of hard-fought, personally typed words, Larry included CDs and a little something extra to put his mind at ease: "My greatest fear was that someone would get my system and put together an ad that should've been a little better than it was, and that it would go to press," Larry says. "And then, it would either come back on me, or they wouldn't be getting the results that they deserved."

Larry designed an ad evaluation process in which his clients go through the process of writing the copy and laying out their ads and then send them to Larry. "I review the ads pre-publication to make sure that we catch any weaknesses or response killers before an ad gets out there and the client is making payments on it every month for a whole year."

Larry launched his first product as a joint venture with Bill Glazer and Dan Kennedy. How did that come about? "I had been doing monthly consulting with Dan, so I just asked," Larry says. "I figured the worst they could say was 'no.'"

Joint ventures ended up being a very good way for Larry to promote his products, especially because he didn't have a lot of money to invest in his business. "When I started, I was very strapped for cash and wasn't very happy to hear Bill Glazer tell everybody in the audience that it would take a minimum of $40,000.00 to launch an information marketing business," Larry says ruefully. "So, I got some advice from Dan Kennedy about how to make it brain-dead simple for people to accept doing a joint venture with me.

KEY CONCEPT Joint ventures can be a great way for you to launch your new info-marketing product; however, you'll need to do the work necessary to make it easy for your hosts to promote your products to their customers.

"I knew that the vast majority of info-marketers have some sort of CD interview every month, so I made an interview template to make it brain-dead simple to interview me. All they had to do was ask me the questions and listen to the answers, add whatever input they had, and the interview would be done."

Larry soon discovered that he needed to stand out from the pack to get his fellow info-marketers to respond to his JV invitations. "Initially, I thought that by just e-mailing them and faxing them, they'd be so delighted to hear from me that they'd immediately respond," he chuckles. "What I found is that these guys are really busy, and you've got to stand out from the clutter. Some responded to the e-mail or fax, but I got a better response when I started FedExing packages. I love to end with a question because it opens up some dialogue. I end my letter with something like 'What would be the best information we could give that would have tons of value for your members?'"

Larry used joint ventures to find out which markets would be most responsive to his program. "Not all markets perform equally well or as you think they're going to perform. By doing joint ventures, I was able to differentiate ones that would be very responsive to my system from ones that turned out to be not very responsive to it," he explains. "There's a code on the name line of the order form that tells me which joint venture each order is coming from. I learn something from every JV I do."

Chapter 21

Joint Ventures and Using Them to Launch an Info-Marketing Business

O NE OF THE UNIQUE THINGS THAT HAPPENS WITHIN THE
information marketing community that doesn't happen
in any other business or industry to the same extent is
that competitors work together to sell each other's products. In
the "normal" business world, you rarely see two competitors
coming together to create a product they can each sell to the
other's customers. However, in the information marketing
world, these "joint ventures" are common. Joint ventures allow
two people to work together to create revenue where there was
none before.

A good option for starting your information marketing
business is to work with an information marketer who is already
serving the market and the customers you are seeking to serve.
At first you might think your product would be completely
competitive, but the idea is to create a noncompetitive product.

Refer to the example of Larry Conn's business in the
previous chapter. He created a product teaching people how to
write Yellow Pages ads and offered it to Joe Polish's customers.

Joe already taught about Yellow Pages ads and included a few examples within his kit directed toward carpet cleaners. However, Joe's kit was a lot broader than that, and the Yellow Pages ad strategy was only one of about 30 different strategies Joe taught. So, Larry's product that spoke only to Yellow Pages advertising didn't compete with Joe's product. Instead, Larry's offer enhanced Joe's product because people who really liked what Joe was teaching and wanted a little more information or detail about Yellow Pages ads could use Larry's product to get those details. Larry and Joe's joint venture is a great example of how two people working together can create a product out of nothing and money out of nothing.

Let me back up a little bit and go through how this joint venture process works. You start with a host info-marketer. This host is someone who already has a product and a market and is selling products and services to that market.

It's a challenge for expert info-marketers to keep up with the level of demand customers have for new products and services. Suppose a customer comes to an info-marketer and buys her introductory product and then buys Product A two months later, Product B six months later, and Product C four months later. That info-marketer has had to create quite a few products, and when her customers have purchased all her products and still want more, she may not be able to create another new product.

If you come along with a product idea, a way of serving some of the host info-marketer's customers in a more elaborate or detailed manner, she may be interested in helping you sell some of your products to her customers. It doesn't take money out of your host info-marketer's pocket. She probably wasn't going to create that product herself. If she's able to work with you on a revenue share basis to offer your product to her list, then it's easy money for her without having to invest any time into product development. For you, you get to generate sales without having to invest money into advertising.

The most common revenue-sharing agreement for joint ventures between a host and a product's developer is each partner receiving 50 percent of the revenue. The host who promotes your product to her list will usually pay for any marketing expenses and any costs of distributing the sales materials to her list. Those are the typical investments on the part of the host. The person who is providing the product will pay for all product fulfillments. This person will create the product, pay for any graphic design, and do anything else necessary to ship a finished product to the buyers, including the box the product is shipped in.

KEY CONCEPT A 50/50 split is the most common revenue-sharing formula for joint ventures, with the product's creator paying for the costs of product creation and fulfillment.

While a 50/50 split is common for home study products, there are different standards for continuity programs. The revenue split for monthly continuity programs is closer to 25 percent for the host and 75 percent for the product's creator. This revenue split recognizes that the product's creator has ongoing expenses of fulfilling the continuity program.

You may be worried that a 50/50 revenue split on home study products is a large amount of the revenue you generate. However, chances are you would have invested that amount or more on advertising, direct mail, and internet traffic generation strategies to sell your products upfront. With a joint venture, you are working with someone who already has done that work, already has a relationship with a list of customers, and often will be able to give you ideas and strategies on selling the product that you wouldn't have thought of because your host has more experience with the market. Your joint venture partner is paid for generating sales, and so you pay nothing out of pocket if that person doesn't actually generate some sales for you in your business.

Chapter 22

The Key to Joint Venture Success: Make It Easy to Work With You

YOU NEED TO PREPARE SEVERAL IMPORTANT THINGS BEFORE A host info-marketer is going to be interested in working with you. Assuming I have convinced you that using a joint venture is another effective way to launch your information marketing business, let me take you through the steps you will want to take to get your business off the ground.

It's easier to find joint venture partners to help you market home study products or services rather than continuity programs. Most established info-marketers are already delivering one or more continuity programs to their customers. While a product sale is OK, they may become concerned about overloading their customers with too many monthly payments. Products such as a traditional home study course will be more popular with your potential joint venture hosts, and you'll see those hosts embrace such products more readily than another continuity program.

The first step is to create your product sales materials. These can take several forms: sales letters, website landing pages with affiliate tracking, teleseminars, webinars, etc. You are responsible for creating any marketing that's necessary to sell your product to your host info-marketer's customers. For example, if you plan to do a teleconference call with your joint venture partner's customers, then you need to write the script for the presentation and create all the marketing for the call. You want to make it so easy for your host that all she needs to do is send the invitation to her customers and show up on the call. Whatever type of marketing you plan to do, you need to have those materials done before you ask for a joint venture.

If someone came to me with a product and provided half-completed marketing materials, I'd call off the entire deal. I charge tens of thousands of dollars to create marketing systems for new info-marketing products. I'm not going to do it for free for a joint venture partner. If you want to sell something to a joint venture partner, then you need to come prepared with all the marketing necessary to sell that program to your partner's customers.

Now that you've created a product, you've identified some potential joint venture partners, and you've created marketing materials for marketing your product to customers, you need to create marketing to encourage your potential joint venture partners to become interested in working with you. The purpose of this marketing is to communicate to your potential partners why a joint venture with you will benefit their customers, to provide information on your background to demonstrate your expertise, and to give them some information on what they can expect to earn by endorsing your program. Your marketing should answer these questions: How is this program going to help your joint venture partner's customers? What problems does it solve, and in what ways will your program make that info-marketer into a great hero with her customers?

Finally, you will need to follow up with your potential joint venture partners. These people are extremely busy. They're running their own businesses, and they have continuity programs they need to fulfill. They have products to ship, new presentations to create, and seminars to promote. And remember, they got into this info-marketing business so they can enjoy a great lifestyle. They aren't interested in having a bunch of conversations with people who aren't prepared and serious about making a joint venture a complete success.

Even if your product is something they are interested in, they may have trouble fitting it into their schedules. That's why it's important for you to follow up with your potential joint venture partners. If you're creating a joint venture program around a specific date or event, then you need to have plenty of lead time so you will have time to follow up several times. If you don't hear back from them, don't let that slow you down; go ahead and follow up again. And here's one more tip: I often send joint venture proposals via FedEx. I've found this is the best way to get people's attention and to demonstrate you are serious about working with them.

You'll need to create all the marketing materials to promote your product to your host info-marketer's customers. The easier you make it to promote, the more likely your host info-marketer will be willing to work with you.

KEY CONCEPT

While you can have success in reaching potential partners with sales letters, e-mails, or phone calls, it may be helpful for you to join their coaching programs, attend their events, or attend events where you know they are going to be so you can see them in person. Over and over again, I have seen great joint venture programs created between a person who sponsors a coaching program and two or three of that person's coaching members. The reason those coaching members are able to get preference comes down to one thing: relationship. The coach knows them and trusts them, and so is more willing and eager to work with them than with someone who has made a cold call with a joint venture idea.

The key to getting joint venture partners to work with you is making it easy to work with you. You need to create your product, develop all marketing materials for your product, send a sales presentation to potential partners letting them know how they and their customers will benefit from your program, and then follow up until you find the joint venture partner that will make your joint venture program a big success.

Chapter 23

How To Go from Zero to Seven Figures with Zero Advertising

W E OFTEN HEAR ABOUT INFORMATION MARKETERS TAKING their direct mail businesses and transitioning them to work on the internet. Brett Fogle with Options University is doing just the opposite, going from selling e-books online to using direct mail, other media, and joint ventures to build his business into a full-scale information marketing business.

Brett's primary market is people who have identified themselves as being interested in stock market trading or options trading. "Options are hot right now," says Brett. "I started an advisory service three years ago for options, and it didn't really take off. So, I temporarily walked away from trading and delved into internet marketing."

Brett established two criteria for his info-marketing business: 1) He would sell an information product, and 2) the market would be people with a large amount of disposable income.

In just two years, Brett has been able to grow his business from zero to over seven figures in sales per year. "That's with zero advertising!" Brett exclaims. "I've done it exclusively through joint ventures."

Brett approached a well-known internet marketer, Steven Pierce, who was also in the stock arena. He had a very successful product called Fibonacci Secrets™. Pierce turned down Brett's initial proposal, so Brett tried his promotion with a lesser known info-marketer who was happy to do a joint venture deal.

Once he had results to show Pierce, the two were able to launch a joint venture that did very well. Brett leveraged the success of his first two JVs to land more deals. "Joint ventures are a very effective way to get started," Brett says. "For anybody who is getting started in information marketing, and specifically online, I would recommend JVs as the easiest and best way to do it."

For example, Brett has an exclusive marketing deal with a brokerage company that pays a five-figure fee every quarter for referring all his leads to the firm. He also taps businesses that want access to his customers to sponsor seminars and events.

Brett started with e-mail blasts to promote his joint venture program. He provided ads that his partners could send out to their e-mail lists. "Two years ago, that was enough," Brett says. "As things have become more competitive and people are bombarded with more advertisements in their e-mail, it's getting harder to get e-mail delivered." So, Brett decided to try something more creative.

He found that his teleseminars were "incidental" to his success. The real value was in the excuse it gave him to e-mail the customer three, four, or five times. Here is how it works. Brett's joint venture partners send an e-mail that says to "look for an e-mail next Tuesday for a special announcement you're really going to want to see." This initial e-mail pre-sells the message. Then on Tuesday, the JV partner sends an e-mail saying "Here's where you can register for a free teleseminar we're having on

Thursday." The e-mail includes short copy of a testimonial with a strong headline to sell the customers on registering for the call. Then on Thursday, they send out another reminder before the call. They record the call so on Friday they can send another e-mail that says "Just in case you missed it, here's the replay for sale." On Sunday an e-mail goes out letting customers know they have 12 hours left to buy or there are only 20 copies left.

To maximize attendance on the actual call, Brett asks for a telephone number and sends a voice broadcast 30 minutes before the call: "Hi, this is Brett. I just wanted to remind you about our call tonight. It's going to be really valuable, and here's why. In case you don't have the number, here it is again. Also, check your e-mail. I just e-mailed it to you."

> Having a sales telese-minar and a series of promotional e-mails **KEY CONCEPT** ready for any new joint venture made it easy to work with Brett, and it made his joint venture offer effective at generating sales when he was given the opportunity.

Brett has found he receives many of his sales through the product descriptions and calls to action within the teleconference reminder messages. Call registrants read those e-mails for updates or additional details about the teleseminar they've signed up for. Many choose to purchase the product before they even participate on the call. Not only does this method create sales before the call, but it also increases conversions during the call itself.

Chapter 24

The Importance of Product Pricing When Offering Joint Ventures

---

O NE OF THE BIGGEST MISTAKES I SEE BEGINNING INFO-marketers make when they are creating a product for joint ventures is they price it too low. They think that by offering a product for $100.00 or $200.00, they are creating great value for a potential joint venture partner's customers, and they are working hard to give a lot of value for a very low price. However, within a joint venture, if the price is only a few hundred dollars, that does not provide very much revenue after revenue sharing.

Imagine yourself as a potential joint venture partner. If you had a large list of customers and you could work with someone who has a product that sells for $199.00 or someone with a product that sells for $1,199.00, which one are you going to endorse? Well, you're certainly going to look hard at the $1,199.00 product because the sales price will generate a higher return on the time you invest into the joint venture.

Don't be afraid of charging a fair price for your products and services. You might even find that you need to increase your price by bundling in additional value or by creating additional programs to boost your product's value so that joint venture partners are more eager to work with you.

Chapter 25

Simple Changes Multiplied Product Price Four Times

ERSUASIVE-SPEAKING EXPERT SUSAN BERKLEY REVISED HER product to create something that supported a higher price point. A former radio personality and well-known voice on TV and radio commercials, Susan is one of the voices that says "Thank you for using AT&T," and she is the voice of Citiphone Banking.

Susan originally sold her audio product Voiceshaping: How to Find Your Million Dollar Voice—seven audio CDs and a manual along with a copy of her book *Speak to Influence*—for $195.00. She thought this product was so comprehensive that it never occurred to her that she could add on to it and make even more money.

Then she discovered Dan Kennedy and realized that selling a $195.00 product was not going to allow her to maximize her information marketing opportunities. One of those opportunities was to take advantage of her speaking skills to become a platform salesperson. Because platform sales often require a higher-priced product, she needed to add components to raise her price significantly.

Susan renamed her product The Magnetic Speaking Power System, adding a new product, Magnetic Self Confidence, which includes four CDs. She created this product by interviewing experts about the psychological causes of a lack of confidence and the fear of public speaking. These interviews give her program more depth because the psychological component makes it unique.

Then she created a two-session program, called a *vocal makeover*, which was recorded as teleclasses. After that, she added Vocal Vitality, two CDs created with a top speech pathologist about voice care, with demonstrations of vocal warm-up exercises.

To enhance the selling component, she interviewed Art Sobczak of Business By Phone to create Magnetic Telephone Selling Power, a 60-minute CD about selling by phone.

Then she added three bonuses: 1) a certificate for a personal 30-minute, one-on-one teleconsultation with Susan and a written critique of the customer's outgoing voice-mail message, 2) a three-month trial membership in a continuity program, which includes a monthly CD of an interview with an expert on persuasion, communication skills, or voice, and 3) a certificate good for a quarterly review of the customer's voice or presentation. The package, if purchased separately, would cost $1,894.00. Online, it is available for $795.00, or four monthly installments of $205.00.

Susan has sold this program through several joint venture relationships, often adding a special bonus for each group. For Loan Officer Success, she interviewed seven industry superstars to create Billion Dollar Secrets of the World's Most Successful Mortgage Brokers. For Mike Crow's Millionaire Inspector Community, she created Speak to Influence for Young Adults as a relationship-building tool and included a reprint license with a private branding opportunity.

After getting coached by Dan Kennedy on her platform selling presentation, she was excited to sell over $100,000.00 worth of product in 90 minutes. In Susan's words, "It was probably the best 90 minutes I ever had in my life. But the best news is I met many wonderful people who will hopefully remain customers for life."

Chapter 26

Eight Easy Ways to Get Others to Endorse You and Your Products

L ET'S GET INTO SOME MORE DETAIL ABOUT THE DIFFERENT ways you can work with joint venture partners to promote your products to their customers. I'm going to go through a few of the options you have and also outline what you will need to have when you approach other info-marketers if you plan to work with them in one of these ways. It is not necessary that you create all the materials for every one of these joint venture options. I'm giving them to you as a menu and letting you choose which ones you think are the best fit for your market and your potential joint venture partners. For each option, I will give you an idea of what your potential joint venture partners will expect from you when you contact them.

Endorsed Mailing

This is the classic way of creating an endorsed relationship between you and your joint venture partner. In this scenario your joint venture partner sends out a sales letter from you, typically with a cover sheet from the partner that describes you. It gives the info-marketer's endorsement and encourages customers to review the materials enclosed. These types of packages have been around for decades, and I have used many of them successfully.

To create an endorsed mailing package, you will need a sales letter with all the information necessary to promote your product. You also should prepare a letter from the joint venture partner endorsing you to the customers.

Don't forget the envelope! You should have teaser copy on the outside that tells customers what's inside to encourage them to open it. Go ahead and design the envelope while you're creating the other sales pieces to control as many of the variables as possible and to make sure the mailing goes out quickly and smoothly.

For endorsed mailings, you need a minimum of three things: 1) a sales letter, 2) an endorsement cover letter, and 3) an envelope that invites customers to open it.

Endorsed E-Mail

E-mail is a simple way (and today it's the most common way) to endorse a joint venture partner. In this example your partner who has a list of customers and their e-mail addresses sends an e-mail on your behalf that promotes your product, service, or website to the customers. In this case, you will need to have a landing page website for your product for your joint venture partner to direct customers to visit.

In the software on your website, you need to have a way of tracking which leads come from which info-marketer. In the beginning this might be very easy because you might be working with only one or two joint venture partners. As you grow, however, it will become important to have your webmaster install affiliate tracking on your site. Most of the software that creates shopping carts for online purchases also does affiliate tracking.

Affiliate tracking allows you to create a unique link for each of your partners to send to customers. When a customer uses a joint venture partner's link to access your website, that partner gets credit for any resulting sales.

Guest on Their Teleseminar

Another way to reach your joint venture partner's members is for you to be a guest on the host info-marketer's teleseminar. Most info-marketers have a monthly call for their members, either for coaching or as part of their continuity programs, and they're constantly looking for guest experts to talk about particular topics. Your expertise will make you a great guest for an info-marketer's monthly teleseminar that targets your market. Actually having a product to sell will make you doubly attractive to an info-marketer in search of a guest expert.

For these types of opportunities, you should have a call already outlined with the questions you want the info-marketer to ask you so you can provide answers that make the case for why that marketer's members should invest their money in your product. If at the end of the call you're going to give out a website address where customers can go to get more information, you need to have a sales letter with the details of your product set up on that website.

Speaking at Their Seminar

Whenever info-marketers offer seminars, they're always looking for something new and exciting to offer their customers as a way to encourage them to attend. No matter how wonderful an event is, most customers do not want to attend precisely the same seminar a second time. Info-marketers have to keep innovating to create new content or to put new spins on old content to make their events relevant, fun, and interesting so people continue to attend.

You might be the solution to an info-marketer's problem. As a guest speaker, you must create a presentation that provides good information and new insights, as well as makes your product available at the end of the seminar. You need to pay special attention to the design of these programs and make sure you're able to deliver a successful sales presentation as well as impart useful information.

In addition to the materials you will need for your talk, such as slides or a PowerPoint presentation, you should have an order form distributed during your presentation so that customers who like what they've heard during the seminar can take action to invest in the product you are offering.

A word of caution: Info-marketers that host you at their events are going to be very concerned that you might try to work around them to get access to their customers. Do not ask customers to subscribe to an e-zine, give a website address, or direct them to do anything other than fill out the order form and turn it in at the back of the room. If you're in a joint venture arrangement as a speaker, you need to funnel all customer contact through the order form. Your order form is the only way someone can contact you as a result of hearing you speak at your host's seminar. Review your presentation and be careful that you're not including anything that could concern your host.

Product Insert

Another great way to generate new customers for your products is to have an info-marketer insert your sales letter or lead-generation device into a product he is already sending to customers. This can be a monthly newsletter, a home study course, or even a digital download product. Your host info-marketer has already gotten them as customers, so including a sales letter or other materials that promote you won't take anything away from that info-marketer. In fact, your materials will provide an additional resource or tool the info-marketer can use.

If you're going to approach an info-marketer about using a product insert, be sure to have that insert available for her to review. If your sales letter is a long one or is best explained using videos, consider using a lead-generation device to direct customers to a website to get the rest of the story.

Thank-You Page

Here is a joint venture tool you may not have thought of: Why not ask an info-marketer to feature your product on the thank-you page of his sales website? Typically when customers place orders on a website, they fill out all their information and hit submit. Once their credit card is approved, they're taken to a page that says "thank you very much for your order." This is a great place for your host to feature your product.

A benefit of having your offer on this page is that you're talking to your host info-marketer's new customers, the ones who have just purchased something. They are excited about receiving new information, and now they're immediately being invited to go to your website to get even more new information. It's a great way to reach out and get new customers. A side benefit is that most info-marketers don't change their thank-you pages very frequently. Once you get that position, very often you're going to keep it for quite a while.

If you're planning on working with an info-marketer by having her post your information on her thank-you page, then you need some sort of lead-generation advertising that drives customers to your website as well as a sales process that converts them from visitors into customers. If you're going to go that route, you need to work with a copywriter or create those items yourself before you approach potential host info-marketers. That's the first thing they're going to want to see.

Banner Advertisement

An easy way to generate traffic to your website is having a banner ad on a host's website. You will need the following things to do this:

First, you will need the banner itself in the correct sizes for the websites that are going to host your ad. There are dozens of graphic designers online that will create banner ads for you.

Second, you will need a unique link for each host info-marketer so that when someone clicks on a banner ad, the lead is tracked and credit is given to the info-marketer whose banner directed that lead to your website.

Third, you will need a website sales process that converts visitors into customers. This way when your host sends traffic to your website, those visitors turn into customers for you.

Promoting Your Own Event

If you've always wanted to create your own event or there are no speaking opportunities available at a host info-marketer's event, then there's no reason why you can't produce your own seminar for your market. As a bonus, you can invite other info-marketers to sell seats to your seminar. It's smart to approach a joint venture partner with an offer such as "I'm offering this seminar, and I'd like to have you participate by selling registrations to people on your list. You won't have to do the work of producing a seminar, but you'll still get to earn the money."

Let them know you are producing the seminar whether they promote it or not. This way it's in their best interest to promote it and get paid from something they don't have to produce. You can even position it this way: "Your customers are going to attend one way or another. If they register because they heard about the seminar through you, then you get paid." It's a win-win-win: The info-marketer gets paid, his customers get a resource they wouldn't otherwise have, and you get new customers.

Here are the things you will need to have if you decide to host your own event: a date, time, detailed schedule, sales materials, and materials that allow your host info-marketers to promote your event. This takes us back to the top of our menu of ways to work with joint venture partners. You can promote your event through an endorsed mailing, an endorsed e-mail, a teleseminar, or any of the other resources available to you. However you decide to promote your event to another info-marketer's list, you need to have the appropriate materials created and ready to go.

All those resources and tools are the starting point. Once you have created the product and the marketing method your joint venture partner will use to get the message out about your product, then you need to meet the minimum criteria necessary to get your host info-marketer's attention. Your goal is to get info-marketers to pay attention to you so you can begin the conversation about endorsing your product. Just because you have a good product and effective marketing lined up for it doesn't mean your host info-marketer is automatically going to do business with you.

For example, if someone came to me today with everything necessary to joint venture on a great program, it would be several months before I could even send an e-mail to promote the product because I already have a line of people who want to work with me. It doesn't mean that I don't want to work with a new info-marketer or a new program; it's just that I have so many things in the pipeline over the next several months that I can't promote anything else. You might find that's the case with the info-marketers you deal with. But you can't get considered, you can't even get in the door, until you have the product and the marketing materials created.

When info-marketers see your proposal for a joint venture, there are a number of the things they are going to consider when deciding whether or not to work with you:

Number one is past performance. If you have done this joint venture in the past with another info-marketer, it's going to be extremely valuable for the new info-marketer to know how many sales were produced based on the distribution list to which the marketing was sent. This will allow the new info-marketer to judge how many customers can actually be expected to buy your product versus all the other choices they have. Quite frankly, the info-marketer you have approached with your program might have a couple of choices and will be basing the decision partly on which program will generate the most revenue for him. If you have past results, it's important to emphasize them. You may even want to invest in buying Google AdWords to drive traffic to your website so you can prove your site successfully converts visitors into customers. This gives your potential host confidence that you've built a marketing system that will maximize his investment in promoting your product.

In addition to past performance, potential host info-marketers will want to know who else is promoting your products to their lists. In fact, if you are working with other info-marketers, feel free to ask them to help promote you to other joint venture partners. New joint venture relationships often are created by referral. If you're a member of a coaching program and your coach is a friend of another coach, ask your coach to refer you.

It may even make sense for you to become a member of another coaching program if that gives you access to other marketers who can endorse your products and services to their lists. Whatever coaching you get from the relationship is value added. While you may have joined to get access to an info-marketer's list, now that info-marketer is actually helping you build your product, so once it's built, he may be more willing to help you promote it. Understand that your coach has no obligation to promote your product, but the relationship you build with him by attending two, three, or four coaching meetings a year will increase the likelihood of that person endorsing you.

Let me stress again the importance of building relationships. It is definitely one of the ways info-marketers make judgments on whom they are going to endorse. If they don't know you, have never heard of you, they're going to be reluctant to work with you. Build a relationship with them over time because it builds trust so they will want to do business with you. Attending events where you know an info-marketer is also going to be or attending the info-marketer's own events is a good way to build relationships that will serve as a bridge to getting that person to work with you. I have used this strategy myself several times. I spend two or three days at a seminar to meet, talk with, and go to dinner with people who are potential joint venture partners for me and my business. Even though I dislike traveling as much as the next person, I highly recommend doing it. Some travel is useful in building relationships with people who can help you make money.

A final note: Whenever you approach potential joint venture partners, it's important to manage your own expectations. These info-marketers have busy lives, and a quick call back from one of them is unlikely to happen. You need to be prepared to follow up, build a relationship, and work over time to build trust and rapport so other info-marketers are excited about endorsing your product or service to their customers. They need to know you're a great person because what they really want to do is expose their customers to someone great.

Chapter 27

Lee Milteer Discovers Her Calling and Turns It into Millionaire Smarts

FTER PURSUING A CAREER AS A RADIO DISK JOCKEY AND traveling around the world as a professional photographer, Lee Milteer did something practical and went into commercial real estate. But her timing was off. "There was a recession going on at the time, and nobody was doing too much of anything in the commercial real estate buying world," Lee says, "but the great news about that was it forced me to ask myself what I really wanted to do, and that was to be a professional speaker."

After hearing people repeatedly tell her she was "good on television" and "you should be a professional speaker," Lee was ready to say yes when the local university called, looking for a woman to teach sales to college students. "They hired me for three months, and I made $168.00," Lee says. "That's when I realized very clearly that it was time to take the lead and become a visionary of the future."

Lee was still working in commercial real estate, and the company she worked for owned 26,000 apartment units. They were all rented because the recession had kept people from buying houses. Lee knew the tide would change, and one day the economy would get better so people could buy houses again. Then the company would have a problem renting their apartments. "I went to them with the proposal to teach their apartment managers how to actually sell instead of just take orders and fill space, because I knew there would be a time when they were going to have competition again," Lee says. "It took me several months to write the program, and they paid me a big 1,500 bucks. I was moving up in the world."

Lee printed up some business cards and began marketing herself as a professional speaker, providing training on sales, sales image, how to manage, and just about anything else. "If they said they needed it, I said I could do it!" Lee laughs.

She met Dan Kennedy at a National Speakers Association meeting. "Dan is a great motivator," Lee says. "He told me my career eventually had to go from being a speaker to becoming an author and then creating an information product. That really is the path. You have to use where you are now, whatever your story is now, to create products, because gaining customers is where your long-term income has to come from."

After two years, Lee signed up with CareerTrack, which was the largest public seminar company in North America. In the first month, she became the company's number-one speaker and ended up being the top salesperson as well. "I worked for CareerTrack for six years, and I actually spoke in 100 cities a year all over North America and Europe giving public seminars."

Her time with CareerTrack did more than just solidify her reputation as a top public speaker; it changed her life by introducing her to back-of-the-room sales. "We sold a lot of products at the back of the room," Lee says. "I created a program called Success Self Programming. CareerTrack sold over a million copies of that product, and I got 50 cents per sale."

In addition to the income from Success Self Programming, Lee credits the two-audiocassette product with helping launch her career. "The program was all about self-image and how you program yourself for success," she explains. "It got me television appearances with Sally Jessy Raphael, Montel Williams, and CNN, as well as hundreds of newspaper interviews and articles in magazines."

Lee soon found herself doing in-house training seminars for large companies such as AT&T, Xerox, IBM, Ford Motor Company, FedEx, and Disney. She was in high demand, and because her philosophy is to "make hay while the sun shines," she averaged 150 presentations each year. Lee credits her strong work ethic to her childhood as a farmer's daughter: "It seems natural to me. I like to work, and I like what I do."

Lee's hard work paid off. She started getting calls from promoters the likes of Zig Ziglar, Dr. Norman Vincent Peale, and Brian Tracy to do large-venue presentations for audiences of 1,000 to 10,000. "They were looking for female speakers who could sell from the platform," she says. "I can sell, so that helped me."

Lee was already creating products and writing books as part of her public speaking career, and Dan Kennedy pushed her to do more. Then came 9/11.

"When I watched the horrible news of that day in September, I never dreamed how it would affect me personally," Lee says. "Virginia Beach is a long way from New York City, but my phone began to ring. I had speaking contracts with NASA, AT&T, Ford Global, and many other large companies. Two weeks after 9/11, every contract had cancelled. Some said they had to divert training funds to other needs; others said people were afraid to fly. But the bottom line was at the end of two weeks, I had an empty calendar. It was the first time in years that I had any time to myself, and it was shocking and scary."

After months of soul searching about the direction she should take in her career, Lee found the perfect fit with Dan Kennedy's Platinum coaching group. "The people in Dan's Platinum group told him they were having challenges with retention. He diagnosed their problem: They were only teaching half of what creates real success, the marketing and education and how to run a business. The other half is the mindset. Dan asked me if I would like to do a coaching program for the coaches in his Platinum group, and I thought it was a great idea. His call came in June, and by August I was up and running with seven major clients."

Lee was able to design a coaching program that applied to any industry because, as she says, "they basically all have the same problems with coaching people. They need ways to keep their clients in the program longer."

The Millionaire Smarts program is now four years old, and it is also brand-new. Lee explains: "The program has changed dramatically since the first version. In fact, one of the questions I ask myself every single month is 'What can I do to add to the program to give my clients more benefits?' Some months I do not come up with anything new, but there are other months when I have a brainstorm and think, 'Oh, I can do this for them, or I can interview this person, or I can add a transcript, or I can add calls, or I can add more reports, or I can add, I can add, I can add.'"

Lee says that asking questions is one of the most important things she has learned to do in her career and in her life. "When you ask yourself a question, your brain—which is literally a computer—searches for resources and answers to that particular question."

The goal of Millionaire Smarts is to "take a ton of work off of coaches" so they can focus on implementing the strategies that will grow their businesses. Lee helps her coaches by teaching them how to get their clients to move past fear, to move past procrastination, to move past insecurity and feeling overwhelmed.

For example, a recent month's coaching topic was called Time Integrity. Lee describes this concept: "It is all about the kind of integrity you have with yourself. How do you honor yourself as a business owner and as an entrepreneur? What kind of integrity do you have in your personal life with your family? What kind of integrity do you have in using your time well in every aspect of your life?"

Lee also does a series on stress management especially for business owners, professionals, and entrepreneurs. "You have to be a business owner or professional or some type of entrepreneur to appreciate the information in this series," Lee says. "It is definitely not for the corporate world." In this series Lee interviews successful entrepreneurs like Brian Tracy and Dan Kennedy and "anybody and everybody who has a great book out there with a good message for an entrepreneur."

>
>
> **KEY CONCEPT**
>
> Selling a home study course in a box with a 50/50 split isn't the only way to structure joint ventures. If you have a service that will increase the retention of an info-marketer's continuity programs, consider offering it as an additional benefit to help your host info-marketer keep his customers longer.

An interesting component of Lee's coaching program is the way she helps others create their own programs. "One-third to 60 percent of my clients actually started their coaching programs with me as their partner," she says. "So they get to advertise two coaches. They get to advertise their expertise in the such and such industry, and they also have as a partner world-renowned human potential expert and productivity expert Lee Milteer."

Lee further assists her clients' launches of new coaching programs by speaking at her clients' sponsored events. "I actually go in and start their boot camps or conventions with a motivational presentation," she explains. "Later on in the day, I talk about the power and the importance of the association and the mastermind theory and then offer our—because it is an 'our' at this point—our coaching programs to their members. I tell them they are going to get the technical information from the sponsor of the meeting and all the right-thinking information and interviews with famous people and informative articles from me."

Another way Lee's program lightens her clients' workload is by providing materials they can repackage and send out to their own clients. In addition to MP3, DVD, and CD formatted audio-video reports and articles, Lee includes transcripts so they can be included in her clients' newsletters, faxed or e-mailed as a weekly report, or even mailed to key clients. "I actually recommend that all my sponsors print out all the reports in the transcript, put it in an envelope, and send it to their high-paying coaching members once a month, along with a personalized three-ring binder that has their name and contact information on it. This is an interesting thing that always fascinates me but is absolutely true: When people get a monthly homework assignment, they feel like they've gotten something helpful. So they do the assignment, put it in their binders, and then feel a sense of accomplishment."

Chapter 28

Other Sources of
Joint Venture Partners

I 'VE FOCUSED A LOT OF ATTENTION ON OTHER INFO-MARKETERS as joint venture partners. However, there are a lot of other potential partners. In the next two chapters, you are going to read about info-marketers who created joint ventures with individuals outside the information marketing world. They turned to associations and other businesses.

After Claude Whitacre created his product, he began offering his services as a speaker at industry association events. Because he offers a marketing system for retailers, Claude promotes his speaking services to associations that provide services and events for any type of retailer, such as jewelry stores, pool stores, furniture retailers, gift shops, and others.

Each of these industries has its own association that provides services and events for the industry's members. Some niches have several. Claude often gets paid to speak at association meetings, and during his presentation, he offers members of the audience who have enjoyed his presentation to invest in The Unfair Advantage Retail Advertising System, which he sells for

$1,199.00. This allows Claude to continue to run his primary business, go out on speaking engagements to conferences that include his target market for big paydays selling his system, as well as increase the number of members within his monthly continuity program as he sells more systems.

And on top of all that, many of the associations don't think to ask for revenue sharing on Claude's sales. Because they don't realize the revenue generated from those sales, they don't ask. Thus, Claude is able to keep 100 percent of the money. The association wants a compelling speaker that will draw attendees to its event. If Claude provides that, then the association is often happy without a revenue share. And for those that do ask for a share of the revenue, Claude is willing to provide it, for the right audience. You can read his complete profile in Chapter 29.

Speaking at events isn't the only way to work with associations. You can write for their published journals or websites, create special content for their members, be a featured guest on teleseminars, or even arrange an endorsed mailing. The only downside of working with associations is they can be slower than some info-marketers because there is often a committee process to weave through. However, if you have powerful associations serving your target customers, these can be a great way to reach them.

While Claude Whitacre has had great success with associations, Fred Berns uses his "sugar daddy" relationship with an industry vendor to promote his business. Fred helps interior designers get more customers.

Vendors in any industry struggle to get attention from their prospective customers. In interior design, furniture retailers want designers to sell their furniture over any of the other choices the designer has. But when every furniture manufacturer is hosting events and trying to get interior designers to carry their products, how does one break through the clutter?

In this case, a furniture retailer used Fred Berns as an attraction to encourage interior designers to attend its events. For Fred, he got free promotion from the furniture retailer, was paid to deliver the presentations, and was able to sell his marketing system for designers. You can read more about it in Chapter 30.

These sugar daddy relationships can be a lucrative way to structure your info-marketing business's marketing system. For their own business reasons, many companies are willing to promote you and your products, if you give them what they need in their businesses.

> Info-marketers are not the only sources of joint venture partners. **KEY CONCEPT** Approach industry associations and vendors to identify partners you can work with to help them achieve their goals while you build your new info-marketing business.

Enjoy the profiles in the next two chapters, and make a list of the associations you can work with as well as the industry vendors that can become your "sugar daddy."

Chapter 29

How a Vacuum Salesman Created a Business with Zero Marketing Costs

MEET 53-YEAR-OLD VACUUM CLEANER SALESMAN CLAUDE Whitacre.

"I do sell vacuum cleaners," Claude says proudly. "I'm that guy. Right out of high school, I went door to door selling vacuum cleaners in the home."

Of course, Claude's story doesn't end with door-to-door vacuum sales, or you wouldn't be reading about him right now. Claude is one of those people who didn't sit back and wait for success to come to him; he went looking for it. "I went to a Peter Lowe Success Event, and afterward I asked Peter if I could buy him dinner," Claude recalls. "So, we had dinner, and I told him that I wanted to do what he did. I wanted to do public speaking. I didn't know exactly how I was going to do that, but I knew I wanted to speak."

But wanting isn't doing, and Claude continued with in-home sales—until about ten years ago. "That's when I finally decided to do something," he says. "I was going to be a speaker, I was going to speak about something with certainty and with deep knowledge, and I was going to really make an impact because what I was going to say would be real stuff."

First, Claude had to settle on an audience. The logical thing would be to speak to other in-home sales representatives like himself, but he hit a snag. "I don't like them," Claude smiles ruefully. "I've met thousands and thousands of them, and I can count on one hand the number I actually enjoy being with."

Claude decided to target retailers, and the reasonable thing to do seemed to be to become a retailer himself. Because he knows a lot about vacuum cleaners, Claude opened a vacuum cleaner store—but he did a little more than that. During his years of selling door to door, Claude had learned a thing or two about sales. He had studied hundreds of books on the subject and had even begun writing a book of his own. "I had really studied selling and neurolinguistic programming, and I had quite a library, even at that time, of maybe a few hundred books on marketing and mostly selling," he says.

Claude put his knowledge of sales techniques to work in his store, and they worked very well. "The first two years I made a good living, selling close to six figures," he recalls.

But his success had its limitations. Claude remembers a breakthrough moment in his career: "I was selling high-dollar items to a good percentage of the people that came in the store, but I realized that the best I could ever do would be to close 100 percent of the people that walked through the door. That put a limit on my success because the number of people coming in was limited. I needed to learn how to advertise to get people in the door."

Once again, Claude turned to reading. "I started buying books on advertising," he says. "I bought some of Dan Kennedy's and lots of the old classics. It took me a couple of years to really get the gist of how advertising works, how to sell high-end products in ads, and how to make ads produce a profit virtually every time."

Claude's business really took off when he stopped focusing on selling and began marketing. "If you have really good marketing and really good advertising, most of the selling can be done before customers walk in the door," he explains. "I switched from concentrating on sales techniques to concentrating on marketing techniques because rather than exhaust myself trying to convince people to buy, I would much, much rather attract people that *want* to buy. That makes my life so much easier."

With his own store, Claude had a real-life "laboratory" to test his ideas. "Some of them were spectacular successes, and some of them were spectacular failures," he grins. But he has been able to take all his experience to build a sales system that he sells, and he also delivers seminars, produces newsletters, and speaks at boot camps and other events.

Back to the vacuum cleaner retail store. There was one small problem: It was too successful. Claude explains: "I decided about two years ago that I was ready to be the guy that talks about advertising from the standpoint of being someone who really knows how to do it. The problem was I was still speaking only part time. Why? Because my store is so doggone profitable! I told my wife two years ago that we were going to sell the store, but we keep putting it off because it makes us so much money. It's a small retail store, 1,600 square feet, but we're in the top 1 percent, and when I speak at the trade convention for vacuum cleaner dealers, everyone is asking 'Claude, how do you do it?'"

Claude shares how he does it in The Unfair Advantage Retail Advertising System, which he sells for $1,199.00 with back-of-the-room sales. Claude did achieve his goal of becoming a professional speaker, but he doesn't do it for the speaking fees. "I'm always doing it for sales," he says. "I make no bones about it. I don't try to hide the fact that I'm a platform salesman. I'm the guy that gets up in the front of the room and explains ideas, and at the end of my presentation, I offer a system that people end up investing in."

Claude jokes that he sells his system by the pound. "It's huge. It weighs 16 pounds!" he exclaims.

The Unfair Advantage system includes a series of manuals on the different types of advertising, all bound into one large manual. They cover radio, direct mail (which is the bulk of what Claude recommends), TV, and Yellow Pages. In addition, the system includes DVDs and CDs of Claude's $3,000.00 seminar and the first 16 issues of his newsletter. Claude also sells a *Reader's Digest* version of his system, The Unfair Advantage of Small Business Advertising Manual, for $20.00 and his book on CD for $45.00. Everyone who buys from Claude is automatically enrolled in his $39.95 a month newsletter. "I learned that from Dan," he says, "and most of my customers stick." With the 24:1 ratio of the $1,100.00 system versus the $45.00 book, it's not hard to guess which Claude prefers to sell, but he is happy with the success he has with both. "In a room of 100, I'll sell 20 systems and 30 books," he says. "I follow Bill Glazer's advice and always start at the top. I offer the system first and then follow that with the book."

Sometimes Claude offers his book or his newsletter as a free gift, but he finds that those customers don't stick with him as well. "You know, they paid nothing, and that's a different type of customer," he says.

Claude says his newsletter is a good core business for him. "For $39.95 a month, my 200 subscribers get a 12- to 16-page newsletter that's just me, nobody else," he says. "I don't have any contributors. I'm either interviewing somebody, or I'll write about my own program."

Not all of Claude's experiments work, and he shares one of those failures here. "Because a lot of my subscribers say 'Claude, you know, I'm not really a reader,' I thought, why don't I just read my newsletter, record it, and send a CD with the newsletter? I was surprised when I had several people say, 'Claude, don't do that. I read the newsletter, and the CD is the same thing.' I did that one month and dropped it because my customers didn't feel like it was a good value."

Claude has found working with trade associations to be a very successful way to get potential clients in a room for a seminar. He uses an idea he learned from Dan Kennedy and presents a seminar the day before an association's trade show begins. The association pays for the meeting space, promotes the seminar, and lets Claude advertise in its trade journal. In addition, Claude writes articles or provides an interview for the trade journal, which makes his in-person presentation more powerful because the association members feel like they know him. Another benefit? Filming the seminar gives Claude a new product to sell later.

Building relationships with trade associations is a fairly straightforward process for Claude. "First, I join the association," he says, "and then I simply call them up and say I have a seminar about advertising that I give for small-business owners. I tell them I've worked with people who sell, for example, sewing machines, and I get some really good results. I ask them if they would be interested if I paid all my own expenses, and they always say yes because how can you say no to free?"

Working with associations has allowed Claude to grow his list and become well-known in several niches without having to spend a lot of money. In addition, he gets to speak to a very targeted group, so a very high percentage end up buying from him. "After reading my articles for four or five months in the association's newsletter," Claude says, "it's much easier to sell from the front of the room."

Chapter 30

Using "Sugar Daddies" to Deliver Customers into Your Business

A FTER 25 YEARS AS A JOURNALIST, FRED BERNS CAN REALLY turn a phrase. Take, for example, Business by Design. What does that say to you? It might conjure ideas like "to have a great business, you need to have a good design or a plan to follow" or "a good design leads to a successful business." Just about any idea that springs from hearing the name of Fred's company, Business by Design, is right on target. He coaches business owners on how to build their clienteles and increase their profits—and not just any business owners: Fred's clients are interior designers.

It's a big leap from being a journalist to becoming a coach to interior designers, but Fred's experiences in running a news bureau in Washington, DC, equipped him with the communication and business skills he would later use to build his info-business. "Basically, the Berns Bureau was a regional bureau for TV and radio outlets and newspapers all around the world," Fred explains. "So, when the mayor of Phoenix would come to town to testify at some hearing in Washington, we would do a report for the local TV station and radio station in Phoenix. I would sign it off by saying 'Fred Berns, KTAR-News Washington' as if I was their own Washington bureau, when in fact, we were doing this for several hundred stations around the country."

While Fred says the news bureau business was a lot of fun, it was also highly competitive. "There are 10,000 journalists in Washington, and a lot of them were doing what I was doing," he says. "I think there are as many journalists as there are lawyers in Washington, DC, and they're thought of as highly as lawyers—that's exactly why I got out of the business!" he jokes.

Actually, Fred's exit from the news bureau in 1995 was a natural progression for him. "I had begun speaking and giving presentations on how to get free publicity," he says. "I actually was able to give classes because I was a journalist. I met a lot of entrepreneurs who said, 'How do I get my story on MTV?' or 'How do I get my story in print?' I developed a course called Free Publicity: How to Get Quoted and Promoted in the Media. I enjoyed the speaking side of it so much that eventually I sold my bureau to one of my correspondents and moved to Lewisville, Colorado, just outside of Boulder."

After 9/11, Fred found his speaking opportunities on the decline because many companies were cutting back on their conventions and training programs. "I had to do some soul searching," he recalls. "I realized the one group that kept booking me, kept buying my products, and kept hiring me to coach them was interior designers. So, I decided after 9/11 to niche in that industry. Now I am a sales and marketing trainer, coach, and speaker in the interior design industry."

Fred is quick to say he is not an interior designer, "but I can help them with the sales and marketing skills they don't get in design school."

Because interior designers are artists, Fred says they tend to take themselves for granted: "They give away their time; they give away their expertise. They go to design school and learn everything they can possibly learn about fabrics and furniture, and when they are dumped out in the real world and have to start a business, it gets clobbered. So I'm teaching them the kind of business skills they don't get in school and especially need in this economy; they're fighting the battle of trying to come across as a necessity instead of as a frill."

Fred's challenge with his clients is to coach them on how they can present their interior design services as a money-saving necessity. He gives these examples: "Interior designers sell window treatments, and with the right kind of window treatments, you can save about 50 percent on your energy bills. I'm instructing my clients to let people know they can save them lots of money in these tough economic times so their expertise becomes a lot more important and timely. In addition, all the financial gurus are saying your one safe investment, your best investment right now, is in your home, and what you want to do is spend money on your home and enhance the value of your home. Well, who better to help you with that than a design professional?"

With these selling points in mind, Fred encourages his clients to promote their businesses as "interior consultants" rather than designers. The idea is that a consultant can provide homeowners with ways to increase the value of their homes.

Fred's business has three main revenue streams: speaking, books and audio CDs, and coaching programs.

Due to the struggling economy, there are fewer in-person speaking opportunities, but Fred still gives presentations to design associations and design centers around the country and internationally. In addition, he has bolstered his speaking revenue by presenting teleseminars and webinars for the design community. But the biggest boost to his speaking income is due to what he terms a "sugar daddy." Perhaps some explanation would be in order here:

"Because there are not as many meetings now, I find myself turning to 'sugar daddies' more and more," Fred says. "I think that's an important trend for me. For example, Hunter Douglas, the world's largest window fashion manufacturer, has become a big sponsor of mine. Instead of me chasing down speaking engagements, I let them beat the bushes and line them up for me. They have deep pockets and a huge database, and rather than me 'smiling and dialing' and trying to call every design center in America saying 'Hey, you've got to have me speak,' I let Hunter Douglas do it."

Fred has found that aligning himself with a larger organization is a good business strategy, especially in a difficult economy, and it's a win-win: "I can help Hunter Douglas in a lot of different ways," he explains. "I'm writing articles for Hunter Douglas, I'm doing surveys for Hunter Douglas, and they're putting my information on their website and promoting it in other ways. So, in other words, my business-building tips are being made available through Hunter Douglas to their clientele—that makes them look good, and it gives me a lot of exposure."

The story of how Fred connected with Hunter Douglas is one of those "right place, right time" things. "I was going to speak at a conference in Los Angeles, and as I was getting on a plane here in Colorado, I overheard two ladies talking about designs. I said, 'You must be going to the XYZ conference. I'm speaking there.' They said, 'No. We're going to the Hunter Douglas Regional Conference in Los Angeles. We're with Hunter Douglas here.' So, I invited them to attend my program, and they did! I was surprised to see them, but from that point on, we developed a very close working relationship."

Fred built this relationship by offering Hunter Douglas a new way to reach out to its designer clients. "I told them I could bring them a lot of designers knocking on their door because I speak around the country and I write articles and blogs. They liked the idea because it showed their interest in partnering with their clients by having me provide seminars and other information to them about sales and marketing. In other words, Hunter Douglas was able to say to designers: 'We want you to do well in this tough economy, and that's why we have brought in Fred Berns to share his expertise and give seminars and write articles on our website, etc., etc.,'" Fred explains.

Working with Fred has given Hunter Douglas an edge in a very competitive market. "In the old days, Hunter Douglas wanted to showcase its products to interior designers, and the problem was they would have these programs and none of the designers would show up," Fred says. "Now, they have Fred Berns offering a 60-minute program on how to set and get higher fees, and they get a huge audience of designers coming to this event. In the meantime, they can showcase their new products to a much more receptive audience."

Fred says that using sugar daddies is a strategy that more info-marketers should use. "I think it's a good shortcut to success to find a sugar daddy who is interested in reaching out to the same clients you are connecting with on a regular basis and say 'Look, let's work together. I can help you attract more prospects to your website. I can help you stir up more interest in your products, simply by providing sales and marketing tips to your clients.' There are corporate allies out there who are dying to have us help them—and they've got the money. They are throwing this money at advertising; they are throwing this money at trade shows, but they are not really connecting with their end users, and that's where we come in."

Chapter 31

Best Way to Launch Your Info-Marketing Business: Joint Ventures

O F ALL THE WAYS TO LAUNCH YOUR INFORMATION MARKETING business, working through joint ventures can be the fastest way to generate significant new sales and customers. With a joint venture, you are able to benefit from the years that another info-marketer has spent in building a relationship with his own customers. The best part is you don't have to pay that info-marketer unless and until he actually generates a new sale for you. It's a great low-investment way to get started in the information marketing business.

You need to invest in creating your product and all your product marketing before you approach potential partners. It may sound like a lot of work, but this is common within business. Typically you aren't going to sell many new products without first creating a product as well as the marketing for that new product. This is where the joint venture launch model differs from the teleseminar model. With teleseminars, you don't have to create the product until you start delivering the teleseminars. But to get the additional sales from having your joint venture partner promote your product to her customers, it may be worth doing the work necessary to create your product first. (Also, there is no reason why you can't conduct your own teleseminar series to create your home study product and then use joint ventures to promote that product.)

Referring back to the **Information Marketing Business Pyramid**™ I introduced in Chapter 3, joint ventures allow you to generate new customers for your Introductory Product without a large investment of marketing money. With this new customer list, you can use upsells to move them up your **Information Marketing Business Pyramid**™ into your more profitable products and services.

The primary downside of using joint ventures is that you do not have control over the time line. The person endorsing you, the one whose customers you want to work with, is the one who controls when he promotes your products. I still have to track down several people who promised they would do a joint venture with me. They've been busy, or the timing hasn't been right—for whatever reason, it hasn't happened yet.

The point is this: Whenever you're dealing with other people to promote your business, you will have a profound loss of control over the relationship. But don't let that discourage you from trying this method of launching a business. For many info-marketers, the revenue gains and the reduced expenses of creating an info-marketing business on their own are well worth giving up some element of control so that another info-marketer can promote them.

If you like the idea of launching your info-marketing business through joint ventures and would like additional instructions, more examples, and detailed how-to checklists, then check out the **Information Marketing Business Pyramid**™. You can get more details at **InfoMarketingPyramid.com**.

The **Information Marketing Business Pyramid**™ provides several items you'll find useful after reading this chapter:

- Sample letters for approaching potential joint venture partners
- Sample endorsement e-mails
- A teleseminar outline you can adapt for your own joint venture call
- Sample joint venture agreements
- Order forms you can adapt for your own business
- Additional details on working with associations to promote your products
- And a whole lot more . . .

Visit **InfoMarketingPyramid.com** for additional details on how you can use joint ventures to launch your info-marketing business.

Launch Your Info-Business with a Provocative Diagnostic Survey

Chapter 32

How a Family-Owned Jewelry Store Created a Shining Info-Business

I F A DIAMOND IS A GIRL'S BEST FRIEND, THEN IT FOLLOWS THAT A girl's jeweler needs to be her best friend as well. Cindy Ritzi with Wm. Ritzi & Co. Jewelers is on a mission help jewelers create best-friend relationships with their customers through improved communications, a unique product for jewelry owners, and consumer education.

Cindy joined the family business right out of college and has been the owner of the 128-year-old company since 1995. During her 30 years in the jewelry business, she has built strong relationships in her community. Cindy's hometown of Ormond Beach (near Daytona Beach), Florida, has nine jewelry sellers, all within three blocks of her store, so she knows the value of good marketing. "We do a lot of community service, and our unique selling proposition has always been that we are the jewelry expert or authority in our area," she says.

Cindy wrote a series of sales letters for a specific segment of her business: Rolex watch repair. "I did a tremendous amount of business in a very short period of time," she says. "I knew there was something to this."

A year later, Cindy attended her first Glazer-Kennedy Insider's Circle SuperConference. It changed her life—and her business. She already had an "inkling of an idea" for an info-business based on the marketing she was doing for her jewelry store, but the conference gave her an "explosion of ideas" as well as a once-in-a-lifetime opportunity.

"The SuperConference was in Chicago that year. They were giving away a free business makeover with Bill Glazer, and I put my name in the box—along with the hundreds of other people," Cindy smiles. "I had a gal from my business there with me, and when they went to do the drawing, I looked at my friend and said, 'I'm going to win.' She looked at me and said, 'I know— you're winning that.' It was the most bizarre thing. It was like this feeling came over both of us, and there's no way to explain it. Of course, the girl called my name, and I had won that business makeover!"

Bill came to the Daytona area and conducted Cindy's business makeover. "It was fabulous," she says. "Bill came in for a morning session and talked in general about marketing and then specifically about the information I had sent him. He went over changes and corrections I should make, and he had redone my newsletters. At the end, he asked if anyone had any questions, and I said I had questions about information marketing. He told me he owed me another consult, so I was able to call him later with very specific questions about how to deal with my jewelers."

Cindy's consultation with Bill led her to purchase a partial list of the 24,000 independent jewelers that would be her prospects. She developed a ten-question survey in which she asked what Bill calls the "painful" questions, such as "How many hours are you working?" and "Is your business up or down?" "The survey led the prospects to the answers of how we could help them," Cindy says. "We offered a free gift for completing the survey, and it was very successful. We had a 7½ percent response rate."

To convert a survey responder into a customer, Cindy took the thoughtful step of including handwritten comments on every survey before sending them back to the prospects with a compilation of the survey's results. "Giving them personal comments showed them we were seriously interested in helping them," she says.

Cindy packaged her jewelry store marketing ideas into a kit that sells for $297.00. The kit provides an analysis of the jeweler's current marketing and some steps to follow to improve it. From those surveys, 112 jewelers invested in her program.

With all she has going on in her life, Cindy is grateful for "a very supportive family," which includes her husband, three sons, and her semi-retired father, who still offers his insights gleaned from his years in the jewelry business. "He's very interested in what we're doing, and our youngest son works in the business with me and helps with a lot of the computer stuff," she says. "And I still have my brick-and-mortar store. I'm at the store about three days a week, and the rest of the time I have an office at my house where I'm doing the writing and other details for my info-business."

Chapter 33

The Single Most Profitable Marketing Tool for Info-Marketers

MANY YEARS AGO, MY WIFE, KORY, AND I WERE SITTING at our table eating dinner. The dining room was immediately adjacent to the living room in the small yellow house we were renting at the time, so sometimes we watched TV while we ate.

The news anchor was excitedly reading the news stories when an image of the house across the street from us flashed across the screen. "Police officers shoot dog at Eddie Road home."

"What? That was across the street! The police are shooting across the street from our home?"

We tuned in and found out the police had been serving an arrest warrant, and a dog had attacked them. To defend themselves, one of the officers had shot the dog and killed it. But the police didn't get the guy they had come to arrest.

There I sat. In a terrible neighborhood with my family, living across the street from someone who was getting arrested.

We had a swing set in our backyard where I played with my 18-month-old daughter all the time. The only comfort I had was at least there was one less killer dog in the neighborhood.

My wife and I lived there because we had no choice. We were married young, and my wife was pregnant before our first anniversary. We had to grow up quickly. That meant we had to put off homeownership and rent while we saved money for a down payment.

That evening I noticed a letter in my mail for a "No Money Down" real estate course. Several months before, I had called in response to an infomercial I had seen on television, but I hadn't bought anything. The operator had taken my name and address, and I'd been receiving mail every week since. That night I pulled out my credit card and bought the product.

Within a month of receiving the product, my family was in a new home in a better neighborhood. I really owe that information marketer a lot because he repeatedly followed up with me. He was there, on the night I was ready, to provide me with exactly the information I needed to solve my problem. And solve it he did.

When I originally called in response to the infomercial, I became a lead. That info-marketer had a follow-up process that continued to keep contact with me. He sent me sales letters, postcards, and information about upcoming seminars in my area. Each week I received more information that allowed me to become more familiar with the info-marketer and grow to like him. Then, when I was ready to change my circumstances, his sales material was there.

I learned later that everything I received was part of a structured sales sequence. Each item was written from the beginning to build on the one before it. In fact, each step was continuously tested against other possible marketing pieces. More fortunes have been made in the info-marketing business with direct mail than any other media. Yes, that's right, more than have gotten rich via the internet and certainly more than social media.

You read about Cindy Ritzi and her info-marketing business for jewelry stores in the previous chapter. Cindy launched her info-marketing business for jewelry stores using a direct mail lead-generation letter. Then she followed up with a sales sequence to those who responded. While the gambit she used to generate a lead was unique, the sales process she used has been around for more than 100 years. I have outlined the process for you in Figure 33-1.

KEY CONCEPT The diagnostic survey is a successful way to generate leads from a mailing list. With these leads, you have the opportunity to follow up with a marketing sequence to convert them into new customers for your info-marketing business.

In the info-marketing world, much is written about internet marketing, about using e-mail follow-up sequences and websites that convert prospects into customers. All those tools are important. In fact, the publisher of this book, Entrepreneur Press, published another book I co-authored with Bob Regnerus, *The Official Get Rich Guide to Information Marketing on the Internet*, that gets into the details of how to create internet sales processes for your info-marketing business.

However, most of the gurus who teach "'how to get rich on the internet" eventually begin using direct mail, seminars, and telephone seminars to convert prospects into buyers. The magic happens when you integrate these techniques into one cohesive marketing campaign.

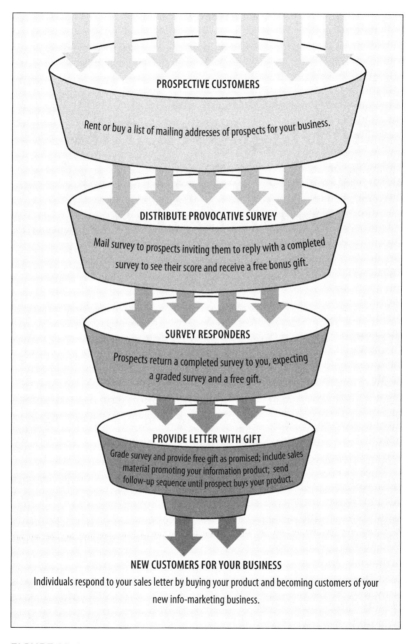

FIGURE 33-1. This funnel illustrates how to use your lead-generation diagnostic survey to move prospects to customers.

Chapter 34

The Diagnostic Survey: Making Them Feel Uncomfortable

THE DIAGNOSTIC SURVEY IS JUST ONE OF SEVERAL LEAD GENERATION devices. You've probably seen a tear sheet. It looks like a clipping out of a magazine or a newspaper with a yellow sticky note on it that says something like "Try this, it works. J." As you grow your info-marketing business, you'll want to test several different lead generation strategies. However, the diagnostic survey is a great place to start.

This tool allows you to use your prospects' natural curiosity to get them engaged with answering the questions. And the questions themselves force your prospects to confront whether or not they are adequately solving a problem they have in their lives.

Here are the questions Cindy Ritzi used in her diagnostic questionnaire to generate leads for her jewelry store marketing product. As you read through the questions, notice how they point out frustrations and inadequacies that would lead a

Jewelry Store Survey

Do you have strong competition in your immediate area from any of these businesses? Check all that apply.

- ❏ Big Box Retailers
- ❏ Jewelry Chains
- ❏ Pawn Shops
- ❏ Antique Stores
- ❏ Other Independent Jewelers
- ❏ Non-Qualified Jewelry Sellers
- ❏ Other _____

How many marketing systems do you have in place to contact existing customers or consistently acquire new clients?

- ❏ 0
- ❏ 1–3
- ❏ 4–8
- ❏ 8–10
- ❏ 10 & above

How were your revenues this year compared to last?

- ❏ 0–5% increase
- ❏ 5–10% increase
- ❏ 10–17% increase
- ❏ 17%–increase
- ❏ Flat or down

Jewelry Store Survey, continued

How much time do you spend working in your business weekly?

❏ 20–30 hours _____

❏ 31–40 hours _____

❏ 41–50 hours _____

❏ 50+ hours _____

Do you have a yearly marketing calendar? Yes _____ No _____

How many times per year do you have contact with your current customers?

❏ 1–3 times _____

❏ 4–6 times _____

❏ 7–12 times _____

❏ 12+ times _____

Do you collect information about your customers, such as

Name _____ Address _____ Phone _____ E-mail address _____

Purchase info _____ Repair info _____ Last visit _____

Do you provide educational information or materials to your customers? Yes _____ No _____

What is your biggest marketing challenge today?

❏ No access to resources _____

❏ Creating materials and writing ads _____

❏ Finding the time to work on it _____

❏ Marketing consistently _____

❏ Other _____

jewelry store owner to want to invest in a product to learn better marketing.

A diagnostic survey built one of the fastest-growing information marketing businesses ever, E-Myth Worldwide. Michael Gerber's worldwide bestselling book, *The E-Myth*, was written based on the sales presentation Michael perfected by speaking in front of groups around the country.

That book encouraged a lot of business owners to call E-Myth Worldwide to discover how they could create better systems within their businesses. When a business owner called, he was provided a free consultation with an E-Myth representative. This consultant

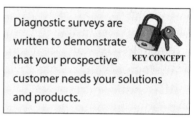

Diagnostic surveys are written to demonstrate that your prospective customer needs your solutions and products.

KEY CONCEPT

asked a series of questions, a diagnostic to determine the extent to which the business owner needed to work on the systems in his business.

The business owner was given a choice of answering Strongly Disagree, Disagree, Agree, or Strongly Agree to 18 questions; here are a few examples:

- I spend most of my time evaluating and innovating the way my business operates.
- I spend most of my time creating long-term plans for my business.
- I don't spend much time performing administrative or operational tasks.
- I don't spend much time directly supervising employees.
- I am achieving the profits I would like.

By facing these questions, business owners were forced to confront everything wrong in their businesses. Before taking the survey, it was easy for a business owner to dismiss the need for help and coaching. After taking the survey, the need for investing in building business skills became apparent. Thus, Michael's consultants were able to sign up a lot of business owners to the E-Myth Mastery seminars and coaching program.

E-Myth Worldwide really grew when the company began outbound telemarketing with its sales professionals going through the diagnostic questionnaire with each business owner they called. They were able to sign up thousands of business owners into coaching programs using this technique.

While attitudes about telemarketing have changed the effectiveness of that approach, the diagnostic survey is a proven sales tool for information marketers. Few others force your customers to confront their faults and insecurities the way the diagnostic survey does.

Chapter 35

Your Diagnostic Survey: Turning a Prospect into a Customer

DAVE DEE IS A REAL-LIFE PROFESSIONAL MAGICIAN. THAT'S magical in and of itself. Many little boys dream of becoming a magician (or a pro baseball player or an astronaut or . . .), but few follow their dreams into adulthood and make them happen. Dave Dee is exceptional, and so is his story.

Dave begins, "I always had the dream of being a professional magician, ever since I was 8 years old, but everyone told me I couldn't do it, that it wasn't practical. You know, when people say that kind of stuff, it really gets into your head. You begin to believe it. So I took the traditional route. I went to college. I got a job in radio advertising sales after college. But I still dreamed of being a professional magician."

Dave's dream didn't take off until he learned a little something about marketing. As Dave tells it, "I was a good magician, but I wasn't very good at booking magic shows. I was doing about three shows a month. But then I learned direct marketing, and I went from doing three shows a month to averaging 30 shows a month in less than three months!"

It turns out that Dave had a mentor named Dan Kennedy. Dave purchased Dan's Magnetic Marketing program and ended up booking 57 shows in his fourth month of direct marketing. This got him to thinking. "I realized that what I had actually done was trade time for dollars," Dave says. "I was living my dream, but I was limited by what I could do. I couldn't really do more than 57 shows in a month, nor did I want to. And then the other thing that got me thinking was what if something happened to me—what happens if I break my leg or get sick—if I can't go out and do the shows, I'm not making any money whatsoever."

That's when Dave's mentor stepped in. Dave recalls, "Dan Kennedy said to me, 'You should package how you did your marketing to book so many shows and sell it to other magicians.'"

Dave took Dan's advice and placed a small ad in one of the four trade magazines for magicians. Before long, he was getting requests for information, and soon he had made his first sale. "At first I thought this information business would be a nice little residual income in addition to my shows," Dave says, "but sitting at home getting checks in the mail was a lot better deal than working."

It all started with a tiny $65.00 ad. "I didn't have a lot of money at the time. In fact, I was in debt, so I had to be very cautious," Dave explains. "I picked the number-one trade magazine for magicians and placed my ad that said something like 'If you wanna book more magic shows, call . . .' I had a toll-free recorded message that offered a free report, which was really a sales letter."

Dave's marketing process was simple, but effective. He ran an ad offering a free report. People called the toll-free number to get the report. Dave mailed the report, which was actually his sales letter that told his story of becoming a professional magician who could book more shows than anyone else in the business. For nonresponders, he followed up with a second letter at Day 14 and a third letter at Day 28. Dave explains, "Some people just aren't going to reply to the first letter they get. They may not read it. They may misplace it. They may be thinking about it. So you gotta hit them multiple times." See Figure 35-1.

The key to Dave's success was connecting with his customers. "The most important thing is to get your customers to identify with you—you need to let the readers know that you understand their pain. Because I was a magician, I knew what their pain was. For example, I knew their parents had told them it wasn't practical, that they wouldn't be able to do it, and that they wouldn't be able to live their dreams. One of the most profound things someone said to me after reading my letter was, 'It was like you were under my kitchen table listening to me talk to my wife.'

"I spoke their language," Dave continues. "I talked about my pain, my struggle; about having a dream but not being able to fulfill it; about having a lousy job and knowing that magicians not as good as me were making more money. So, I hit upon all those emotional hot buttons. This is the key. You've gotta hit upon the emotions. Selling is all based on emotion. So I talked about what their pains were, what their

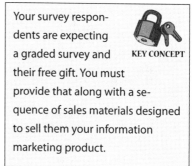

Your survey respondents are expecting a graded survey and their free gift. You must provide that along with a sequence of sales materials designed to sell them your information marketing product.

KEY CONCEPT

frustrations were, but I never gave them the solution. I told them I had the solution, but to get the solution, they'd have to buy my product."

Dave's follow-up letter was similar to the first. "I took that first sales letter and put it on a different color paper," Dave explains. "I cut it down slightly, because the first letter was 16 pages long. Now someone might say, 'Who's gonna read a 16-page sales letter?' But if it hits their emotional hot buttons,

- - page 1 - -

From: Dave Dee

"7 Steps For Making More Money With Your Magic"

* * * * * * * * *

This report reveals how you can make more money and even have more fun as a magician.

PLUS DISCOVER HOW YOU CAN GET THE BOOK YOU JUST BOUGHT FOR FREE, RECEIVE MORE FREE BONUSES, AND DISCOVER HOW YOU CAN MAKE YOUR MAGIC CAREER SOAR – GUARANTEED.

I urge you to get comfortable, ask not to be disturbed, and STUDY this letter - it IS that significant! It introduces something THAT amazing!

* * * * * * * * *

Dear Fellow Performer,

If you are a **Children's Performer**: how would you like to get a steady stream of phone calls everyday from parents interested in your service? How would you like to close over 70% of the people who call? Put an end to the "I'm just calling around for prices" objection? Have a list of names, phone numbers, addresses and birthdays of kids months before their party? How about if this list cost you nothing?

If you are a **School Show Performer**: how would you like to dominate your market even if someone else has been performing in the schools for years? Learn how to get booked over and over at schools, even when they tell you they don't have time for assemblies?

If you are a **Corporate or Trade Show Performer**: how would you like to attract prospects who are interested in using a magician for their event and are pre-disposed to hiring *you* ? Have qualified prospects calling *you* and asking for your help?

If you are a **Performer of *any* kind**: how would you like to stop wasting money on advertising ? Finally have a proven, systematic way to get quick results from every dollar you invest in ANY kind of advertising, marketing or promotion? Develop a constant stream of new prospects?

(please go to the next page)

FIGURE 35-1. Here are the first pages of each of Dave Dee's three-step sales letter sequence selling his magician marketing tool kit. Notice how each letter is slightly different; however, they are almost the same.

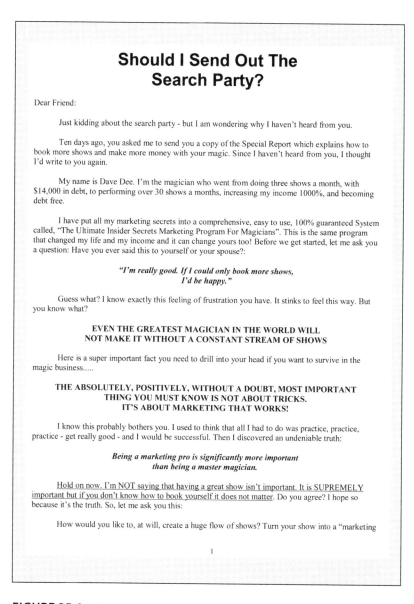

Should I Send Out The Search Party?

Dear Friend:

Just kidding about the search party - but I am wondering why I haven't heard from you.

Ten days ago, you asked me to send you a copy of the Special Report which explains how to book more shows and make more money with your magic. Since I haven't heard from you, I thought I'd write to you again.

My name is Dave Dee. I'm the magician who went from doing three shows a month, with $14,000 in debt, to performing over 30 shows a months, increasing my income 1000%, and becoming debt free.

I have put all my marketing secrets into a comprehensive, easy to use, 100% guaranteed System called, "The Ultimate Insider Secrets Marketing Program For Magicians". This is the same program that changed my life and my income and it can change yours too! Before we get started, let me ask you a question: Have you ever said this to yourself or your spouse?:

"I'm really good. If I could only book more shows,
I'd be happy."

Guess what? I know exactly this feeling of frustration you have. It stinks to feel this way. But you know what?

EVEN THE GREATEST MAGICIAN IN THE WORLD WILL
NOT MAKE IT WITHOUT A CONSTANT STREAM OF SHOWS

Here is a super important fact you need to drill into your head if you want to survive in the magic business.....

THE ABSOLUTELY, POSITIVELY, WITHOUT A DOUBT, MOST IMPORTANT
THING YOU MUST KNOW IS NOT ABOUT TRICKS.
IT'S ABOUT MARKETING THAT WORKS!

I know this probably bothers you. I used to think that all I had to do was practice, practice, practice - get really good - and I would be successful. Then I discovered an undeniable truth:

Being a marketing pro is significantly more important
than being a master magician.

Hold on now. I'm NOT saying that having a great show isn't important. It is SUPREMELY important but if you don't know how to book yourself it does not matter. Do you agree? I hope so because it's the truth. So, let me ask you this:

How would you like to, at will, create a huge flow of shows? Turn your show into a "marketing

1

FIGURE 35-1. In the second sequence, he starts off with a list of reasons why the reader wouldn't have responded to the first step. Later in the letter, he continues with the same copy as in Steps 1 and 3.

If You've Wanted To Get My Marketing Program For Magicians But Simply Couldn't Afford It, Here's Some Exciting News.

Dear Friend,

You've received information from me three times, gently encouraging you to take advantage of my special offer to invest in the "Ultimate Insider Secrets Marketing Program For Magicians".

I suspect the only reason you've NOT responded before now has to do with the amount of money required for you to get my Program.

If times are tough for you right now, I understand.

That's why I wanted to write to you one last time and make you a very special offer, that'll take the "money stumbling block" away.

Before I reveal what it is, the following is a review and summary of the benefits you'll <u>absolutely</u> receive if you accept my very special new offer:

If you are a **Children's Performer**: How would you like to <u>get a steady stream of</u> phone calls everyday from parents interested in your service? How would you like to close over 70% of the people who call? Put an end to the "I'm just calling around for prices" objection? Have a list of names, phone numbers, addresses and birthdays of kids months before their party? <u>How about if this list cost you nothing</u>?

If you are a **School Show Performer**: How would you like to <u>dominate your market</u> even if someone else has been performing in the schools for years? Learn how to get booked over and over at schools, even when they tell you they don't have time for assemblies?

If you are a **Corporate or Trade Show Performer**: How would you like to attract prospects who are interested in using a magician for their event and are pre-disposed to hiring *you*? <u>Have qualified prospects calling *you* and asking for your help</u>?

If you are a **Performer of *any* kind**: How would you like to

1

FIGURE 35-1. Notice how Step 3 is almost identical to Step 1. The headline and the first few paragraphs are different, but the rest is the same. These are smart and easy ways to add to the life of a marketing campaign by making small changes to the initial letter.

they'll read it from cover to cover and then read it again. It can be 16 pages, 24 pages, whatever."

Dave's second letter was 10 pages, with "Second Notice" printed at the top of the page. He used basically the same elements, changing the headline, font, and paper color. "I also cut the third letter down a little, and I changed the offer up a little bit as well," Dave says. "The first offer had only one option, to pay in full. With the second letter, I gave them the option of making payments. The third offer was a scare: If you don't do this now, the price is going up. I stamped the deadline date to reply on each letter and said 'You only have 21 days to buy. You have 14 days left. You have seven days left.' So each letter was counting down to the deadline."

While Dave no longer works in the magician marketing business he started, he is busy with several other information marketing businesses. Today he teaches others how to start their own businesses. "The one thing I want to get across is that everybody has some knowledge or can access knowledge that other people want. The key is to not limit your thinking. You can do it!" Dave exclaims.

You can do it. The diagnostic survey wasn't popular when Dave created his business. He had to use old-fashioned advertising to generate his leads. However, when you combine Dave's sequence of sales letters along with a survey, then you have a powerful marketing process to transform your list of prospects into a list of buyers.

Chapter 36

Best Way to Launch Your Info-Marketing Business: Diagnostic Surveys

T WO PRIMARY BENEFITS MAKE ME LOVE USING SURVEYS TO launch an information marketing business. First, it is one of the fastest launch methods there is. As soon as you get a survey written, which doesn't take long because a typical survey is only a couple of pages long, you can immediately have it in the mail, generating leads for your information marketing business. Of course, as soon as you start generating leads, you need to get the sales letter completed so you can send it to the individuals who reply to your survey.

Using a survey allows you to get started quickly while some of the other launch methods can take several months. Nothing beats the speed of using diagnostic surveys to launch your information marketing business.

Second, this launch method allows you to test different variables to see which one generates the best response. You do not have that luxury with the other launch models. For example, let's say you're not sure whether your product should be priced at $995.00 or at $1,495.00. You've wrestled back and forth, you've talked to all the experts, but everyone says you need to test the pricing to find out which is best. Well, with the diagnostic survey launch method, you can test. Here is how you do it:

Prepare two identical sales letters and order forms, but on one set list a price of $1,495.00 and on the other set list a price of $995.00. Send half of your leads the $995.00 letter; the other half gets the $1,495.00 letter. Then you can evaluate the results. How many products did you sell at each price, and which one generated the most income for your business? This way you can figure out which price is better.

Sometimes you will find out the higher price generates more sales than the lower price because people believe that the product must be better. Other times, the higher price might generate fewer sales, but still results in more cash for you and your business.

Split testing is another great benefit of using surveys. It's more difficult or even impossible when your customers are together in a room for a seminar or on the phone together for a teleseminar series. In these situations your customers have the opportunity to talk with each other about what they paid for the event.

In the **Information Marketing Business Pyramid**™ I explained in Chapter 3, this is a system to generate sales for your Introductory Product. You can then market to your paying customers as well as to the individuals who asked for their surveys to be graded but didn't choose to buy (your leads and opt-ins) to move them up your pyramid to the higher-priced, larger-margin products and services.

There are some necessities to keep in mind before choosing a diagnostic survey as the best option for launching your business.

First, you must already have or be able to acquire a list of customers within your market. Just because you don't know how to do that, don't rule out this option. List brokers can help find a great list for you. The only caution is don't allow a list broker to talk you into something you know isn't really your market. You also can work with associations, trade journals, or other people who have lists of your target audience. If you offer to share the survey's results, in addition to gaining access to a list, you may find someone to work with you on a joint venture.

Second, this launch method requires a significant investment of cash to get started. You have the distribution of the survey itself, a direct mail piece with the survey inserted that is going to be about $1.20 per mailing. If you are doing a large volume, you may be able to get it under $1.00 each. Either way, you're going to have to invest marketing money to identify who within your market is interested in the product you have to sell.

One way to decrease your investment is to do incremental mailing. If your market has 100,000 people or more, then mail only 5,000 at a time and space the mailings every two weeks. This gives you the opportunity to evaluate the results of the list and generate a few sales from your first mailing before it's time to invest in the second mailing of 5,000. This can save you the pain and frustration of discovering the hard way that the list is not as effective as you thought it might be.

Keeping in mind that you will need to acquire an industry list and make a significant marketing investment, using a diagnostic survey to launch your information marketing business can generate good results in a short period of time.

If you are considering the diagnostic survey launch method for your business, you will benefit by reviewing examples of the materials you will need. The **Information Marketing Business Pyramid**™ includes

- examples of diagnostic surveys,
- sales letters to use as follow-up to the surveys,

- additional insights on what to do after you have received the returned surveys, and
- how to turn product buyers into continuity program participants so you can make sure your initial sale sets up a series of sales from you to each customer.

All that and more is included in the **Information Marketing Business Pyramid**™. Check it out at **InfoMarketingPyramid.com**.

Making a Big Splash in Your Industry with a New Event

Chapter 37

How to Launch an Info-Business with a Three-Day Event

IKE CROW BELIEVES IN THE "WAVE THEORY"—IF YOU GET in on a growing industry at the beginning, your business is going to follow that wave of growth.

Mike had gone into the real estate business with his father and uncle and soon discovered the home inspection industry. "The industry was new," Mike says. "I believed it was gonna grow, and as it grew, any company there at the beginning would grow with it. Sure enough, we did grow, but at a certain point, the industry matured, so we had to find a way to continue our growth using other means." Mike found those means when he discovered coaches.

"Brian Tracy, Jay Abraham, Dan Kennedy, Bill Glazer, and a number of people were out there teaching people how to market their businesses," Mike recalls. "We saw Dan Kennedy at a Peter Lowes seminar back in the early 1990s. I had taken my wife and kids with me because I wanted them to have a feel for the information, to know that it wasn't just me, that there were thousands of people involved."

Mike was shocked when his wife bought in to the idea. "My wife was the one who said, 'I like what Dan Kennedy is saying; we need to get his stuff and do this.'" They purchased Dan's program, started using his principles, and began getting results. Their business started growing.

Soon Mike realized that every industry seemed to have a coach. "One of the industries I work with is real estate agents," he explains. "I sponsored Rick Deluca to do a free half-day seminar for real estate agents. As I sat there and watched Rick present some really good information, it occurred to me that you don't have to be real slick, you don't have to be real polished, you just have to be genuine. You just have to have good information."

Nothing he saw was specifically geared toward home inspectors, so Mike adapted materials from various coaches for his niche and grew one of the largest home inspection companies in North America. He ended up selling the business for an amount his accountant said the buyer would "just laugh at and walk away." After working for the new owner for three years, Mike decided it was time to leave: "I was working inside a large corporation, and they did everything tremendously different. Quite honestly they tore apart what I had built. We had a peak, efficient business, and piece by piece, they got rid of it. So, I resigned."

That was in 2003. Mike recalls, "At that point I was sitting on my back patio with a nice bank account wondering what I was gonna do now. That's when I decided I could teach other home inspectors to do what I had done."

Mike's story takes a different turn at this point. While most people will put a kit together, sell it for a while, invite people into a coaching program, and then have a large, three-day event, Mike held his three-day event first.

"We did things completely backward," he laughs. "Other people did small, half-day events, but I said, 'Let's just start this

FIGURE 37-1. Mike Crow conducts a lot of customer acquisition campaigns by sending postcards to the entire population of home inspectors through rented lists. Once the home inspectors call for a free report or go online and submit their information, Mike is then able to follow up with a sales campaign to sell them products and coaching.

thing off with a bang.' I had the money, so we went straight to a three-day event. We advertised and sold people into it—teleseminars played a huge role in that process. I didn't want to travel all across the country, so in our initial series of advertisements and e-mails, we offered a teleseminar. At the end of the seminar, we gave participants two options: They could sign up for 3 Days of Secrets Revealed, and/or they could join the Dream Team. If they joined the Dream Team, they received

What you need to know...

- How to Make $700 More Per Week By Targeting Upscale Homes
- How To Make Your Advertising Money Work Harder and More Effectively For You
- How To Stop Wasting Money On Ads And Quit Being The Prey Of Advertising Reps
- How To Educate Your Customers So They Want You to Inspect Their Homes When They Call
- How To Keep Your Current Agents Coming Back! They'll Never Look For Another Inspector Again!
- How To Get Agents To Refer You Like Crazy!
- 70% Of Your Clients Will Come From Referrals
- How To 'Wow' Your Customers and Why This Will Insure Your Success!
- How To Never Waste Another Dollar On Useless Advertising!
- What A USP Is and Why It Will Make All Your Advertising and Marketing Hugely Successful!
- The Easiest Way To Almost Instantly Double Your Business!
- How To Double Your Profits On Almost Every Job!
- How To Say Good-bye To 'Pressuring' Customers - Learn How To Get Customers To Want Your Services!

That's Only a Fraction of My Marketing Secrets!

3 Days of Secrets REVEALED

The Most Powerful Three-Day Conference You'll Ever Attend

Come discover the strategies highly successful inspectors are using to increase their revenues and profits.

Truly successful professionals are more productive and more profitable than you ever imagined. They are in control of their businesses and their lives; they choose how and when they work. They enjoy lucrative, predictable incomes. They never have to sell. They never cold call. They never spend money on marketing and advertising that does not produce immediate, verifiable results every time. Their clients consider them their consultant for life. And they enjoy a steady stream of new clients, as well.

How do they do it?

They learned the secrets of building a successful, reliable, 100% referral-based business. You can too.

By attending the **3 Days of Secrets Revealed** you'll learn new, highly profitable business systems that will help you transform your business into one that generates substantially higher revenue while requiring significantly less time.

Bottom Line:

This is the Best Investment of Time and Money You'll Ever Make!

100% Guaranteed

We guarantee that these business-building systems and strategies, along with the training and coaching you receive, will add 1 to 5 inspections per month to your bottom line. If you decide this event does not live up to our promise, we will immediately refund your tuition. Simply turn in your materials and ask for a refund after the last session on Day 1. No explanation necessary. Your tuition will be cheerfully refunded, plus we will reimburse you upto $500.00 for your travel expenses. Or, if you stay for all 3 days and decide you can't at least make 10 times your tuition by implementing my strategies, you can turn in your materials and we will cheerfully refund your entire tuition.

So what are you waiting for? Take advantage of this "Better than Risk-Free" offer now.

Call now 1-800-211-3981

or www.MikeCrow.com

FIGURE 37-2. Mike Crow Postcard to sell registrants to his seminar.

Identify the safest, fastest, most effective, and most profitable route to growing your home inspection business.

You'll see vivid, tangible, bottom-line results in just weeks. It's transactionally impossible not to have a tremendous breakthrough. You will discover:

- How to **take your business to the next level** in size, profits, and position in the marketplace.
- How to get the **maximum results** from your time, money and effort.
- How to make your business so **radically different from your competitor's** that you effectively have a monopoly over customers.
- How to **acquire more new customers** without spending thousands on advertising or a sales force.
- How to **increase your bottom line exponentially**, not gradually.
- How to **unearth thousands of dollars** buried in your business.
- How to **isolate and quantify a select group of result areas** that hold the key to breakneck, exponential growth.
- How to **optimize your business strategy** by testing, measuring, evaluating, and systematizing.
- How to **leverage your marketing** so you control downside risk while retaining unlimited upside potential.
- How to **think like a marketing genius.**

At the conclusion, your business will have undergone an amazing transformation. You will have created an integrated business growth plan specifically for your business – one that identifies and prioritizes opportunities, recognizes risks to avoid, and arms you with superior techniques no one in your industry is using!

Growth rates of 50%, 100% or even 500% are not out of the question!

I am certain that by applying this incredible business-building system to your business, you will become infinitely more productive, effective, customer focused, and profitable.

How much can your company make from this program? I'd love to say you'll double the size of your business. But let's say you only **increase your profitability by 15-20%,** you only **raise your average sale by 8%,** your ads only **pull 5% more inquires,** your office schedules only one more customer out of ten, what would that mean to your business over a month ... six months ... a year ... forever? Is that enough to justify trying this program?

Of course, these claims are just rhetoric until you see tangible results for yourself in your business. I know of only one way to convince you, and that is to offer you my "Extraordinary Guarantee."

My "Extraordinary Guarantee" is that I will enthusiastically assume all the risk.

I promise that when you attend **3 Days of Secrets Revealed** and in good faith apply what you learned every week, it is improbable if not statistically impossible – that you won't have a **major breakthrough.** I guarantee that your breakthrough will be **worth 10 times your investment in just a few months.** If you don't

believe that by the end of the first day. You can turn in all of your materials and my team will refund all your money plus up to $500.00 air fare, car rental and/or lodging. I will even give you until the end of the third day and if you don't think this is true just turn your materials in and my team will give you a complete refund for the seminar. **Best of all, your profits don't stop** after six weeks or even six months. After completing the **3 Days of Secrets Revealed** you will **walk away with applications, knowledge, and ideas for the rest of your life** – in

> *"I attended the first 3-Days of Secrets Revealed and immediately used only a few of the tactics and concepts Mike teaches. I doubled my business – my free time also doubled, and it moved my business from not worrying too much about where my business is going to come from, because it is very highly and very directly focused on marketing my business it has worked for me, on top of that the coaching calls keep me focused and stay focused. I highly recommend you spend some time with Mike Crow."*
>
> **Dean Forrest, All Valley Home Inspections**
> **Cottonwood, Arizona**

So what are you waiting for? Take advantage of this "Better than Risk-Free" offer now.

Call now toll free **1-800-211-3981** and put the most powerful business-building tool ever developed in your hands – Alternatively, you can sign up on our website at www.MikeCrow.com

FIGURE 37-2. Another postcard Mike Crow created to sell registrants to his seminar.

my Big Bang marketing kit, free entry to my 3 Days of Secrets Revealed, and coaching with me on a monthly basis over the phone."

Mike video-recorded his kickoff event, 3 Days of Secrets Revealed, and that became his first kit. In addition, he offered coaching. "I'm a big believer in continuity," Mike says, "and I wanted to make sure we had people sending us money every single month."

Chapter 38

Anatomy of a Successful Info-Marketing Seminar Business Launch

---

IKE CROW'S STORY ILLUSTRATES ONE OF THE BEST ways to launch a brand-new information marketing business, an in-person seminar. An in-person seminar is a powerful way to launch your info-marketing business.

Let's consider the results Mike had after his event:

- A group of satisfied customers who attended the seminar and had a great time
- New continuity customers in Mike's Dream Team program, investing to receive ongoing coaching and resources
- Video and audio products sold to those who weren't able to attend the seminar

Seminars are a great way to launch your info-marketing business. Figure 38-1 diagrams how this system works.

Your goal is to charge a registration fee for your event that allows you to put a large number of people in the room while also breaking even or generating a profit. This way, you have

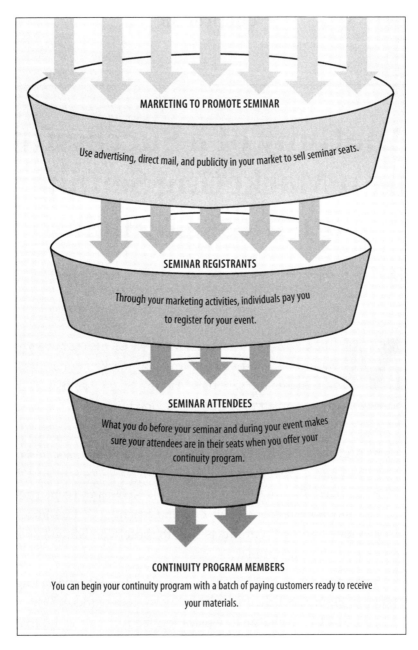

FIGURE 38-1. How to use a seminar to generate customers for your continuity program.

little or no marketing expenses for the products and services you sell during the event.

I've planned more than 100 events in my career in several different industries—for physicians such as anesthesiologists, dermatologists, and ob/gyns; for paramedical professions including occupational therapists, speech language pathologists and audiologists, and oriental medicine practitioners; for industries such as movers and warehousemen, financial service centers, and motorcycle dealers; as well as for CEOs of companies that generate hundreds of millions of dollars in revenue.

While there are differences in these groups, the events are almost identical to produce. Providing information, facilitating human interaction, and creating an engaging environment are the same for any event, and you do them using the same steps every time.

Choose a Date

Give yourself 9 to 12 months to produce an effective event. While there is always a strong urge to get on with it, events require adequate time to produce them correctly. Plus, you must give yourself enough time to promote your event, especially if it's your first one. Plan for plenty of time to get the materials created and distributed well in advance of your event.

As far as which dates to choose, avoid religious holidays of all kinds. Facilities often will steer you toward their open dates with discounts, so triple check for federal holidays or religious holidays that could give your attendees an easy excuse to skip your event. Should you host your event on a weekday or a weekend? There is no set answer. Typically, if your audience is comprised of business owners, weekday events are best. If your attendees are individuals or professionals, weekends are generally more convenient for them.

Choose a Location

If your event is nationwide, I always recommend having your event in Florida. I live here, and I believe it's the best place to hold your event. Several cities have great airports and meeting facilities, so you can move around within the state for years if you want variety.

As far as other cities go, Dallas, St. Louis, Indianapolis, Memphis, and other big cities in the middle of the country offer an inexpensive alternative to top tier cities like Chicago, New York, and Las Vegas. While the top tier cities are exciting, they offer many distractions. It's difficult to build a relationship with attendees if they can't walk through the casino without spending an hour at the blackjack table.

If you live in or near a city with a decent airport, consider having your event there. What you give up in convenience for your attendees, you gain in convenience for you. As a local business, you'll likely find a hotel that's eager to work with you because you may have several meetings bringing attendees into the city. Also, you can visit the hotel and walk through the meeting facility without having to travel. That home-field advantage may be good to have for your first event.

Create Marketing Materials and Pricing

This is the most important part of your event planning. Give yourself four to six months to sell seats to your event. In addition to what I cover in Chapter 42, profiles in this section illustrate a few examples of the marketing others have used to fill their events.

You'll need to create or rent a list of your target market, create and send direct mail, host teleseminars that promote your event, and work with joint venture partners to sell seats. If you are new to all this, consider hiring a professional sales copywriter with experience in event marketing to help you create a marketing campaign.

Don't be cheap. The power of hosting your own seminar is that attendees will pay $995.00, $1,495.00, $4,995.00, or more to attend an event about something they are interested in. This allows you to invest a significant amount of money in marketing to build awareness of your company within your market and to sell seats.

Every market is different, and what your market is willing to pay will be unique. It's impossible to quote you one price that I know will work for you as well as everyone else. However, I highly recommend you offer a fee that's at least $995.00 to $2,495.00. If this seems high to you, that's OK; even if you get only 40 people in the room at $995.00, that funds $39,800.00 in marketing you can do to make sure everyone in your market knows who you are. If you charge $1,495.00, your marketing budget leaps to $59,800.00 with only 40 people in the room.

Create a Budget

Work with your host hotel to identify the costs for your event. When in doubt, don't spend it. While you may be tempted to "wine and dine" your attendees, this isn't necessary and may actually hurt sales at your event. Plus, it sets up an unreasonably high expectation for your future events.

That said, many hotel contracts require you to buy a minimum amount of food and beverages to book the meeting space. Negotiate these down as much as possible. It's as easy as asking them to lower the requirement.

Two places I do suggest investing money for food and beverage are to host a reception and a luncheon for attendees where you can promote your coaching program. Other than those two events, I would offer only water, coffee, and perhaps sodas to attendees unless the hotel requires you to provide more. As long as there is a restaurant at the hotel and perhaps a few nearby dinner options, you don't have to feed your guests. Keep these dining choices in mind as you plan your event.

Other significant expenses are audiovisuals and videography. If you are audio recording your event with a paid tech on site, your investment could be as little at $1,500.00 a day. If you plan to videotape your event, you'll need a nice backdrop and a stage to make sure the video camera can see you clearly over the audience. Plus, you'll need a camera operator, someone working the sound, and another person troubleshooting the slide presentations. Full production can easily cost $7,500.00 a day for your event. While you want to get several proposals and negotiate the best deal you can, if you are selling your product for $995.00, then you only need to sell a few to recover your production costs. Also, getting just one or two new coaching clients will completely pay for your event.

Other than those investments, I recommend you plan your event's budget to allocate as much as possible to marketing the event. The more people attending your event, the more people you have the opportunity to sell into your coaching program. Consider if you can afford allocating all your registration fees toward marketing your event, paying for food and beverage, and covering your audiovisual costs. This way, you can enter the event at break-even, with registration fees covering your event's costs. Then you can count the revenue you generate from your coaching program as your profit from hosting the event. Too many people try to pocket their marketing money and then suffer from not having enough people at their events. Cut the food or the audiovisuals before you cut your event's marketing budget.

Execute

You will have many details to track as you pull together your event. However, most will take care of themselves once you've committed to a date, location, and budget.

It's easy to get intimidated by the thought of creating your own event and speaking on stage for two or three days. If so, perhaps one of the other info-marketing launch models is for you. But before you choose another model, keep in mind that hosting a live event isn't as difficult as it may sound.

There are additional details, instructions, and examples in the **Information Marketing Business Pyramid**™. The lessons learned, step-by-step instructions, and easy shortcuts will save you a lot of time, money, and aggravation as you launch your information marketing business. For more information, visit **InfoMarketingPyramid.com**.

Chapter 39

You Can Still Make Big Money from Small Audiences

I F YOU NEED SOME ENCOURAGEMENT TO USE A SEMINAR TO LAUNCH your information marketing business, Fabienne Fredrickson is the one to ask. Three years after hosting her first seminar, she has gone from a low six-figure income to running a multimillion-dollar business.

"I owe a lot of my success to the fact that we did seminars," Fabienne says. "I was at a Glazer-Kennedy event in November 2007. Events expert Bari Baumgardner was there, and I walked up to her and said, 'I want to do a seminar. I want to do it with you, and I want you to teach me what I need to get started.'"

Nine months later, after conducting three preview calls to publicize her first event, Fabienne had 42 people in the room, and she couldn't have been happier with what many might have considered was a small attendance. "I see a lot of people with illusions of grandeur about their first seminar drawing 200 or 300 people," Fabienne smiles. "I've yet to see that happen."

Fabienne was happy with the turnout for several reasons. First, after paying for space rental, audiovisuals, food, event planning, and seminar materials, she had cleared $12,000.00. "Not bad for a weekend's work," she says. But that $12,000.00 was only the beginning.

The real money came from what happened after the seminar. "I don't know many people who actually offer a mastermind group at their very first event, but I put it out there, and we ended up getting 12 people into the mastermind at $10,000.00 each!" Fabienne exclaims. "That $120,000.00 was a huge uptick in my income and in my positioning in the marketplace. I also sold the workshop in a box after the seminar, and in one week I sold 60 of them. I made a cool $60,000, so all in all, I made about $200,000.00, doubling my income that year with just one event."

Don't get caught up in thinking you need to have 100 or 200 people in your event to make it a success. Fabienne had only 42 people at her first event, but she was still able to turn that event into $200,000.00 of revenue for her business.

Chapter 40

Building an Event that Launches Your Continuity Program

NOW THAT YOU'VE DECIDED TO HOST AN EVENT, YOU HAVE TO figure out what you are going to do with your attendees. The best length for a national meeting is two to three days long. Most find the three-day format gives them the best opportunity to teach enough information, build a relationship with the audience, and have time to offer a coaching program. It may seem like a long time if you've never held an event, but trust me, those three days will fly by.

Let me walk you through the steps I use when I'm designing an event for a coaching client who is launching an info-business with a seminar.

Outlining the Content

It all starts with identifying the content and the training your audience will love. Build your seminar by outlining the content you will provide during the event. For this discussion, let's assume your first event will be national in scope, so you are going to plan for it to last three days. But this exercise works the same whether your session is three days long or three hours long.

Map out the morning and afternoon for each day of your event on a sheet of paper, either in a word processing file or in a spreadsheet. Then start to create an outline for what you'll teach during those sessions. If you are also building a product out of the seminar's recordings, consider building in breaks every two hours so you can have natural breaks on any DVD videos you'll create.

Give thought to the flow of the teaching at your event, and plan to deliver the content in a logical sequence that delivers a great experience for attendees. Also, don't feel you have to cram ten days' worth of content into three days. It's easy to overwhelm people with too much. It's all the better if you distill several years of experience and lessons learned into an actionable game plan your attendees can learn within three days.

Would you like to have a few outside speakers present to your group? It's fine to have two or three guest speakers to provide some of the content. However, if your primary goal for this event is to launch your coaching program, then you need to feature your knowledge and build a relationship with the audience as much as possible. One benefit of having an outside speaker or two is they can sell products to your group. Typically, the event's host and the speaker split revenue from sales 50–50. Having a guest speaker offer a product will help generate more revenue from the event for you. Still, most info-marketers are opting to have few, if any, outside speakers at their first events to give themselves the greatest opportunity to offer coaching and build great relationships with their audiences.

The decision on when to offer your coaching program will vary based on the rest of your schedule. For a three-day seminar, plan to offer your coaching program for the first time on the afternoon of the second day, with applications due by lunch on the third day.

Plan to host a reception on the evening of the second day for anyone who is interested in the coaching program. During the reception, your job is to walk around the room, spending three to five minutes with as many of your attendees as you can. Ask each person about what she is looking for in a coaching program, discuss each individual's goals, and let each prospect know how your coaching program will help in achieving those goals. Your objective is to knock as many fence-sitters off the fence and into your coaching program as you can. However, to your guests, it should look like you are simply making the rounds and talking with everyone.

On the third day, host a luncheon promoted as a "quick-start event" for everyone who has joined your coaching program. You can use this time to give them an outline of the dates, any of the logistical details, and some encouragement about how much they'll enjoy coaching. Also, this provides an incentive to many of your attendees to join coaching so they don't get left out of the luncheon.

An important part of any educational environment, especially in adult education, is engagement. Get your attendees working on and discussing with each other what you are teaching. Set aside time each day for your attendees to begin working on and thinking about what you've taught them. Some of your options include posing a question and giving them time to work independently on their answers, distributing a case example for them to read and diagnose, or asking them to review an example and guess why it was so effective.

Encourage sessions for group discussion where attendees discuss and critique each other's work products. This fosters networking and connections within the group.

These exercises allow your attendees to leave with some of their homework done, and I think they feel a real sense of accomplishment that builds to "Well, if this person can do this much in two or three days, imagine what he could do with me over the course of a year." It's better to teach your attendees six things they understand and are ready to implement than to skip the exercises so you have time to teach ten things they don't understand well enough to implement.

Finally, you'll want to sprinkle in some things to make your event interesting and fun. If you have a few stories you can tell, include those throughout the event to break up your teaching. You also can ask attendees to keep track of their "aha" moments so they can share them with the group on the third day.

Your advance planning will help you or anyone you hire to create your event's marketing, and it'll make it a lot easier to produce your training materials. While investing time to create a plan may not look easy, it is definitely the shortcut to success when it comes to launching your information marketing business quickly.

Chapter 41

Foreclosure Can Be a Good Thing . . . Just Ask Ted Thomas

PILOT TED THOMAS WAS FLYING HIGH IN THE REAL ESTATE business until changes in the tax law threw him into a tailspin. He eventually crashed, having to file for bankruptcy. But that didn't keep him down. Like a phoenix, Ted found a way to rise from the ashes of his burned-out real estate career to become one of the most successful information marketers in the industry today.

Ted's first career was as an airline pilot. He worked for Aloha Airlines, and from there he went into the real estate business in California. He bought apartment houses and office buildings all over the West. During the 1970s, Ted built a company that owned over $200 million worth of real estate. That all changed abruptly in 1986.

"In '86 they changed all the rules," Ted remembers. "You couldn't write off real estate anymore, and so all the commercial real estate we had bought—and I owned 1,800 apartment houses in Phoenix alone—dropped anywhere from 25 to 35 percent in value."

In less than a year, Ted had lost everything. "With the stroke of Congress's pen, it all just went away," Ted muses. "I went from the clubhouse to the outhouse in six months. In 1986, I was living in the country club, right close to the clubhouse. Just like that, it was all over. I lost my house to foreclosure."

But Ted didn't let that foreclosure stop him. "I redirected myself. Believe it or not, losing my house to foreclosure is what got me into the foreclosure business!" Ted exclaims. "I started looking at my situation, and I said, 'Gee, I wonder if anybody else is as stupid as me.' So I went down to county records to find out. It turns out I lived in a very wealthy county, Contra Costa County, right across from San Francisco. And 75 people a week were going into foreclosure!"

Ted pulled himself out of bankruptcy by purchasing foreclosure houses and reselling them. Putting his marketing savvy to work, he even used direct mail to buy and sell houses. "This was back in the 1980s," Ted says. "The *San Francisco Examiner Chronicle* called me for an interview because they couldn't believe I was buying houses using direct mail. At first I turned the interview down. The guy called me back in a couple of days and said, 'Look, we're going to do the article, so if we can interview you, we can make sure it's accurate.' So I did the interview. That's when people started calling and saying 'Can you teach me how to do it?' Bingo. I was in information marketing."

Not one to start small, Ted began charging $1,000.00 per day, and his typical consulting took five days. From there he branched out into writing reports that outlined his steps to follow, and that led to a book. "In 1988, I did a big, thick book," Ted says. "It was 450 pages, and I self-published it. It sold for $100.00. Back then, no one could sell a book for $100.00."

Ted put his strategies into a book, and one of those books landed on Howard Ruff's desk. Howard Ruff was a gold investor

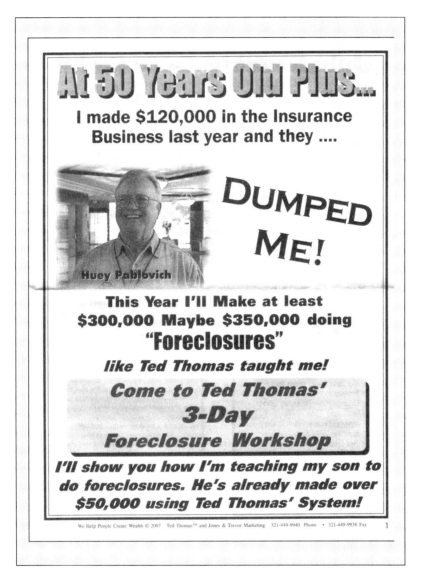

FIGURE 41-1. Ted Thomas positions learning his information as an escape from his prospect's frustrations. In this page Ted appeals to anyone frustrated with his current job and scared about getting laid off by his company.

who wrote a newsletter that went to a list of 300,000 people. "Howard Ruff called me up and said, 'Ted, I read your book, and it's really good. Could you make this into a seminar for my clients?' I said, 'Yeah, it'll probably take me two or three weeks,' and he said, 'Oh, it'll take three weeks just to write the mail piece.' Stupid me, I said, 'What's a mail piece?' I didn't know!"

Ted had something else to learn, too. When he asked Howard how they would split the money from a seminar, he was shocked when Howard said 70/30—with only 30 percent going to Ted! As the author, Ted thought 70 percent might go to him. "I didn't know that it cost money to market a seminar," Ted remembers. "But the payoff was huge. Howard charged $5,000.00 for a three-day seminar. Nobody did that in 1988!"

Nobody but Howard and Ted. For the next ten months, they had 50 people at each seminar, each one paying $5,000.00 for the privilege. They took in $2.5 million, with $800,000.00 going to Ted. "Did that get me out of bankruptcy or what?" Ted laughs.

Howard had a few more lessons for Ted. Like sequential mailings: "Howard said, 'Look, you mail once, they like it, you mail it again. They like it, you mail it again. You just keep doing it.'" Another tip from Howard was to record the seminars and sell tapes. "We mailed our seminar offer to 50,000 people," Ted says. "Only 500 people bought at $5,000.00, so Howard had the idea to record the seminar and send a notice that people could buy the tapes. We made another $150 million that way."

Today, Ted is still in the real estate business, using the same techniques he sells in his information marketing business. His success has inspired many others to copy his formula. "I have kept doing real estate, buying houses and wholesaling them, and I still use direct mail and the system I created. I still do the same old system. I still sell it, and I've been selling it since 1988."

Ted continues to build his business, offering everything from books to manuals to directories to CDs to DVDs. "I have a video

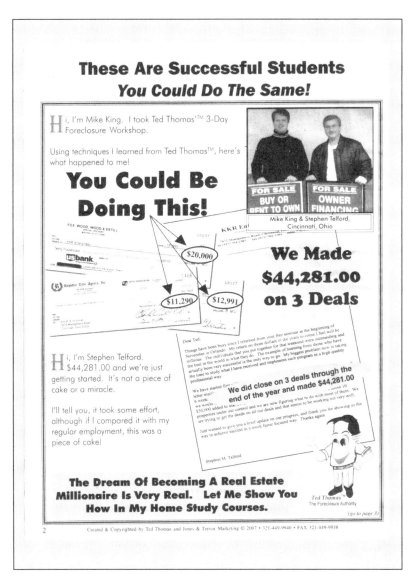

FIGURE 41-2. Ted Thomas uses a lot of graphics in his sales letters. On this page, Ted uses arrows, then introduces larger, darker, circled numbers, and finally summarizes the total of the three checks in a starburst. These are designed to catch the eye of prospects who are quickly skimming the sales letter to get them to read more about the success story Ted is illustrating.

library that would cover the wall in your office. It's that big because I don't do anything without a video camera running," Ted says. He also does four live events a year that bring in $250,000.00 to $500,000.00 each.

One of the ways Ted has marketed his live events is by partnering with other info-marketers to get them to offer an event to their lists. For his first event, he was able to get 600 people to attend. That number went down for subsequent meetings because others began copying the strategy, so Ted backed off from it for a while. He fine-tuned the idea and tried it again three years ago, this time charging a higher fee and keeping the events smaller and more unusual. He has held seminars at airports with jets flying in the background and at the CBS News studio so attendees can see firsthand how a news station works. "You've gotta change your approach every few months because everybody copies it," Ted says. "I'm going to keep doing meetings; I just have to do change-ups to keep it interesting."

Ted turns every live event into videos and then audios and on down to transcripts for sale. Attendees at his live events get to see how Ted repackages his materials and sells them again and again.

All that reselling has landed Ted in his own piece of paradise on the east coast of Florida. He lives on Merritt Island, where Ted says, "If I threw my pen out the window, it would land in the water." Ted shares his island with 5,000 alligators, two of which live in the lake on Ted's property. He also gets to watch osprey and four-foot cranes that like to wander around in his backyard. When he tires of bird watching, Ted has front row seats for shuttle launches from Kennedy Space Center, which is seven miles due north of his swimming pool. "I can sit by my pool and watch them go. It's unbelievable!" Ted exclaims.

FIGURE 41-3. On some pages, Ted Thomas uses many graphic elements, while other pages contain mostly text, delivering his sales story. The combination of both styles appeals to the widest possible variety of readers' preferences.

Ted draws inspiration from his idyllic surroundings to produce 40 or 50 mail pieces a year. He does the copywriting and develops the marketing plan, and then he has staff execute it for him. "I map it out for my staff—what goes to what list, and then they're able to get it done," Ted says. "And to a certain extent, they can tell me what part of the list is reacting and what part we should mail a particular piece."

Chapter 42

Filling Your Seminar with Paid Registrants

Ted Thomas's story in the previous chapter illustrates the power of using seminars to build an information marketing business. And you can see the lengths Ted goes to when he promotes his seminars to generate large numbers of attendees and build the income he has enjoyed through his information marketing business.

The single most important thing you must do to have a successful seminar, and thus a successful info-marketing business launch, is to promote your event. If you don't have attendees in the room, then you're not going to be able to generate the sales necessary to launch your information marketing business. That makes marketing your event the pivotal piece of this type of information marketing business launch.

In the next few pages, I'm going to give you an outline of an effective event marketing plan, along with the things you should consider as you plan your approach to launching your event.

If you have time and expertise and enjoy copywriting, then you can easily create all these materials yourself. If you are not a copywriting expert, consider hiring a copywriter who has experience filling seminars. You should check the references on her client list to make sure she is someone who has filled seminars in the past and to decide if her past experiences will help with your particular market. The nice thing about hiring a copywriter is the speed you'll gain in developing your marketing materials. While you're busy building relationships with people who can promote your event, you will have someone creating copy so that by the time it is written, you will have people in place to help you distribute it. Hiring a copywriter can give you leverage and help you get things done quickly.

Let me give you a timeline for marketing your event and list the things you should be thinking about as your event approaches. This will give you a starting point for creating a successful seminar to launch your information marketing business.

Early Planning Is Your Shortcut to a Successful Event

Although 9 to 12 months out may seem like a long time to plan an event, I witness too many info-marketers cutting their marketing cycles short. It decreases the number of attendees they are able to generate and thus the number of coaching customers they're able to get from those attendees. Of course, there are many reasons for trying to cut it short. One may be because you can't afford a large amount of marketing. If that's the case, then you will need to do your marketing over a shorter period, but if at all possible, invest in a longer marketing cycle that will allow you to do more promotions and get more attendees in the room.

Your Big Event Idea

What is the one big idea that will make attendees want to flock to your event? What is it that's going to capture their imaginations and make them say "Wow! I've been waiting for this for a long time." What is it that's going to get them to do anything they can to get to your event? That big idea, that big concept, that big title is one of the pivotal things that's going to grab the attention of your potential audience members and get them to want to come to your event. That big idea is one of the first things you need to create, and 9 to 12 months out isn't too soon.

Marketing Plan

You want to create a marketing plan that runs for four to six months in advance of your event. The marketing plan should include a sequence of direct mail to people you've identified as potential attendees, e-mail marketing to any lists you have or lists you can obtain, social media campaigns, joint venture partners, or any other partners that will agree to promote your event. Also consider if advertising is an appropriate method for getting leads for people who will be interested in registering for your event. Take all those ideas and create a marketing plan out of them. When are you going to send marketing pieces and over which time periods? What are the deadlines to get those pieces created?

Secure Location

Identify the city and the hotel or other venue where you plan to host your event so you can begin publicizing your dates and location. Most info-marketers choose to tell prospects the city for their events but do not reveal the actual location except to someone who has registered. You don't want interlopers who try to show up for free, hang out at the bar, and network with your attendees. It also helps to prevent vendors or other businesspeople from setting up their own meetings in a room next to yours.

However, early in the process, you will want to have the meeting location determined for your own planning purposes and the city confirmed so you can include the location city in the marketing materials you send as part of your event's promotion.

Finalize Speakers

If you're going to invite guest speakers, confirm those individuals as early as possible so you can obtain their biographies and sales information to promote their sessions in your marketing materials. One of the big benefits of having additional speakers is that what they're covering might attract attendees to the event who might not otherwise be interested. You want to be able to feature all speakers in your marketing materials to attract as many potential attendees as possible.

Recruit Sponsors and Vendors

Are there companies or other individuals marketing to your customers that would like to be part of your event? Very often sponsors can help by providing money that gives you financing for marketing or your event's other costs. They can help you promote the event to their customers and can bolster the credibility of your event by showing you're not the only one promoting this event to your market. Having sponsors shows you are a member of a team of major companies within your industry. Displaying your sponsoring companies' logos and recognizing them as sponsors of your event show you are a real player in the marketplace and your event is where your customers are going to receive great information.

Give some consideration to what companies would be appropriate sponsors. When you approach them, it's really as simple as asking. A lot of companies are already accustomed to marketing through sponsorships. You'll need to explain your event, the types of attendees you are attracting, and how your event will help them further their goals. Your sponsors want the same things you do: exposure in the marketplace and an opportunity to make money.

Build Relationships with Promotion Partners

Who else in your industry and market would be a good promotion partner for your event? Letting individuals know you are creating an event to meet certain customers' needs you've identified and working with them to help promote the event can be a great way to get the word out, and it's also cost effective for you. It may be worth giving 50 percent to even 100 percent of the registration fee to your promotion partners to encourage them to sell tickets to your event. It's not always necessary to give that much of the registration fee, but it certainly is worth it if you can use those partners to generate registrations that don't cost you any marketing investment.

Give some thought to other vendors, magazines, or trade journals in your market, trade associations in the industry, and anyone else who might provide a way of promoting your event to the marketplace. Take advantage of these great and sometimes untapped resources for getting seminar seats sold that won't require you to invest in more direct mail marketing.

Execute Your Event's Marketing

When you're within four to six months of your event, it is time to distribute your marketing materials to potential attendees. This is when you need to get your attendees to mark your dates on their calendars and save them for you and your event. You want to publish your dates ahead of all the other distractions and opportunities that can take attendees away from your event.

If you can get them locked in with a registration fee and a plane ticket, that's all the better at this point because that makes them committed to you. Anything else that comes up for those dates they can brush off with "Oh, I'm already booked for that week." This is crunch time to make sure you get your event on your attendees' calendars.

Provide Marketing Materials to Your Partners

For any partners you build a relationship with, either as sponsors or as promoters for a split of the registration fees, provide them with the marketing materials they need at this time. Send them sample e-mails, sample faxes, ads they can put in their publications, sales letters to distribute, scripts they can use on the telephone, and articles and other materials they can include with their own marketing media, including their newsletters. Send these items to your partners as early as you possibly can so they can start promoting the event on your behalf.

Establish Response Deadlines

Deadlines are the single most important response booster you can add to any marketing campaign. When a seminar is four to six months out, it's easy for potential attendees to say to themselves "You know what? I'll set this aside, and I'll make the decision whether or not I'm going to go to this a month ahead of time." It's really easy to put it off. By the time your event approaches, a potential attendee might have five other things she wants to do and will decide "Oh, no. I'm not going to bother going to that seminar."

You want people to make the decision as far in advance as possible that they are going to attend. One of the best ways is by taking away discounts and bonuses as the event gets closer. For example, if you have a registration fee of $2,500.00, you can offer a price of only $1,500.00 to anyone that registers four months in advance and then $2,000.00 to anyone that registers two months in advance. These are called expiring discounts.

If you aren't interested in discounting your registration fee, you can offer deadlines with expiring bonuses. For example, you can host a special early bird reception the night before the event for everyone who registers before a certain date. Getting this special access to you in advance of the event will encourage attendees to register early. Once the discounts and bonuses expire, stop mentioning them in your marketing materials. You don't want someone to make the decision to not register because it's too late to receive a particular bonus or discount.

Using expiring deadlines in advance of the event will encourage your attendees to register early rather than having all of them come in at the last minute.

Use Multiple Contacts over Various Media

Throughout your marketing plan, use every media you can afford to contact your potential attendees. You will want to use direct mail, e-mail marketing, social media, and every other way you know to get your attendees to pay attention. Invest in your event's marketing because that's what's going to generate the attendees, allowing you to populate your first coaching program for your info-marketing business.

Increase Your Marketing to a Fever Pitch

In the three to four months before your event, you should have all your marketing materials climax so that everywhere someone goes in your marketplace, he is seeing someone writing about your event, hearing others talking about it, getting asked "Are you going to . . .," and it becomes clear that your event is "the place" for everyone to go.

Teleseminars to Promote Your Event

Consider using a series of teleseminars to help promote your event. It could be two or three teleseminars, either with you making a presentation or with you interviewing one or two of the speakers you have invited.

Your goal isn't to provide a lot of teaching, but instead to sell your seminar. Review the problems your attendees are facing, discuss the challenges within the industry, and then present what's going to be revealed at the seminar. During the teleseminar, ask individuals to register for your event, reminding them of any bonuses or discounts that are about to expire. Teleseminars are a great way to get people to block out time on their calendars and then dial in at a certain time so you can explain the reasons why they need to register for your program. Use teleseminars as a tool for generating attendance at your event.

Keep Your Registrants Excited

Just because someone has registered doesn't mean you can ignore him. Many registered attendees, for whatever reason, choose not to show up at an event. You need to keep your registrants excited and happy about showing up at your seminar.

One tactic I've used to keep registrants excited about my seminars is to publish a series of articles. The articles discuss challenges in the industry, the top mistakes people are making, and what I'm going to reveal at the seminar. I send these articles to my registrants so they stay excited about attending my seminar.

The point is that I keep in contact with my registrants, I keep focusing them on the challenges they're going to be able to solve as a result of coming to my seminar, and I keep them engaged with me during the weeks leading up to the event. It's also a great way to highlight any special events or bonuses or to remind them about anything they need to know about reserving their hotel rooms or transportation.

At a minimum, if you are using a copywriter to write sales copy for your event, have that copywriter create a series of e-mails designed to keep registrants excited about your meeting.

Home Stretch

In the last two months before your event, you want to continue your marketing pitch and keep after getting new attendees.

Telemarketing

Consider a telemarketing campaign to reach out to your potential attendees on the phone and get them interested and excited to register. The purpose of calling is to make sure they've received the event's marketing and to ask them to register. If you're marketing to consumers, you have to comply with any do-not-call laws, both on the federal level as well as on a state level. But telemarketing can be a great way for getting attendees to come to an event. Often you'll discover that a lot of people are trying to decide whether or not they should attend. By giving them a call and talking to them about the event, you can move them from undecided to paid registrants.

When you call, begin the call by asking a few questions such as "Are these problems you would really like to get solved once and for all?" and let them say yes. "Does this event look like a great way to get the information you need to solve those problems?" and presumably the answer will be yes. "Well, great. Are you ready to go ahead and register? That way we can secure your seat and the special discounts available at this time so you don't miss out on any of those." By asking these questions, you will be able to move prospects forward to getting them registered and confirmed.

Telemarketing is an effective marketing media. Consider doing it yourself if you have the time or hire someone on a commission basis to sign up new attendees. However you choose to do it, reaching out with telemarketing is a great way to build attendance for your event.

One Final Push

Continue your marketing during the last month leading up to your event. Consider adding a special bonus for all attendees as part of your final campaign to renew interest and gain more attendees in the last few weeks leading up to your seminar. Many info-marketers get quite a few additional attendees during the last month or so before their events. Some people just want to wait until the last minute, and you don't want them simply to forget. Keep up the pressure, keep up the marketing, and get the latecomers to go ahead and sign up.

Finalize Your Presentations

One of the things you want to make sure you do during the last month before your event is to give final consideration to the presentations you're going to make. Review your outline and add any additional content you may need, and create slides or other visual aids to help engage your audience in your topic. Create or review the order forms for the programs you're going to sell as well as those for any of your speakers. This is important: Make sure you see every order form from outside speakers before they are produced. You should review the offers and the pricing to make sure your speakers are honoring the agreements they have made with you.

This chapter has provided a quick outline of what you need to do to market your event. Of course, there are many event marketing strategies and secrets, and I certainly haven't covered them all here. I encourage you to take a look at how other info-marketers are promoting their events and then adapt the strategies that are appropriate and effective for your market.

Chapter 43

Offering Your Coaching Program to Generate Maximum Sales

OU'VE GONE THROUGH ALL THE WORK TO PLAN YOUR EVENT, filled the room, and created a great training program. Now that you are on stage with a group of happy attendees staring back at you, how do you offer your coaching program to get maximum sign-ups?

Your coaching program offer should flow naturally as part of your seminar. Don't make an announcement that you are transitioning from the lessons to a pitch for your coaching program. This presentation should flow naturally from your other sessions.

Begin the afternoon with "hot seats." These are where individuals in the audience apply for the opportunity to come up to the front of the room, explain their situations, and get help. You should let everyone know about this opportunity at the beginning of the event and ask them to complete a brief application if they want a chance to be in the hot seat.

Plan to do three to five hot seats in the hour before you offer your coaching program. Invite the selected attendees to the front of the room, one at a time. Have each one sit on a stool, with you also seated on a stool, half facing the hot seat and half facing the audience. Then ask each hot seat to explain what he needs.

Once an attendee has explained his story and you've asked any necessary questions to elicit the relevant facts, ask the audience to provide feedback and input. After a couple of audience members speak, you will provide your recommendation.

These hot seats allow your audience members to see your coaching services in action. They hear the problems and watch you deliver real-world solutions to solve those problems.

The people in hot seats will want to join your coaching to get help implementing the plan you created for them on stage. The attendees who didn't get to be in the hot seats will want to join so they can get you to help them with their individual problems.

If you have any existing coaching members, invite them to participate on a panel discussion with you. Let them know in advance that you'd like their help in demonstrating the value of the coaching program by talking about their successes. Most coaching members will be happy and excited to talk about their experiences. On stage, ask them to share their stories and their recent breakthroughs. This provides proof that your coaching works. If you distribute a schedule to your attendees, you can label this session "Real Life Breakthrough Examples You Can Emulate."

After the hot seats and the coaching members panel discussion, it's time to roll out your coaching program presentation. On the schedule you can name this "The Shortcut to Accomplishing All Your Goals Within 12 Months." You should start this session the same as any presentation within the event. Again, you do not want to announce that you are about to make a sales pitch. This session, like all the others, is about how you can help your attendees achieve success.

This session can last for 30 to 60 minutes. During this time, you will list the benefits of participating in your coaching, tell your story of how you've benefited by being in groups, and explain what your attendees can get out of coaching themselves. Here is a quick overview so you can see how easy it is to create your own presentation:

- All the knowledge in the world is nothing without implementation. It's easy to get caught up in the day-to-day tasks and lose sight of the important goals in your life. You need a way to keep yourself motivated throughout the year.
- I have had several attendees throughout this event coming to me and saying "This is great, but I would love to have access to you to answer questions and get help on an on-going basis."
- In response, I have created a way for you to get access to me throughout the next year, to get the help you need, to provide answers, and to keep you motivated.
- Emphasize: This is an implementation program, not about getting more information but about quickly applying what you already know to generate results for your life.
- Present the coaching program and what it includes.
- Emphasize: It's not just access to me. The entire group will provide help, advice, and resources through the master-mind process.
- Let them know about the special reception to celebrate the next 12 months for anyone who is interested in the coaching program.
- Give them the deadline of lunch tomorrow to turn in their applications.

During the time you are planning your event, it's well worth attending a few other events so you can see how other info-marketers offer their coaching programs. In the end, everyone has her own style and does her own presentation. I've presented the common elements here as a guide for you.

Chapter 44

Best Way to Launch Your Info-Marketing Business: Seminar

WHENEVER YOU CREATE A BRAND-NEW BUSINESS, YOU FACE inherent risks, but as long as you understand those risks, you will be able to manage them so you can continue to thrive and succeed. Although a seminar is more complicated and takes several months to implement, this method does have several benefits you should consider.

When you speak from the stage in front of an audience, you're able to build a much better relationship with that group of potential customers than by using any other mass media. When someone receives your sales letter in the mail, he isn't able to hear your voice or see your mannerisms or really gauge the nonverbal communication you're able to deliver when you're in front of a room. And when you're in front of the room for three days, you're able to share a lot of stories, review several case histories, demonstrate that you are the expert, and show you are there to help your listeners. As a method of building a bond with a group of customers, there is nothing better than a live seminar. You're going to have a group of raving fans who love you and love your information, and you'll have the best possible chance of building a group of paying coaching members.

Another benefit is you can generate a profit on the seminar itself. Even if you break even, it is a way to launch your coaching business without any marketing costs. If you were going to launch a coaching program without a seminar, you'd spend several thousands of dollars in marketing to generate buyers. Also, you might not get a "critical mass," that is, enough people paying the fee to justify your creating all the materials for the coaching program every month. If you're trying to fill your coaching program using direct mail, your prospects may not read your letter for several weeks, and even if they're interested, it's easy to set it aside and wait for later. A seminar gives you a deadline when people need to act, and an event draws interest and lends credibility to what you have to offer.

Hosting a seminar really is one of the best ways to create continuity programs and fill them with subscribers very quickly. If you were trying to fill a coaching program by using direct mail or other methods, you might have a few members join one month, a few join the next, and then maybe another group join four months later. Meanwhile, you would be trying to deliver the program, paying all your expenses, and doing marketing— all at the same time. It's very easy to get spread thin, making it difficult for you to do everything necessary to promote and run your coaching program.

By using the seminar launch method, you're able to focus on the seminar for a number of months, fill it, deliver it, and then afterward, follow up with a group of attendees who decided to join your coaching program. It provides a smooth transition to another product without your having to do so many things at one time. So, hosting a seminar to create a coaching business is a great way to make efficient use of your time and to put as many continuity subscribers into your business as quickly as possible.

The final benefit of hosting a seminar is that it allows you to create a product while you're delivering your seminar. You can record the audio and/or the video from your sessions and package those recordings into a product that is the solution to your customers' problems and a cure for what's ailing your industry.

Seminars complete a good portion of your **Information Marketing Business Pyramid**™ (see Figure 44-1). During the seminar you'll record your Introductory Product. You'll launch your Group Coaching Program by filling it with seminar attendees so you can complete that block of your pyramid. Plus, you will have the opportunity to deliver more extensive presentations that you can later break out into High-Priced Products to fill that block. That's not all; if you are ready, you can offer to provide services to your seminar attendees to give them the opportunity to get their needs implemented more quickly and to generate more revenue for you. This builds the Implementation Services block of your pyramid. While a seminar is a large investment and will require a lot of work to produce, it provides you with a great launch toward completing your **Information Marketing Business Pyramid**™.

At the end of your seminar, you will have a new product: videos, audios, and handouts. The seminar itself will have forced you to become prepared, to get up and deliver the presentation, and to create a product. I have known info-marketers who have worked for a year with no product to show for it. By having a seminar, you will work for 9 to 12 months, and at the end of that time, you'll have a great relationship with your customers, a coaching group, a product you can sell, and perhaps even some money left over from registration fees. Those are the benefits.

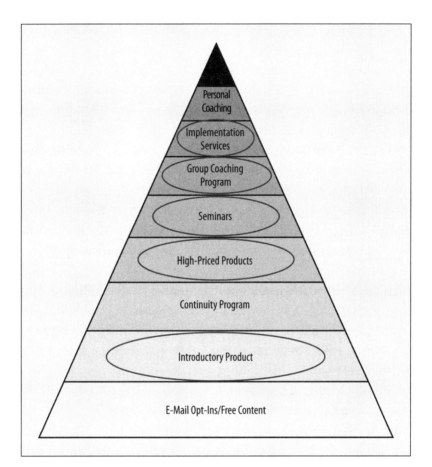

FIGURE 44-1. Your Information Marketing Business Pyramid™ after your first seminar.

Now let's turn to other areas to consider when using a seminar to launch a coaching business.

First, you need a long lead time to promote your seminar. In Section II, we talked about the teleseminar launch method. Using that method, you can go from startup to paid customers in a couple of months. The seminar method is going to take 9 to 12 months. This may seem like a long time; however, if you're able to put a full complement of coaching members into your program at one time, the efficiency and economy of scale may offset any delays in getting your business started.

Next, there's a larger financial commitment. For example, when you sign a meeting space contract, typically you're guaranteeing a minimum amount of revenue to a hotel for the meeting space it is setting aside for you. You can minimize that obligation by booking a small meeting room and limiting your attendance to only 50 attendees; this reduces your risk of having to pay the hotel for unsold guest rooms and meal functions. Another large expense is your marketing costs. Between your risk of failing to meet your hotel contract's obligations and your marketing investment, you will have a lot of money at stake.

To grab a number from the air, you should consider investing $25,000.00 to $40,000.00 for your seminar. To put that investment into perspective, if you were buying a Subway franchise, your investment would be around $200,000.00. From that investment you could expect to generate $50,000.00 a year in income.

In information marketing, you need only five to seven coaching members to generate the same $50,000.00 of profit for you in a year. And you can generate that same profit for less than one-quarter of the franchise investment. Plus, you should be able to sell 12 to 20 people into your coaching program, thus generating many times what you could from any Subway store.

If you are interested in using a seminar to launch your information marketing business and need additional assistance, take a look at the **Information Marketing Business Pyramid**™, where I provide additional examples, more insights, and more detailed strategies than I am able to include in this book. If you want to check out that resource, visit **InfoMarketingPyramid.com**.

Create an Info-Marketing Business to Generate New Customers for Your Service Business

Chapter 45

How Using a Little Horse Sense Improves Results

I GREW UP AROUND HORSES. LUCKY ENOUGH TO HAVE MY OWN horse, I rode for years, competing in hunter jumping shows and dressage. Through this experience, I learned how to read a horse's body language. A skin twitch gives me insights into a horse's thoughts that are missed by most people.

When my daughter, Samantha, was 8 years old, she had horse fever. She loved spending time at the barn and taking riding lessons. While my parents still have thoroughbred horses, I don't have any, so my daughter took lessons at a farm on the outskirts of town.

One day when my wife was out of town, I took Samantha for her lesson. I brought my folding chair, a book, and a cold drink. I was prepared to relax under a shade tree while my daughter had her lesson.

The riding horses at the farm are kept in a pasture for most of the day. The caretakers even feed the horses in the pasture, dumping their grain and hay into field buckets so the horses don't have to go to the barn at all. The only time these animals go to the barn is for riding lessons. Horses are quick to figure this out.

Imagine eating a snack in a sunny field, minding your own business, when you see a child walking up to you with a halter and a lead rope. Sure, she's also got a bucket with a handful of feed, but that halter means an hour of work. What would you choose? An hour of sweaty work or an afternoon of eating in the pasture?

That gets me to the problem. As Samantha walked toward the horse, it lifted its head and trotted away to the other end of the pasture. Before Samantha could walk over there, the horse doubled back to where she was grazing before. You'll never chase down a horse that doesn't want to get caught.

My daughter returned to the barn without a horse, crying, covered in sweat and with an empty feed bucket. I was yanked away from my peaceful spot under the shade tree and drafted into service.

My years of horse sense paid off. I taught Samantha my horse wrangling strategy. It's less about horse catching and more about horse *attraction*.

Although you walk into the pasture with the same tools— halter, lead rope, and a bucket with a handful of feed—you do it in a different way.

I taught Samantha to walk past the horse. You cross its path, about 10 feet in front of it, as it grazes. But you always keep your eyes straight ahead, never looking at the horse. When you get about 12 to 15 feet past the horse, you stop. Just stand there, looking ahead.

Horses have the intellect of a 3-year-old child, except with less patience and more curiosity. As we stood in the sun, looking ahead toward a clump of trees near the fence line, I asked Samantha to count to 25. Before she got to 16, the horse walked up to us and nuzzled Samantha on the shoulder.

I asked Samantha to give the mare a handful of feed. This gave her a moment to slip the halter over the horse's ears. We led the horse through the pasture and to the barn for the lesson.

Customers are skittish creatures. Just as horses are conditioned to look out for predators lurking in the bushes, customers are trained that marketers are predators. At the first sign of someone selling something, they slam down the phone, trash the envelope, or fast forward the TiVo®.

Are you tired of chasing your customers from one end of the pasture to the other? The difference between chasing customers and having them come to you completely changes the results of your marketing and the profitability of your company.

Using information products as the "handful of feed" to attract your customers can make it a lot easier for you to close the sale. The tools are similar, but the approach is different. Instead of chasing customers, you attract them to you.

Chapter 46

Harmony Tenney Combines Sales Ability with Radio Advertising

H ARMONY TENNEY IS ONE OF THE MOST SUCCESSFUL RADIO
station advertising sales representatives in the country.
She built that success by creating a how-to kit for her
customers so they would know how to get the results they
wanted from their ads. When the results poured in, so did
the customers' testimonials, and Harmony was on her way to
building an info-business.

Today, Harmony has info-products that target different
niches: lawyers, business owners, government, and nonprofits.
Her products teach her clients how to use radio advertising to
grow their businesses and programs "like wild fire," she says.
Not only does she teach how to create radio ads that get results,
but she also helps her clients not get caught up in some rep's
"sale of the week."

Harmony has been in radio for 12 years, so she knows the
ins and outs of the business. She describes one of her bad habits

this way: "I always try to make the path behind me easier for someone else to climb." But sometimes a "bad habit" can be turned into a profitable product. Harmony began work on a book on how to sell radio advertising better, but then, she says, "I realized that the bigger market is how to buy radio advertising."

Harmony's radio advertising info-product began as a $9.95 audio book in 2001, and then she expanded the book into a six-CD audio book with transcript that sold for $99.95. "I realized that while there are many radio reps out there, the 'inverse' market of small-business owners that need to learn how to buy radio (so they drive the process rather than a rep that may not have a clue) is much greater," Harmony says. "That's when I developed my small-business info-product."

Now instead of Harmony having to cold call on small businesses to invite them to invest in radio advertising, these business owners approach Harmony because they want her radio advertising information product.

Business owners in Harmony's community become prospects to invest in radio advertising when they invest in her information product. This allows her to avoid wasting time with business owners who have no intentions of ever investing in radio advertising. The revenue from her information product sales allows her to do more advertising than other radio reps, eliminating the need for cold calling.

While this product provides the information a business owner needs to know to invest in radio ads, it also helps the customer see Harmony as an expert. That trust leads many product buyers to invest in radio advertising with her.

And while Harmony no longer cold calls to sell ads for her radio station, she says, "Every now and then I'll see a business that I want to do business with, and I'll approach them."

Chapter 47

Recover Your Marketing Investment and Get New Customers for Free

THE MOST DIFFICULT AND EXPENSIVE PART OF ANY BUSINESS IS acquiring new customers. Sorting through the potential customers to identify the ones that are interested, willing, and able to buy is time consuming under the best conditions. That's the bad news.

Here's the good news: With information marketing, all the hard work is done for you, and it's underwritten by your clients.

Figure 47-1 provides you with a visual of how Harmony Tenney used information marketing to sort through all the business owners who could have become her customers to identify the few that were interested in learning how to acquire customers through radio advertising.

Instead of disappearing like a tree in a forest, your information product allows you to stand out like a cell phone tower, dozens of feet above the trees, with a red light blinking. In marketing it's all about getting noticed. If someone doesn't pay attention

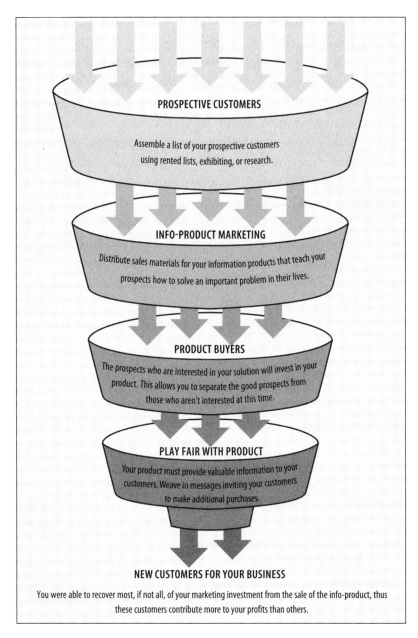

FIGURE 47-1. How Harmony Tenney uses info-marketing to create new radio advertising customers.

to your sales message, it doesn't matter how good it was or how elegantly it was delivered; no one heard it.

Allow me to give you an example from a recent Jump Start Coaching call. (I conduct these calls monthly for members of the Information Marketing Association.) Amy asked for help on her website design business. She creates websites for toy retail stores, but the store owners don't recognize the opportunities they are missing when they have a website that doesn't sell merchandise.

I recommended that Amy create lead-generation advertising for the toy retail industry describing how to automatically increase the revenue of any toy store without increasing the number of employees or the square footage of the store. I told her she should run this advertising in industry trade magazines, attend annual meetings of toy store retailers, and work with franchisors within the industry.

For any of the leads that responded, she would offer a product that teaches toy store retailers all the functionality they need on their websites to tap into the toy market around the world instead of being limited to only the people who come into the store. This product would provide case examples, work sheets, and detailed how-to information.

Amy had all these things with her existing clients, and she could use them as successful case examples in her new product. I also told her she should include an offer for any toy store that invested in her product to apply the full amount of its investment toward the cost of having Amy's company create the perfect toy store sales website for that business.

Now, instead of being just another website supplier, by virtue of this information product Amy becomes the leading toy store internet marketing expert. If you owned a toy store, who would you rather have create your website, one of several website providers or the leading expert in internet sales for toy retailers?

As an information product publisher, you are instantly seen as an expert in your industry rather than being one of many competitors offering services to customers. Even if no one purchases your product, this increased exposure and visibility from your product's marketing allows you to charge higher prices for your services and generates a steady stream of new clients.

When I discovered information marketing, I had already created home study courses for my association clients to market to their members; however, I had never created a product that I owned and marketed for myself. My first product taught associations how to implement all the membership marketing strategies I was using for my consulting clients. I assembled my processes in a step-by-step manual, together with some examples, and made it available to the same prospects to whom I had been marketing my consulting services.

But wait, wouldn't that reduce the number of consulting clients? If someone buys your systems in a product, they don't need to hire you for consulting, right? No, in fact, it does just the reverse.

Yes, it seems like you would lose clients if you taught them exactly what you planned to do in your services and then provided them with examples and step-by-step processes for doing it. However, it actually generates more clients. Plus, the clients this method generates are better clients because they understand the process you are going through and have taken the time to learn what is necessary for a successful implementation.

Sure, some people who invest in your product will be able to implement what you teach them on their own. That's terrific for them. In the majority of those cases, you'll find they wouldn't have hired you as a consultant anyway. They were determined to get it done themselves. Your product provided them a valuable shortcut, and you generated revenue from customers that never would have hired you.

Think of it this way. If you provide a high-value product or service, it's difficult for many of your customers to understand exactly how it works and what you do. By selling a product that provides your customer with a complete understanding of your processes, the theories behind those processes, and several successful examples, it is much easier for that customer to appreciate the consulting services you are offering.

Selling services without an information marketing business is like proposing marriage without dating. It makes you look desperate and undesirable. It's through the dating process, making small commitments and keeping those commitments, that you are able to escalate the relationship to a larger commitment.

Once you've created your information product, you must market it. That is the beauty of this process. If you were marketing your own services, you'd have some type of ad promoting your services and inviting people to contact you. Now your advertising can focus on your product and the shortcuts your prospects will receive when they invest in it. Then, instead of those ads generating a small number of clients, they'll generate product buyers. These buyers will help you recover your advertising investment so you can greatly expand the size and number of your ads. And these product buyers will become great customers for you.

Your product should provide all the information your customers need to solve the problem you promised it could solve. In my case, I gave all the information necessary for an association to produce an effective membership marketing campaign. In Harmony Tenney's example, she provided everything an advertiser needed to produce an effective radio commercial.

In addition to that, you may also include clients' success stories, which illustrate that your strategies work as well as demonstrate that you accept clients. Invite customers to provide their work to you for evaluation. This gives you the opportunity to explain how to make it more effective, further encouraging them to engage you to perform services for them. And within your products, it's fine to include an invitation to contact you, saying something like "Here at XYZ, we reserve some time every year to help our customers implement the strategies we teach within this product. For more information about becoming an XYZ client, contact ____."

And then there is follow-up. By investing in your product, your customer has demonstrated he is interested in solving an important problem. Feel free to have someone call your buyer, conduct a diagnostic to prequalify, and then offer to help in a more direct manner. Your info-business builds a terrific list of prospective customers.

There's an important difference in marketing your services with information products. Instead of approaching your customer trying to get her to buy, you offer a product. Then as she is pursuing solutions to problems, your customer begins to pursue you. Now instead of you selling the customer, the customer is selling herself on you.

This is a crucial positioning change. Clients are reluctant to hire a consultant who is available. The assumption is if the consultant were any good, he wouldn't have time to take on any new clients. In many ways, by marketing your services directly, you are demonstrating to your prospective clients that you aren't good enough to be too busy to take on clients. The information product cures this problem. You can explain it's because you were so busy and couldn't help people personally that you created this product so others could follow your step-by-step processes themselves.

When you begin to implement this for yourself, it is easy to be overwhelmed. It's like learning anything new. You may feel frustrated and not know how to begin. However, by following the steps outlined in this book, you can create a profitable and effective new customer acquisition program. A lot of other people have done it; that proves you can do it, too. All you need to do is get started.

Chapter 48

One Person Can Do It All with the Right Marketing Tools in Place

---

Y OU COULD SAY JEANNA POOL WAS BORN TO CREATE A BUSINESS for solopreneurs. The number "1" has special meaning for her. "I'm an only child, and both of my parents were very successful entrepreneurs. But the one thing I saw them struggle with is they traded hours for dollars. And of course, I saw the yo-yo of them marketing to get clients, then being so busy with those clients that they stopped marketing until the clients were gone, and then having to rush back into marketing to get new clients. It was the whole feast and famine kind of thing."

Jeanna earned a degree in design and marketing and always knew she wanted to do graphic design as well as something in advertising and marketing. She gained experience by working at ad agencies and design firms before opening her own graphic and web design business six years ago. Remembering her parents' struggles, Jeanna decided to focus on one-person businesses that continually deal with feast and famine when it comes to clients and workload.

"The majority of my business has been doing marketing programs and designing things for other people," Jeanna says. "I decided I wanted to package my expertise and knowledge and begin leveraging my time versus working one-on-one with people. That's why I authored the book *Marketing for Solos* to change the way small businesses market themselves."

Getting her book written was easier said than done. Like most business owners, Jeanna had a hard time finding the time to do it. "Basically, I checked into a hotel for two long weekends, back-to-back, and just wrote," she laughs. "I moved the TV out to the hallway and unplugged the phone!"

With the hard work of writing behind her, Jeanna embarked on the even harder work of promoting her book. She used direct mail to her own in-house client list as well as to meeting planners she had met through speaking engagements. "I hosted a huge book-launching party here in Denver for all my past clients and colleagues and friends," she says. "I also carried my book everywhere and gave it out as a business card."

Following the success of her book, Jeanna launched a ten-week coaching program called The Marketing Mentoring Groups Program, which sells for $1,997.00. "It's a ten-week boot camp where I can work with a small number of people and basically keep them accountable and walk them through exactly what to do for marketing their services," she explains. "It's geared for people who sell their services face-to-face to other people."

Jeanna markets her Mentoring Groups Program in her e-zine as well as through direct mail and e-mail to the customer list she has built from her web design business, public speaking engagements, and book promotion activities.

The first year, Jeanna did two boot camps. "Last year I did just one because it is a lot of work!" she laughs. "I'm transitioning into leveraging my time, so I'm packaging the program into a home study course."

Customers who complete Jeanna's ten-week program graduate into a monthly continuity program with a beginning level priced at $39.00 and a top level at $197.00. The continuity programs offer benefits including a monthly call, call-in times, interviews with experts, and a newsletter. Jeanna also includes a critique of a logo or a newsletter, an idea she got from Yanik Silver. "I send out a CD where I basically take a flier or a newsletter or a logo and kind of tweak it and critique it," she

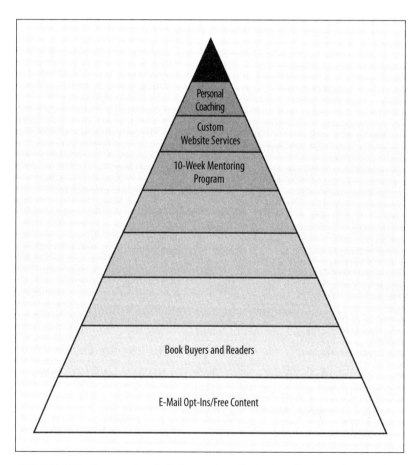

FIGURE 48-1. Jeanna Pool's Information Marketing Business Pyramid™

says. "For customers who are doing their own design, I just give them some design tips to keep in mind."

Jeanna's mentoring program generates projects for her web and graphic design business. "That's one of the sneaky little reasons to do it," she smiles. "We'll be on the module about marketing activities and tools to use, and I'll tell them they need a website. So they'll say 'OK, Jeanna, do our website for us.' Or they'll need direct mail or lead generation, and I'll do that for them."

Figure 48-1 shows how Jeanna built her own **Information Marketing Business Pyramid**™to move her prospects from book buyers to coaching clients to engagements for custom website services.

Jeanna says she has been fortunate in that she has always been able to charge a lot for her design work. In addition to good fortune, it could be due to the fact that she gets results. "I've gotten 95 percent of my clients ranked several times on the first page of Google," she says. "The reason is because of all the good content on the sites."

Chapter 49

Attracting Customers for High-Priced Products and Services

THIS EXAMPLE ISN'T RELEVANT FOR EVERYONE READING THIS book, but it's important that you see how powerful information marketing can be as a customer acquisition tool. Harmony Tenney asked her small-business owner clients to pay for her information products. This allowed her to recover her marketing costs and identify prospective clients. Sometimes, however, it works out better if you don't charge for your info-products, but allow them to do the difficult customer prospecting for you.

After the first edition of this book was published, I was approached by an executive from one of the five largest consulting companies in the United States This company has more than 25,000 consultants, its minimum contract is $500,000.00, and the people who run it aren't really interested in a consulting project that's smaller than $1 million. Because of my agreement with this client, I cannot disclose the company's name or markets, but that's not important for this illustration anyway.

No matter the transaction size, it's important to maintain deal flow, to have a steady stream of new customers coming to the company for work. I was able to design an information marketing business that allowed my client to create that deal flow. Figure 49-1 provides a visual example of the high-priced consulting services sales process I designed.

It is terribly difficult to make sales calls and push for clients to invest in high-priced consulting services. One of the challenges is you have no way of determining who within your prospect list sees themselves as having the type of problem you can fix. The elegance of the sales process I created for this client is that it established credibility, authority, and expertise at the beginning of the process with a simple monthly newsletter. Just the fact that you can publish a monthly newsletter will impress many of your prospects. Then by offering the opportunity for engagement through a webinar, your prospects will get to hear your voice and begin to feel like they know you. Finally, the self-diagnostic is an easy, nonconfrontational way for them to find out if they have problems you can fix. For years we sent these diagnostics in the mail and invited prospects to return them to be graded. Now the process can be posted online and automated.

Because of the value of the clients it was targeting, this company chose to mail the newsletter and host the telephone seminars without charge. Because this company had a prospect list of about 5,000 people, its investment to produce, print, and mail 12 months of newsletters and to mail marketing for four quarterly telephone seminars was about $100,000.00. This investment was easily recovered with its first client. Using this process was far more efficient than taking consultants from billable projects to conduct nonbillable sales calls on prospects that weren't interested.

Note that this process works even if you aren't a big company charging $1 million for your consulting services. Don't

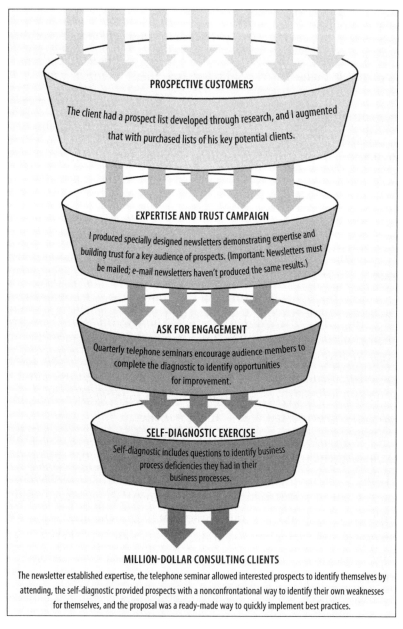

FIGURE 49-1. High-Priced Consulting Services Sales Processes

be intimidated by the large numbers. In fact, I used this same process to get my own consulting clients many years ago. At that time I had only 250 prospects. I printed my newsletter on my copier and had my receptionist mail it out. Almost every newsletter generated new clients, many worth $15,000.00 to $30,000.00, and some worth over $100,000.00 to me in paid services, all for an investment of less than $100.00 per issue.

Chapter 50

Capture Additional Customers with a Variety of Products and Services

AN AUTHOR OF 24 BOOKS PUBLISHED OVER 20 YEARS (TWO OF them best-sellers) contacted me for consulting services. He owns a marketing agency that performs services for some of the largest corporations in the country. His challenge is he's sold hundreds of thousands of books, but only a few of the readers have ever become his customers.

I had read his books and was a fan of his writing. But I had long since realized where he'd been going wrong all those years.

I created a chart similar to Figure 50-1 depicting his business based on the **Information Marketing Business Pyramid**™. As you move to the top of the pyramid, you are increasing the price of the products you sell and have fewer customers. In this case, the author had fans who hadn't yet purchased a book, and he had hundreds of thousands of people who had purchased a book. The only other thing he offered for sale was his company's services. There was nothing in between.

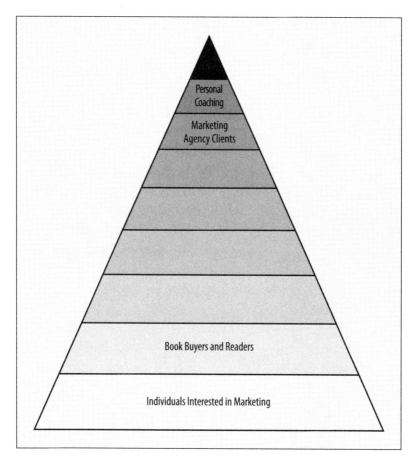

FIGURE 50-1. A broken Information Marketing Business Pyramid™ with a huge jump from book buyer to becoming an agency client.

Figure 50-2 illustrates what I recommended this author and business owner create to enable him to get more agency clients at the top of his pyramid as well as generate more money from customers who would never become clients of his agency. In this business model, his new books would ask readers who wanted more details, additional examples, and step-by-step instructions than you can include in a book to invest in an information

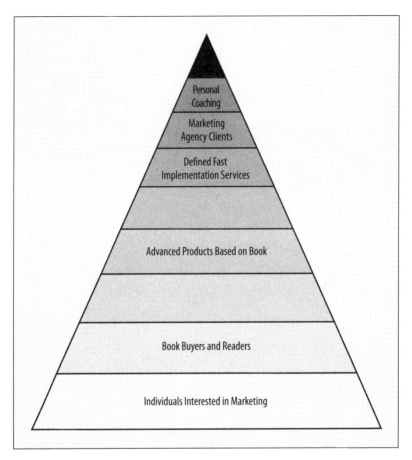

FIGURE 50-2. A healthier Information Marketing Business Pyramid™ with additional ways book readers can become customers and gain more price points.

product. Even if only 5 percent of book buyers invested in his $997.00 information product, that would generate another $12 million to this author.

For his info-product buyers, I worked with him to create a marketing service he could systemize and have some of the junior members of his firm implement for customers. We worked out a price of $9,997.00 for his fast implementation services. If only 10 percent of his product buyers invested in these services, it would generate another $12.4 million for his business. The advanced products together with the defined services could generate over $24 million in new sales for his business. And all of it would be an easy-to-ship product or services that junior staff could implement. Plus, having these stepping stones would encourage more customers to move up to his full marketing agency services.

Unfortunately this author didn't come across the concept of information marketing until after he'd already published his first 20 books, but he's gotten this system implemented for his most recent book.

Even if you aren't a book author, you can still use this template for your business. Too many businesses offer products at one price level. This myopia isn't limited to companies charging high-priced consulting. Think of the magazine industry. Magazine publishers offer magazine subscriptions and rarely offer their subscribers higher-priced products or services. What if Barnes & Noble offered manuals and home study courses priced at $997.00 or even $4,997.00? You wouldn't have to sell many of those to equal a whole lot of $24.95 book sales. But if all Barnes & Noble had were expensive products, the stores wouldn't generate much foot traffic.

In the end, this is just another way to quickly build the **Information Marketing Business Pyramid**™. See Figure 50-3.

As your customer ascends through the pyramid, you generate increasing cash flow and profit for your business. This allows you to invest a lot more in generating new customers, and you may just put a few of your competitors out of business.

Your information products can be paper and ink, audio CDs, DVDs, in-person seminars, coaching programs, or some combination. The most important step is to get started.

Map out your current product offering. How can you improve it by adding less expensive products or more expensive

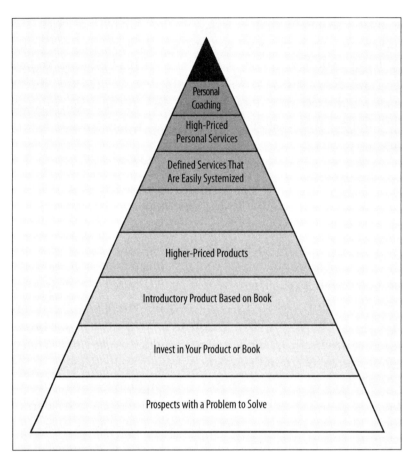

FIGURE 50-3. Full Information Marketing Business Pyramid™ giving your customer or opportunity to ascend to higher price points.

services? Answering this will allow you to escalate your pricing and generate more profit.

You will find more details and examples about creating an information marketing business as an add-on to your existing consulting business in the **Information Marketing Business Pyramid**™. Check it out at **InfoMarketingPyramid.com**.

Transitioning from Launch Mode into Growing a Successful, Sustainable Business

Chapter 51

What To Do If Your Product Launch Strikes Out

MY FIRST INFO-MARKETING BUSINESS LAUNCH WAS A FLOP. That's right, you're reading a book authored by a guy who failed the first time he launched an info-marketing business. However, I have found I always learn more from my failures than I ever do from my successes. Let me tell you what I discovered.

For many years, I did membership marketing for trade associations. I helped associations generate more members in a month than they had generated in a year or many years. I took the processes I delivered through my personal consulting and packaged them into a product. I included manuals, home study courses, sample systems, and templates, all together in one great package for associations to use in creating their own membership marketing programs. With my product all ready to go, I locked myself in a hotel room for a week so I could work nonstop to create lead-generation ads and follow-up sales letter sequences. (This was before e-mail was popular, so my marketing was through the U.S. mail or via fax.)

My free report was titled *The 7 Deadly Mistakes Associations Make, How to Avoid Them and How to Simply & Easily Increase Membership Within Your Association!* (While I called it a free report, actually it was a sales letter.) The first half of the report detailed the problems in the association industry and what most membership marketers do wrong. The second half talked about marketing systems and how the readers could acquire a complete marketing system for their own association so they could fix those mistakes and create new members—all for only three easy investments of $497.00.

I was excited because I had packaged into a box everything I knew about growing associations. Now instead of providing consulting services to one client at a time, I had a product to sell. I had done the work once to create my product, and now I was about to sell it over and over again. My work was done, and the money was going to roll in.

I contacted magazines within the association industry, placed my ads, and excitedly waited for the magazines to get published. When those magazines hit the streets, I started to generate quite a few leads. It was exciting because I could see the process working; people actually were requesting my free report! Now it was time to begin using my sequential sales system.

First, I mailed the free report, and then each prospect received six different follow-up mailings in sequence over several weeks. I set up a simple manual process since there weren't computer systems to track leads at that time. I trained a college student to print out all the mailings at the same time and then file them until it was time to send them out. At the time I was starting my first info-business, I used expandable pocket folders with 31 pockets labeled 1 to 31. The college student would print out all the follow-up mail pieces for a lead, put them in addressed envelopes, and then put each mailing in the numbered pocket corresponding with the date when it was to go out. For example, if the free report went out on the 6th and a follow-up piece was to go out three days later, he would put the follow-up mailing in the pocket labeled 9. When the 9th came around, he would grab everything out of that pocket and drop it in the mail. He did the same thing for each subsequent mailing until the lead became a customer. When we made a sale, he would go through and pull the rest of the mailings for that customer out of the follow-up file. That is how we kept up with lead-generation follow-up sequences before I invested in today's software packages that do it all automatically.

As it turns out, there was very little response to my sales sequence. I was terribly disappointed. I had done all this work, created my product, created ads, created a sales letter, created a follow-up sequence, built systems to execute it long before there were computers to help systemize all of it, and it flopped. After all that work, I sold one customer. That's it, only one. And while it was encouraging that somebody had bought my product, it was not enough to be considered a business.

If your first try at launching your info-business fails, do more market research and consider trying again with a different launch method. **KEY CONCEPT**

As a member of the Glazer-Kennedy Insider's Circle, I had the opportunity to call in and speak with Dan for 15 minutes. I told him about my business flop and how I had sold only one of my kits. His advice to me was terrifying. He told me to contact each individual who had responded to my ads but didn't buy to find out why he didn't buy. "Just call and ask," he said.

I was scared to death. I wanted no part of calling potential customers. These people had rejected me. I had given them opportunity after opportunity to review my sales letter, I had sent them all these follow-up sequences, and now, after all that, they had chosen not to buy—and I'm supposed to call them and ask why? Maybe they were mad at me. Or maybe they thought I was an idiot. It was terribly disheartening, but I did it.

Plus, in addition to those calls, Dan had recommended that I host a teleseminar, inviting my leads from my failed business program as well as other potential customers to ask me questions about selling association memberships. While answering a caller's question, Dan told me to follow up my answer with my own questions: "If there was more information about this topic, how would you want to receive it?" and "What are some things you want to know about membership marketing?"

Once I started calling my prospects and talking with them during those question and answer sessions, it became abundantly clear why my first product had flopped. My customers didn't want a system in a box. They wanted a seminar. I had chosen to sell a boxed product because that was the way I wanted to deliver my product. I had looked at the market, and at the time there were lots of seminars, but nobody was selling a boxed system. So I thought it would be a great way to get information. My customers wouldn't have to leave their offices, and they wouldn't have to send their employees to a seminar. "I bet a box is just the thing. A complete marketing system in a box is exactly what the association industry needs" I thought. Well, I was wrong. I discovered that the reason there weren't existing marketing systems within a box is because the market didn't want marketing systems in a box; they wanted to attend seminars. Association leaders were familiar with seminars, and that's what they wanted. As soon as I started offering seminars, I became successful.

Here are two lessons I want to teach you from my experience. Number one, don't be afraid to contact your leads who don't buy and find out why. If you have only e-mail addresses because your leads are coming through a website opt-in system, then invite those potential customers to a teleseminar once in a while. You can offer your teleseminar for free, or you can charge a nominal fee. But either way, get them on the phone and invite them to ask you questions. As they ask questions, provide them with answers and then go ahead and ask them your own questions. For example: "Well, you've looked at the marketing materials; what did you think?" or "I know you visited the website, and I'd like to get your opinion on the product (or the video or report) you saw. Can you tell me what you think?" By asking questions of your leads, you'll glean insights about your marketing system your buyers really cannot provide you. Your buyers are buyers; they love your product, they love you, and they are going to give you positive feedback. The real information will come from nonbuyers.

Asking nonbuyers about your marketing is much more powerful than trying to evaluate your efforts by looking at metrics for your website. Metrics are important. They do have their place. It's very important to monitor the number of people who visit your site, the number of people who visit your site that choose to opt-in, and the number of people who choose to opt-in versus the number that buy, and to watch those ratios over time so you can change your marketing to make them increase. But metrics won't tell you *why* your website visitors didn't buy. The only way to uncover the why is to contact your leads and ask them.

The second lesson I want to teach you is this: If your first attempt at a business launch isn't successful, don't be afraid to consider a different launch method. If you have information your market wants, you just need to find a different way to deliver it. Choosing a different launch model that targets your market's preferences might be just the thing to turn your first unsuccessful launch into a successful information marketing business.

Chapter 52

Easy-to-Follow Guide to Fast Product Packaging

U SING ONLINE VIDEOS, PDF DOWNLOADS, OR EVEN ONLINE audio is a great way to deliver a product to a customer, especially for the info-marketer. A customer comes to your site and makes a purchase, and you send out an e-mail with a user ID and password to access the site. It couldn't be any easier. Plus, there is no fulfillment cost.

If you choose to use digital delivery, you can skip this chapter (unless you're curious). This chapter is about creating a printed product that you actually ship out to your customers. What difference does it make?

In most markets, you'll generate more satisfied customers from a shipped product than from one that's strictly online. And as you are starting out in your business, I recommend that you go with the most dependable delivery method. If you learn later that your customers want an online product, then it will be easy to post your product on a website to allow access. Your webmaster can set that up for you with few hassles. But let's discuss the reasons why printed products often outperform digital ones.

With printed products, a piece of you actually enters your customer's home or office. You become part of your customer's everyday life, and this person has a visual reminder of you. It's a much more intimate way of building a relationship with your customer than online delivery. With printed products, image is everything, and so you should pay particular attention to how you package your product.

Unfortunately, product packaging decisions come at the worst possible time. Immediately after you have gone through all the work to create your product, you have to make dozens of decisions about how that product will look when your customer receives it. For example, let's assume your product could be

- a three-inch binder with 375 pages in it separated by 13 tabs,
- nine DVDs with the course on video (recorded during a two-day seminar), or
- ten audio CDs with the audio from the course.

The rest of this chapter provides a template you can follow to create your own products that will speed your efforts or allow you to delegate this task to a member of your team.

Binder Materials

One goal of delivering a large binder filled with many pages is to make it look like a substantial reference resource. Customers often judge a book by its cover. If it looks thick, they'll assume there is plenty of great information in there. Of course, above all, you want to actually include a lot of great information in your product. Still, don't forget your customers often make snap judgments based on appearances, so it's good to give them a positive first impression of your product.

I often use binders that have a plastic pocket on the outside. This allows me to have an insert designed to match the DVD and CD covers. When you ask your graphic designer to create your binder artwork, request a cover image, a spine image, and if desired, a back cover. The spine image is an easy detail to overlook, but it makes your product look nice on your customer's bookshelf.

DVDs of Product

When you have a seminar, you'll need to hire an audiovisual company to provide the microphones and recording equipment for the event. This company can also send a technician to video the sessions. At the end of the seminar, you'll receive the recordings of the video and the audio.

To outline the footage for each DVD, I watch the entire two days of the seminar. While I watch, I make notes of what to cut and where to begin and end each session for my product. I make my notes based on the little time clock on the front of my DVD player that shows the hour, minute, and second of the current image.

Before the sessions begin, I often make announcements about breaks, sponsors, or lunch; I cut those out of the product. Also, there are exchanges with the audience or other parts of the program that I often choose to leave out of the finished product. I just make a note of where those items begin and end. I then give that information to the videographer who shot the video at the seminar.Because he keeps a copy of the video and audio for himself, he is able to do the editing for me. Within about two weeks, I receive DVDs and CDs that serve as my master copies for duplication.

Many people forgo the work of watching the video and making editing notes. It does take a long time, but it results in a higher quality finished product. For those who choose not to invest the time and money into editing their products, I will admit that editing the audio and video has no impact on price or sales. Your customers can't evaluate the video before they make the purchase. Many people say it doesn't matter because it can't impact sales. While I choose to do that work to produce what I consider to be a higher quality product, many others will tell you it's not a smart investment of time. I leave that up to you.

DVD Packaging

As a sample, here is a close-up of a DVD case I created for Barry Lycka. The outside case is the first thing your customer sees; however, it's just one of the three important pieces for you to consider: 1) the outside of the DVD case, 2) the inside of the case, and 3) the DVD labels. See Figure 52-1.

Your DVD case needs to sell your customers on watching the program. They may know you, and they may have invested a lot of money to obtain your product. However, your DVD packaging is the perfect opportunity for you to restate all the smart reasons why they purchased your product to begin with.

This case includes a prominent photo of Dr. Lycka, establishing him as a celebrity expert. It has copy points on the front cover that tell customers what they'll learn from watching the DVD. Plus, there is more sales copy on the back cover, along with a long biography.

All this will affirm your customer's smart choice of investing in your program. When your customer opens your DVD case, your DVDs are on the right side of the case, so there is an opportunity to put a message on the left inside cover of the case. I often provide an outline of the contents on each DVD along with the disclaimers and copyright notices.

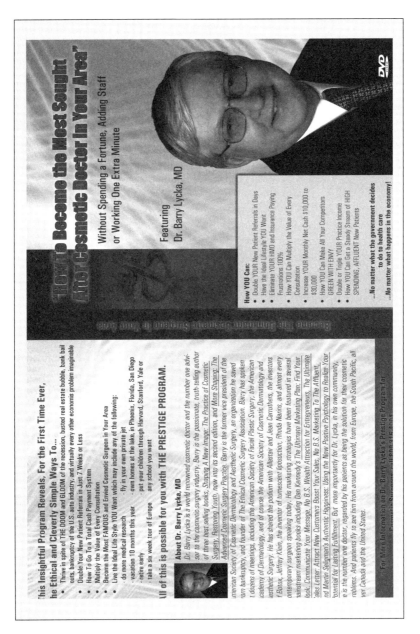

FIGURE 52-1. Example artwork for a DVD video case.

As far as the DVD labels go, it's still important to entice your customers into watching the program they have invested in. One detail to remember to include when you are having DVD or CD labels created: Include the term "CD-R" somewhere on the label because eBay.com allows only the copyright owner to sell CD-R audio products. So, if you have someone duplicating copies of your product and making them available on eBay.com, it's easier to get those auctions removed if your CDs and DVDs are labeled CD-R.

A couple of notes that apply to all these DVD case items:

- Put your contact information on everything; you never know what will get separated or passed on to others. If your contact information is on it, it's easier for a future customer to find you or for your current customer to redis-cover you.
- The DVD case and DVD labels should make the info-mar-keter into a celebrity; including the photo and biography reinforces expert status.
- Always be selling: Make sure you reinforce the impor-tance of the content in your products with teaser copy on the packaging and labels. Plus consider promoting another product on the DVD insert or with a note on the packaging.

Avoid Confusing Your Customers

I believe DVDs should be packaged in a rectangular-shaped package, similar to the height and width of the packaging of DVDs your customers buy at Wal-Mart. I package audio CDs in square packages, similar to the size of gem cases used for the music CDs Walmart sells. This has been described as "old school." That may be, but I've overheard confused customers calling because there was no picture on their TVs when they put the audio CDs into their DVD players, and they can't understand why something shipped to them in a DVD case is actually an audio CD, or worse, something with MP3 files that should be loaded into their iPods or MP3 players.

You are welcome to disagree. Many prefer using a clamshell case because it's a see-through plastic case that holds up well in the mail. Clamshells are less expensive, and there's less to design: Your graphic designer need only create a label for the CD because it will show through the case.

Audio Files

When I'm creating audio CDs of a seminar, I ask my video editor to create the audio for the CDs from the edited video. This way, I don't have to edit the video and then provide similar specifications based on the audio files.

Whether you are getting audio from a live seminar or you have audio from a teleseminar you recorded, you'll typically receive the audio files in an MP3 format. This is convenient for your customers to listen to on their computers. One detail to consider: These MP3 files are typically an hour or more long. If you have them duplicated onto CDs, there will be one long track. This requires your customers to push and hold the fast forward button for a long time to find a particular section of your program. Ask your CD duplication company to create tracks on the disks every five minutes or so. This way it's more convenient for your customers to find the content they need.

Audio CD Packaging

Your audio CDs get the same three items as your DVDs: case cover, inside materials, and CD label. As you can see from this gem case cover layout, the contents of the audio version are identical to the DVD. See Figure 52-2.

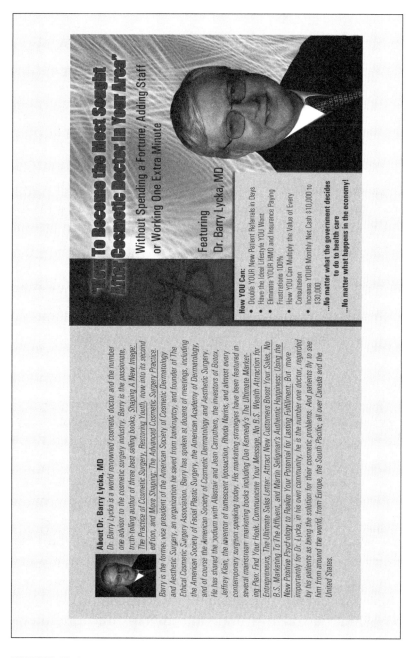

FIGURE 52-2. An example label insert for an audio CD gem case.

A couple of notes:

- Even though I package these in an audio CD gem case, I like to include audio CD logos on the packaging and the disk labels to prevent confusion for my customers.
- There is less room for copy because the packaging is smaller; you'll have to edit down the copy from the DVD case to make it fit on the CD case.
- DVDs hold about two hours of video while audio CDs hold about an hour and 17 minutes of audio. Therefore, you will often have more audio CDs than DVDs for the same hours of content. Plan for that difference in your labels.

The Information Marketing Association Buyer's Guide includes a list of audiovisual companies, teleseminar providers, duplication and fulfillment companies, as well as graphic designers. You can get more information at Info-Marketing.org.

"Read This First" Letter

Getting a box full of stuff can be overwhelming. Your money-back guarantee makes it easy for overwhelmed customers to ask for a refund rather than begin learning from your product.

It's useful to include a brief letter reselling them on the product in their hands and giving them a single place to begin consuming the product. This way, instead of getting overwhelmed with the sheer volume of information, this letter puts them into action, consuming one component of the product. The hope is that completing one component will make them comfortable and lead them into the next section.

Whenever you ship any media to your customers, always include a quick letter reminding them how smart they are to have acquired this information and how it will benefit them.

Then include specific instructions on where to begin. Even if you are just shipping a book, include a cover letter to tell your new customer to open to page x, scan the table of contents, and then turn to page y and begin reading.

Graphic Designers, Duplicators, and Fulfillment Companies

While you can produce your binders, CDs, and DVDs yourself, it's better to outsource this work to professionals. Graphic designers, duplicators, and fulfillment companies have equipment to produce a large amount of product and ship them efficiently. Also, they are working when you are on vacation, on a business trip, or doing a seminar. Plus, they have warehouses to stockpile small inventories of your product so your product can be shipped immediately each time you make a sale.

Even though I could easily produce CD labels or DVD case covers on my own computer, I choose to outsource this work to a graphic designer. It always looks better when a professional does it, and it's a small investment compared to the work necessary to produce a product. If I were going to send a salesman out to do sales calls, I'd want to make sure he was well dressed, had his hair brushed, and was looking sharp. Same with my products: I want them to give a positive first impression.

Contact several providers to become familiar with the range of services and their prices. No one provider is best for every info-marketer. Shop around and find the best person for you.

Chapter 53

Social Media Myths Revealed and How You Really Use It in a Business

I T MUST BE A LAW. NO BOOK CAN BE PUBLISHED IN 2011 UNLESS IT includes an extensive discussion of social media marketing. This chapter will generate the most criticism of this book, I promise you. I understand that all of us desperately want social media to deliver the customers and business growth all those social media gurus promise. But if you are investing money and time into building your business, you want to use the marketing methods that have the best return on your investment, not the one that is merely the most fun.

The following description shows you the effectiveness of social media as well as its limitations.

Have you ever gone to your local chamber of commerce member socials? Very often they are evening receptions, and they have a sponsor that provides food and an open bar. Many business owners in the community go to chamber of commerce events to network.

When you go to this event for the first time, what do you do? You walk in the room, you're confronted with all these people you don't know, and you scan all the faces to find a familiar one. The moment you find someone you know, you walk across the room and say hi to your old friend. Let's call him George. You say, "Hey, George, how are you doing? It's great to see you. I'm so glad to see you at this event."

In the process of connecting with George, Sally walks up to George because Sally also recognized him. What's the natural thing to do? George is going to introduce you to Sally. Now you have met someone you had not met before. While you're talking to Sally, someone comes up to you that recognized you, and so you introduce them to George and Sally. Then another person comes up to Sally that neither you nor George knows, so everybody introduces each other. The group gets bigger, and the number of people you know grows each time you attend a meeting. That is the essence of social media. It's connecting with the people you know so you can meet the people they know and broaden your network.

How can meeting people by using social media be bad? It's not bad. Social media can do some great things for you.

First, you can use social media to do market research. By looking at social media sites and the groups and the forums where people are interacting within those sites, you can see the questions people are asking, view the common answers, and even engage in discussions and build a reputation as a problem solver. That type of market research can be extremely valuable, and I highly recommend investing time in social media to conduct your market research and find out more about the customers to whom you are going to be selling.

Another benefit of social media is it can generate leads. As you are posting on forums, as you are interacting with people you know and the people they know, other people are going to see you and want to become your customer. That is a great method of generating leads and can have value to you as a businessperson, similar to the way you might generate leads and gain customers at chamber events.

But contrary to all those people who are selling how to get rich by using social media, I've worked with dozens of people who have bought every product and invested hundreds of hours in Twitter and Facebook, and now they are not on those sites anymore, at least not on a professional level. They have automated all their posts and spend 30 minutes a month updating

 Social media is useful for market research and for lead generation. As a marketing strategy for a business, there are more effective ways to invest your time.

KEY CONCEPT

what goes out automatically to their friends and followers. Social media, just like the chamber event, is an effective tool for a while; you meet people, but after some time goes by, you notice it's the same group every month, and you no longer get new customers every time you go. The effectiveness declines over time.

This book is focused on what works in 2011. If I recommend something to you, it's because I've seen it work consistently or I've worked it myself. It's not a theory or something I have heard has worked for a friend of a friend, and it's not some cool whiz-bang strategy big corporations have tried. After all, what happens at Zappos with its millions of dollars in startup venture capital is not that relevant to you and me as we launch our businesses from home.

In this book you're holding, you have proven strategies that have worked hundreds of times in different business niches. If you follow these templates, they will work. Social media may be great, but as of now, it is not as effective a marketing tool as others. Follow the launch models I have provided you. Certainly, use social media to get the word out about your seminar, to publicize your product, and to generate leads for your sales process. But follow the models and the templates I have given you, and they will help you grow your business. Then, for the most part, save social media as a pleasant distraction and a great way to catch up with your old friends.

When someone has a method of using social media to launch an info-marketing business that has been repeated a couple of times to prove it works, I'll be the first to let you know.

Chapter 54

The Information Marketing Money Machine™

WITHIN THE INFO-MARKETING WORLD, DOZENS OF SYSTEMS teach how to create a business from scratch. Within this book I provide you with five ways to launch your information marketing business. These systems give you a good understanding of how to efficiently invest your time to launch a new business.

What these launch formulas *don't* show you is how to use your time once your business is launched and growing. What you do to create your business is very different from what you do to run it.

Without a process, many of us become experts in only one essential part of our info-marketing business. Some people love doing teleseminars, so they immerse themselves in that one method of customer acquisition and product creation. For others, seminars become their only go-to customer acquisition method. They end up traveling all around giving seminars. This may work for them, however, it requires manual labor, and their businesses become dependent on their traveling. And then there are folks like me who love creating products so much that it's easy to forget that we have to go out and sign up new customers to buy the products we create.

Enter the **Information Marketing Money Machine™**. I've been developing this system for several years based on my personal experience, consulting services,

> Once you launch your business, you'll need to transition from "launching" to building a strong long-term business. Too often when a new info-marketer starts becoming successful, she assumes she knows everything and stops learning. It's crucial that you avoid this so you can transition into running a successful long-term business.
>
> **KEY CONCEPT**

and work with hundreds of info-marketers. See Figure 54-1.

FIGURE 54-1. Information Marketing Money Machine illustrates how the components of your business manufactures profit for you.

The **Information Marketing Money Machine**™ has three main sections. To build a strong business, you and your team must spend a similar amount of time on each section to build your own strong money machine. This way, you will build a business that is balanced and that gives you the lifestyle you hoped to create when you first started.

The three sections are 1) Customer Acquisition, 2) Backend Marketing/Fulfillment, and 3) Operations. While you may delegate much of the actual work involved in any of these focus points, you must continue to monitor and spend your time improving your business within each of them.

Customer Acquisition is a focus point for info-marketers because their entire business depends upon it. This section is made up by the "Business Models," "Lead Generation," and "Sales Conversion" parts of your money machine. No matter how loyal your customers are, eventually they won't be your customers. It's essential that you have processes that add new customers to your list. Info-marketers who ignore this focus point for a while suddenly find their profits have declined. Then it's difficult to create new customer acquisition programs because they don't have the time or the money to invest in testing new models.

Equally important for info-marketers is the Backend Marketing/Fulfillment focus point. This is made up by the "Product Creation," "Backend Sales," and "Relationship" sections of your machine. Dan Kennedy says it all the time: "We make a sale to get a new customer." Once you have that customer, your products and system should build a relationship with him so that he wants to buy more from you. If you are just starting out in info-marketing, you don't worry about this much. The goal is to get the product completed and shipped so you can improve your customer acquisition systems. As you grow, you have to spend more time on this focus point to create products and systems so that one product naturally leads your customer to invest in another.

Now, regarding the Operations focus point, just a couple of months ago, a successful info-marketer told me, "I shouldn't have to spend time on that stuff; my gift is coaching."

I had to explain, "Coaching is an essential service your business provides; however, it's not the business. Even if you delegate a lot of the day-to-day work, you must focus on operations to generate a good lifestyle for yourself and allow you to do more of the work you enjoy."

The Operations section of your machine is illustrated by the legs that hold up the machine and keep it running. They are "Business Systems," "Team Members," and "Accounting/Legal." I readily acknowledge that the Operations focus point is the least exciting part of an info-marketing business. However, many info-marketers use technology and strategies designed to give them leverage, only to end up working long hours trying to keep everything running. The leverage spreads them thin, makes them busier than ever, and eventually prevents them from doing the customer acquisition and value-building work necessary to grow their businesses. Instead, they get busier and more frustrated. Still, the Operations focus point is useless without new customers and a good relationship with your current customers.

Together, these three focus points enable you to create a perfect lifestyle business. New customers coming in every day. Products and systems that build a long term relationship with those customers. And an operations infrastructure that gives you the freedom to do more of the work you enjoy.

Chapter 55

Quick Reference Guide for Essential Info-Marketing Operations

---

MOST INFO-MARKETING EXPERTS AGREE: THE BEST WAY to launch a new business is to get started immediately. Too many times when first-time info-marketers begin by laying out all the administrative details, they spend so much time on those details that they never get around to actually launching their businesses.

Yet while it's important to launch your business quickly and start making money, a time comes when you must take inventory of the operational and legal requirements of running a growing business. Your success makes you a target, which makes you vulnerable. However, you can put legal defenses into place to protect your assets, products, and customers.

Here is a quick listing of several compliance issues to be aware of as you grow your info-marketing business.

Copyright

Protect your newsletters and products from people stealing them and presenting them as their own. A copyright creates a protection under federal law for your products and sales materials. You need to include copyright notices in your products and sales letters and have documented agreements with all your writers and content providers.

Registering your products with the U.S. Copyright Office is the only way for you to fully protect them. The best part is it is a quick and easy process. Most importantly, it provides you with statutory damages and attorney's fees. These penalties and fees can be a terrific deterrent when you are pursuing people who are stealing your work. Even if you never recover those damages, the threat can often be enough to stop continued infringement.

You register a work with the U.S. Copyright Office by completing a simple form and sending it in with $30.00 and a couple of copies of your work. For a newsletter or a teleseminar, you'll need to do this within 90 days of publication.

Fair Use and Permissions for Copyright Protected Work

Did you come across a killer sales letter you want to adapt to your business? Or have you seen an order form you want to edit into your own? It's always better to ask for permission. That letter or form could be copyright protected, exposing you to legal liability.

Even if something is protected under intellectual property laws, your unauthorized use may still be legal. This is because there are exceptions to each of the laws protecting creative work—situations where authorization is not required. For example, under copyright law, a principle known as fair use permits you to copy small portions of a work for certain purposes such as scholarship or commentary. Under the fair use doctrine, you can reproduce a few lines of a sales letter without getting permission. However, to prevent hard feelings, it's always best to ask.

Always get permissions in writing; relying on an oral or implied agreement is almost always a mistake. You and the rights owner may have misunderstood each other or may remember the terms of your agreement differently. This can lead to disputes. If you have to go to court to enforce your unwritten agreement, you'll have difficulty proving exactly what the terms are. Business advisors strongly recommend getting written permission agreements and advise against relying on oral agreements.

Trademarks

Trademarks protect distinctive words, phrases, logos, symbols, slogans, and any other devices used to identify and distinguish products or services in the marketplace.

There are, however, areas where both trademark and copyright law may be used to protect different aspects of the same product. For example, copyright laws may protect the artistic aspects of a graphic or a logo used by a business to identify its goods or services while a trademark may protect the graphic or logo from use by others in a confusing manner in the marketplace. Similarly, trademark laws are often used in conjunction with copyright laws to protect advertising copy. The trademark laws protect the product's or service's name and any slogans used in the advertising while the copyright laws protect the additional creative written expression contained in the ad.

Most often, trademarks are words or phrases that are clever or unique enough to stick in a consumer's mind. Logos and graphics, such as the Nike swoosh, that become strongly associated with a product line or service are also typical.

Product Disclaimers

One of the many things info-marketers need to do to protect themselves and to fully and properly educate their customers is to routinely include publisher's legal notices and disclaimers in info-products and publications, literature, order forms, seminar materials, etc.

Data Security

You must put several safeguards in place to protect credit card numbers and other personal data in your possession. Credit card numbers cannot be visible to employees after the transaction. You must create processes to hide the number in computer records and cross out the number in permanent paper records. Also, you must be extremely careful if you choose to share credit card information between two companies. You are taking responsibility for the other company's ability to safeguard your customers' information.

Essential Documents

There are some documents you must have to protect yourself as a business owner. Plus, when they are done correctly they can help you run your business more efficiently.

- *Employment manual.* For info-marketers who have employees in their businesses, it's essential to create an employment manual to provide the details of your relationship between your business and your employees. Even if few of your employees are in the same city, it's important that you document the relationship with a manual. This is your key protection tool if you get into a dispute with an employee. While you can hire an expert to create a manual for you, inexpensive templates for your state are available online.
- *Policy manual.* While your employment manual spells out the relationship between you and your employees, a policy manual allows you to outline essential elements of how your employees should interact with each other and your

customers. Policy manuals are good for defining dress codes, business hours, and policies ranging from rules on bringing food to the office to your expectations for e-mail communication decorum.

Insurance

You need to consider these three types of insurance coverage as your business grows:

1. *General Business Insurance Coverage.* Think of this policy as homeowner's coverage for your business. This inexpensive coverage will replace your computers and give you some resources if a disaster strikes your business. These could include tornado, fire, or hurricane. These policies replace your business equipment, give you money for business interruption, and often give you money to replace documents lost during a disaster.

   Some info-marketers think they don't need this coverage because they work out of their homes and believe their business records and equipment are protected by their homeowner's insurance policies. Homeowner's policies specifically exclude business property. These policies aren't going to cover data loss, destroyed inventory, or business interruption. Plus, they won't replace your computers and other equipment if they are used primarily in your business.

2. *General Business Liability.* You'll want basic "slip and fall" coverage in case someone claims you injured him. Suppose someone attends your seminar and falls over a chair. Or your product falls off a shelf and hits someone in the head. Liability insurance covers these types of claims.

3. *Consultant's/Publisher's Liability.* As a growing info-marketer, you should consider specific coverage for the types

of claims that could come from your coaching, teaching, or product-publishing activities. Someone could implement something based in part on your recommendations through coaching or products. If this customer is unhappy with her results, she can sue you, even if she didn't correctly implement your advice.

You can obtain each of these insurance coverages from a commercial insurance agent. If you don't already have an agent, ask your homeowner's agent or auto agent for a referral to someone in your area.

Sales Tax

Info-marketers *are* responsible for sales taxes and are subject to penalties and fines for the failure to collect and remit them. The law is clear that you must collect and remit sales taxes for any state in which you have a presence. Therefore, you should contact your home state to register, receive a sales tax number, and begin remitting taxes on sales made to customers within your home state.

In addition, if, for example, you have a conference in Chicago and sell products at that event, you are required to register with the State of Illinois and collect and remit sales taxes. Some states consider a sale exempt from sales tax if you generate the sale from the front of the room and ship the product from your office the following week. You should contact the department of revenue for the state where you hold your event to get the details about its laws and to determine if you should collect sales tax on your sales.

Disaster Recovery

Disasters strike in many ways; hurricanes, floods, fires, or tornados affect businesses somewhere in America every week.

Add to that the threat of former employees deleting records, and disaster can strike anyone. It's easy to get lulled into a false sense of security, especially when you are using online applications to run your business. After all, those companies have mirrored servers and lots of backups. However, you could be just one disgruntled employee away from having those records disappear.

Execute a backup for your system. At least weekly, download databases from online service providers and back up all your websites to your own server. This way if your service provider has a problem, you can restore your data with a new provider and continue your business while your regular provider diagnoses and resolves its problems.

Chapter 56

The Money Collecting Machine for Your Info-Marketing Business

A N ESSENTIAL PART OF YOUR INFO-MARKETING BUSINESS IS THE ability to accept payments through credit cards. You'll get a check every once in a while, and as you are starting out, there is nothing wrong with accepting payments through PayPal or Google Checkout. But as you grow, you will need to accept credit cards. It's easier for you and more convenient for your customers.

From the mid-1990s until the end of 2009, getting a credit card merchant account was relatively easy. You contacted your bank or one of the hundreds of online providers, asked them for "credit card merchant services," and signed up. Instead of one of those terminals, they provided you with a user ID and password so you could log in to your online interface, and you were all set. If you wanted to connect your new merchant account to a shopping cart, you simply followed the directions from your shopping cart provider, and everything was connected and working.

Beginning in 2010, spurred on by new regulations from MasterCard prompted by the residential and commercial credit crisis, banks became more stringent about the merchants they accepted.

Merchant services providers, as a rule, do not understand the information marketing business. Our businesses have an FIC code we assign to ourselves from the table of codes provided by the Internal Revenue Service. Most merchant account providers code info-marketers as a "publisher." Publishers typically have relatively consistent revenues. Certainly there are spikes when they come out with a new product, but the revenue generally falls within a range.

An info-marketer's revenue can vary greatly from one month to another. For a while you sell kits for $500.00 or $1,000.00 and continuity programs for $50.00 or $100.00 per month, and your revenue falls within a normal range. But then you decide to hold a boot camp. Your registration fee is $2,500.00, and 200 people sign up. Suddenly you have $500,000.00 in sales! This large spike of revenue sets off warnings in the loss prevention department of your merchant provider. You have marketing expenses to pay, so you look in your checking account, but you don't see a deposit for the registrations you have processed.

Not only are the deposits for the boot camp missing, but there aren't *any* deposits. Because your seminar changed your credit card processing pattern, your merchant services provider has put a hold on all your transactions and is holding your money.

Because merchant services is the primary way you will receive your money, you should be prepared to deal with people who do not understand your business and are, in general, suspicious of you. Your $30,000.00-a-year merchant services loss control agent works all day in a cubicle, and it's his job to protect the credit card company from thieves who rack up a bunch of charges on customers' cards, don't deliver anything, and then take all the money out of the checking account and skip town.

As an info-marketer you need to understand that people don't know how your business works. That's why you must develop a strong relationship with your merchant services providers. You need them to trust you. You need them to be willing to work with you when you have revenue spikes in your business.

Look at your business from the merchant services providers' perspective. They consider processing merchant services to be a loan to you. Your boot camp customers have a right to charge back their $2,500.00 registration fee on their credit card for up to six months after the transaction. At five months and 28 days, your customer can call the credit card company and say, "This is not a legitimate charge. I do not want to pay it." The credit card company has to give the customer a credit, and then it has to look to you to collect the $2,500.00. If the credit card company believes there's a chance you won't be around in six months, then it is not going to deposit your charges into your account. You know you are trustworthy, but your provider has to consider the worst-case scenario. It is your merchant services provider's job to protect the bank, not grow your business.

It's entirely possible you'll never have a problem with your merchant account provider. You can walk into your local bank, sign up for an account, and run your business for years without incident. But often when an info-marketer's business begins to grow quickly, merchant account providers can become conservative about how much money they are willing to deposit into an info-marketer's checking account.

Through the Information Marketing Association, I negotiated a special relationship with merchant service providers to provide hassle-free credit card processing to help info-marketers get paid quickly. If you'd like information on that program, you are welcome to check out **InfoMarketingMerchantServices.com**. No matter which provider you choose, this is a relationship you'll need to build for your business and a vendor you'll need to communicate with on an ongoing basis.

Chapter 57

Automating Your Business So You Can Set It Up and Forget It

O NE OF THE MOST POWERFUL ASPECTS OF THE INFORMATION marketing business is you can automate many of the business functions. New prospects can visit your website, provide their contact information, and receive your sales materials without your direct involvement. You can be at the beach, hiking in the mountains, or enjoying time with your family while your marketing system is selling your prospects on buying your products.

This automation requires you to learn about some software systems you may not be familiar with and, unless you want to do it, to find someone who can set up these systems for you.

Whenever you create a multistep marketing sequence, you need a way to

- capture a prospect's name, address, and e-mail address;
- identify which ad or joint venture partner sent this lead to your website;
- send follow-up e-mails to your lead automatically;

- prompt you or a member of your team to mail any snail mail follow-up steps to your prospect; and
- know when that individual chooses to buy so you can take him out of the marketing sequence and put him into the next sequence you do for your customers, such as a welcome sequence or a backend sales sequence.

Keep in mind you have different customers in all different stages of your marketing sequence. Some convert to customers right away while others need to go through more steps of your marketing sequence before they buy. It can get unwieldy very quickly. Luckily, several software solutions can help you address this situation quickly and help you manage your processes.

InfusionSoft

InfusionSoft is a software system designed for information marketers. It is the best solution for tracking client data and for processing one-time online sales as well as offline sales. Information is easy to upload, store, search, download, and modify. Clients can be entered with multiple addresses, telephone numbers, e-mail addresses, etc. Follow-up sequences to send materials to your prospects to convert them into customers can include e-mails, fulfillment, and timed step-mailings. These follow-up sequences are excellent ways to provide the regular contact with clients that all direct-response marketers strive to achieve. Once you create the best follow-up sequence for your customers, you can put everything into InfusionSoft, and this program will take care of tracking which prospect needs which step of the sequence and getting it implemented for you.

With the record-search feature, clients can be found with minimal data, which is helpful when removing bad addresses from a mail campaign. A member of my team was able to find a client with only the first letter of the first name, first two numbers of the address, and three digits of the ZIP code visible on the returned envelope.

The contact merge feature is simple and useful when contacts appear multiple times, which happens when lists are uploaded from different sources. "De-duping" can be done on the entire list, on new imports, or on contacts that haven't been checked recently, and they can be checked by a single criterion, like e-mail address, or by multiple criteria, such as name, address, and/or e-mail address. Once the duplicate contacts have been identified, merging is easy and quick. Contacts can also be merged manually when a specific contact is found in the system more than once. During manual merges, you can choose specific information from each record that will be merged into the client's final record.

InfusionSoft's use of web forms for user-initiated online purchases is outstanding. Each form generates its own unique link that can be integrated into your e-mails and/or websites. Once a transaction is completed, an action sequence is initiated that can send customers an e-mail, take them to a success or a thank-you page (or a failed transaction page for declined orders), put them into a group, remove them from other groups, and do a variety of other useful functions.

InfusionSoft is a high-quality program that has lots to offer direct-response marketers. While initially the sheer enormity of its potential can be quite overwhelming, customer support is available, both online and offline.

I've been using InfusionSoft since 2005. I've tried other systems when I've created businesses in partnership with other info-marketers. While there is quite a bit to learn and it may be intimidating when you first try to learn how to use it, no other program gives you the flexibility you need to grow your business. For a free product tour, auto responder test drive, and online demonstration, visit **InfoMarketingCRM.com**.

Chapter 58

Juggling Responsibilities While Launching Your New Info-Business

O NE OF THE THINGS I RAN INTO WHEN I WAS CREATING MY information marketing business is I was trying to do it while running another company. New info-marketers often tell me, "I have a job. I don't have time to do all that to launch a new business."

I understand. Before I decided to simultaneously launch a new info-marketing business, I thought running my company was all I could do. I was busy. I had employees. I had deadlines. I had clients. I had meetings to travel to.

I can tell you exactly how many trips I had out of town because it was a goal of mine to reduce the number of out-of-state and out-of-town nights I had. As part of accomplishing my goal, I documented how many nights I spent out of town each year. The first year of working toward my goal, I had 47 nights out of town, down from 68 the year before. My next goals were to get my out-of-town travel down to 30 nights and then 20 nights a year.

When I began my info-marketing business, I was traveling for my primary company 47 nights a year and running my company on a daily basis. When was I supposed to create new products and try to launch new marketing plans in a business where I didn't yet understand all the details? It's one thing trying to run a business with which you are already familiar, but trying to create something brand-new was challenging for me.

You may be in a similar situation. You are reading this book, excited about launching a new opportunity, but soon overwhelm will set in. You'll think, "Wow, there are a lot of details to pull together. I've never done this before, and I'm not sure I can do it. And even if I did know how to do it, I'm not sure I would have the time to make all this happen."

Let me tell you what I did to break through and create a successful new info-marketing business. It was scheduling time, what I call time-blocking. Really, it's a discipline, much like weight loss.

In 2004, I had grown to 237 pounds. My wife's two pregnancies had taken a toll on my waistline. I had gained 20 pounds with each.

Over the course of five months, I was able to lose 35 pounds with a revolutionary diet plan: I ate less and exercised more. Hundreds of diet plans promise weight loss without any work. It's just like those business opportunity salespeople promising you'll get rich without work. While the title on the cover of this book includes "get rich" it doesn't include "without work."

The only diet that works is to plan out your meals and exercise for the week, and then stick with your plan. Whenever I left my eating to a moment-by-moment decision, the habits I had created over the previous ten years took over. I ended up eating more food than I needed.

Instead, I started planning out my meals for the week, at the beginning of the week. Some were meals my wife cooked. Others were during client meetings where I'd choose what I was going to order several days before I got to the restaurant. The first week I planned my meals, it took me four hours. I went through cookbooks, looked up restaurants' menus and their nutritional information online, and created a daily plan. As long as I followed my plan, I limited my calories and lost weight. I even planned little treats at the end of each week. Those treats gave me something to look forward to and savor when I wasn't eating as much as I was craving.

I launched my new info-marketing business in a similar way. At first I planned to get up early in the morning, blocking out 6 A.M. until 8 A.M. to work on my new business. I conducted research, created marketing materials, and did product development. But over time, working on my clients' projects started to creep into this time. I'd tell myself, "Oh, I need to get this project done. I'll interrupt my plan to get this done for today and then get back to my plan tomorrow." But once that starts, it's terribly difficult to get back on track.

Then I set aside every Friday to create my new business. I'd allow myself to be busy all week with my primary business, but on Friday, everything else got ignored while I created my new info-marketing business. Fridays gave me dedicated time to get my business created and launched.

I've often told myself, "I wish I could focus on one thing." It seems like it would be so much easier if all I had to focus on was the new info-marketing business I'm trying to launch. I've seen too many others make the same mistake. They quit their jobs or sell their businesses before they've gotten their new info-marketing businesses launched. They think they can get their businesses launched faster by focusing all their attention on it.

The truth is without their primary income, these new info-marketers will be in a dire situation if their info-businesses don't generate immediate profits. They won't have money to continue marketing their businesses, and their info-marketing dreams will die.

As stressful as it may seem to run your current business, work your job, and create a new info-marketing business at the same time, this is what works. Busy people get things done. Nonbusy people find distractions that prevent them from ever becoming productive.

Stay busy, and plan out your workweek in advance. Plan some distractions you can look forward to. And then execute your plan during the week. If something important comes up, put off all nonessential work projects until next week. Don't put off your info-marketing business startup work.

If you create a work plan and then follow your plan, soon you'll find you are making significant progress toward launching your dream info-marketing business.

Chapter 59

How to Trust Your
Skills and Be Skeptical
of Your Beliefs

NEW INFO-MARKETERS FAIL FOR TWO PRIMARY REASONS. Luckily, both are avoidable.

Every time I tried to start my first info-product, I was paralyzed by a foggy feeling in my brain. In everything else I had so much clarity; decisions came easily, and I had an answer for every question. But for some reason, when it came to creating an information product, I was paralyzed.

Even today when I'm fleshing out the details for a new business I'm starting, I experience flashes of excitement over a new idea followed by a brick wall of fogginess. Is this just me, or have you experienced the same thing? I find I get lost in the fog most often when I get intimidated by all the details of launching a new project.

In May 2004, Dan Kennedy had one of his free call-in days for members to dial in for a 15-minute one-on-one discussion with him. In my confusion-induced fog, I can still remember asking him how to record audio programs. He explained that there are tape recorders and recording studios. The studios are more expensive, but tape recorders work just fine. Radio Shack has a good selection.

I think back at this and shake my head—what a ridiculous question for me to ask! I'd been recording audio for years. I had the opportunity to ask Dan a question, and I chose to ask him about something I already knew? Today, I produce at least ten hours of recorded audio a month. But back then, I was in the fog.

The problem wasn't that I didn't know how to record the audio; it was that I had no idea what I was going to say when it came time to press the Record button. Sure, I can talk for hours, but I was scared that when I faced that red light, I would freeze up. And that's the first reason people fail in the info-marketing business. They forget what they know. Or they think they don't know anything.

I do it all the time. When I'm working through a project, it's easy for me to become overwhelmed with all the details. Right now I'm launching a new product. In this campaign there are affiliates to recruit, train, and motivate; 37 e-mails to compose and deliver to seven different lists; 17 web pages; three videos; two webinars; a 33-page report; and then the actual product. All this to lead to the sale of a $1,297.00 product that needs DVD cases, binders, CD cases, and product packaging.

Within the maze of this project, it's easy to get overloaded. And when I get overloaded, my brain wanders into the fog and I forget everything I know. All I can think is, "I can't do this." Fortunately, I've learned how to recognize when I'm in the fog.

This is the plan I created to get myself out:

When I feel overwhelmed and frustrated and my urge is to stop, I start composing lists. What needs to happen, what do I know how to do, and what do I need help doing? Then, with my list of things I need help with, I determine who I need to ask.

Yes, it's simple. Yes, it's a beginner's mistake, but we all fall into it. We get so caught up in our projects and our lives that we forget what we already know. We think that someone else must have the answer, and we go searching for it. Instead, I've found when I just sit down and separate what I know from what I don't know, I really have more of the answers than I thought I did. I just have to get them out of my clouded head and onto paper.

Over the years I've had the privilege of working with many great info-marketers. I'm proud to say we've had our share of successes. My perspective also has allowed me to witness (and experience) a few failures.

Can you imagine anything more frustrating? You break through all the inertia, you learn how to create a product, you build a sales campaign, and after you unleash your marketing on the world, nothing happens. Or most often, you have just a few buyers (you almost always have at least ONE buyer). It's frustrating.

These failures always have a common theme: I didn't understand the customer. I misunderstood what the customer wanted, and/or I underestimated the amount of work necessary to get enough customers to know, like, and trust me enough to buy.

This happens naturally, especially if you've been running a successful info-marketing business for a while. Once you've created a product or two, it becomes easy. And as an info-marketer, you have a large group of customers telling you how terrific you are. They thank you profusely for helping them. While that's a great feeling, it's easy to begin to believe you've got this thing figured out.

I've found that whenever I think I've become an expert about a market or a topic, this is the time to watch out because I'm about to be disappointed. And I've seen that when info-marketers have the feeling they know their markets and they are confident about what they have to offer, they really have no idea.

When some of your customers are telling you how wonderful you are, it's easy to lose sight of what they really think. Yes, they think you are wonderful, but they also think other things. Plus, the few you interact with are the exception. They are the 20 percent that participate. The majority of your customers are silent. The other 80 percent is out there, and the only way to know what those people are thinking is for you to go to them and ask.

While you are launching your business, you may know exactly what customers what. You offer it to them, and they leap for your products and coaching. That's great. What you must realize is that two years later, you aren't the new person anymore. Their perception of you and your products changes. You have to change with it.

Our belief systems are built over the course of our lives based on what we hear, see, and understand. And to filter out noise, we quickly reject anything that doesn't fit within our belief systems. You see it with new coaching members. You can explain something about their businesses or lives two or three times, yet they still hold on to their old beliefs. Then, two months later, they come back to you and explain how they had an "aha" moment.

As info-marketers, we have to get to the "aha" moment more quickly. We have to be sensitive to what our customers are telling us, what they are saying about our business, and what they believe, but aren't telling us. This comes up in many ways, but you have to be looking for it. If something isn't consistent with what you believe to be true, investigate it immediately. Rather than brush it off, take a deep look.

A quick for instance: I believe the team at my office does a great job. Every week at least one member e-mails a compliment about an experience he has had with my team. However, every now and then I get a message from someone with a complaint. Rather than brush it off as a crank member with a problem, I investigate. Often it is confusion on a member's part. Other times I discover a training opportunity. However, I always embrace information that doesn't fit with my beliefs.

Success is balance on the middle of a beam with the two most common reasons for failure on each end. Reason one, you don't believe enough in your own skill and ability to get you out of your current challenges and break through a seemingly overwhelming situation. Reason two, you are so confident in what you believe about your market that you ignore the reality that's always changing and evolving.

What is overwhelming you? Are all the details you need to launch your business swirling around in a hazy fog within your head? What do you believe about your business and your market? Write it down: Who are they? How old? What is their experience? What do they need? Then look at that list and continue to modify it. Also, instead of listening only to your own instincts and friends, go talk to your potential customers to find out what they are thinking. While it's often humbling, it's important to know so you can get more new customers, keep your customers longer, and keep more money for yourself.

Chapter 60

The Source of All Info-Marketing Breakthrough Success

A COUPLE OF YEARS AGO, MY DAUGHTER FACED THE TASK OF learning the multiplication tables. Yes, 2 x 2 = 4. She had a lot of trouble with the 7s and 8s. The problem 7 x 8 would reduce her to tears.

Samantha had to learn to compute 100 multiplication problems within five minutes. We received a note from her teacher that we needed to work with her because she had completed only 22 of the equations in the little quiz she'd had in class that day.

We made a few copies of the 100-problem page, got her some pencils, and sat her down to practice. She burst into tears. You'd think by her reaction that we had stabbed her with the pencils.

For 20 minutes she refused. She cried. She ruined her page with tears. She'd do three problems and then rip the paper in half trying to erase a mistake.

I helped Samantha out by giving her compassionate advice. I told her that if she had just stopped crying and gotten started, she would be finished already and playing with her friends. It didn't help.

Finally, after 51 minutes, she got through the 100 multiplication problems. See? It's not that hard. Once you get started, you can get them done.

Next day: time to run through them again. The goal was still five minutes. The record time to beat was 51 minutes. We had the same scene as the day before. Tear-soaked papers, rips made from erasing, and lots of frustration. But the problems were done in 34 minutes.

The third day was the last one for the tears. Samantha was determined to get outside, so she got the problems done within 19 minutes and was out the door five seconds later.

It took about 10 tries to get the 100 problems done within 10 minutes. Then she was under seven minutes with two more tries.

When we started setting the timer for five minutes, Samantha would get through all but 7 to 10 of the problems. Then she'd get all of them done but miss two, a different two each time. After about 20 tries, she could get them done within $4\frac{1}{2}$ minutes. I told her to use that extra 30 seconds to check her work, but she never did. I understand—I never checked my work either. I just turned in the test and enjoyed the extra test time to relax.

Once Samantha had run through the entire process, we talked about her experience over dinner one night. She told me that she doesn't even have to compute the problems anymore. Now she looks at 7 x 8 and the answer automatically flashes in her head.

That is how you learn every new skill. First there's frustration. It's the sort of frustration you feel in your skin, almost panic. Everything in your body says, "This isn't right. I can't do this." After you decide that it's not that difficult, you get through it by figuring it out and thinking it through. Then with enough practice, you don't even have to think about it anymore. It's just second nature.

I remember driving for the first time. I'd just gotten my learner's permit after studying all weekend to pass the test. My mom drove us through town and then pulled the van over so I could take the wheel.

I was OK with driving; it was all the other cars that made me nervous. We lived on a busy two-lane road, and those cars coming up the other way were very close. If you looked at it, there wasn't a lot of space between you in your lane and the oncoming traffic in the other.

Now I drive and don't even think about it. You do, too. Have you ever driven for 20 minutes, changed lanes, stopped at lights, made turns, and then had it occur to you that you hadn't been thinking at all about driving? That's the way learning is.

I hear all the time from info-marketers who are having trouble getting their businesses started. I understand the struggle. Most of us are doing a lot of things for the first time. Sure, it's easy to send an e-mail. However, when you are writing it with the purpose of making a sale, suddenly this task gets difficult.

Too many people quit to avoid the frustration. Most of us are busy running other businesses and have employees and family commitments. So, it's very challenging to find time for a task that creates frustration. It's kind of like suffering through your times tables without a parent standing there forcing you to do it.

There is an important source of motivation that'll help you get through this frustration and get your new business launched. I came home one evening and found my wife naked. I don't know about your house, but that's a rare event at mine. But it's not what you think.

My wife was in the bathroom, struggling to look at her backside in the mirror. I had to ask, so this is the story:

My wife had been working out with some friends at the gym. Evidently when you work out, your boobs shrink. I have no scientific proof, but that's what I've been told. They all got to talking and decided to draft one of the women from the workout class to investigate cosmetic surgery. This way they all could get the facts, and only one of them would have to go to the appointment.

The cosmetic surgeon did a thorough examination. The draftee from the workout group had come in asking about a breast enlargement, and the doctor also showed her how she'd benefit from some liposuction around her thighs. She was really fit, had been working out for several years, but there were still some stubborn places that weren't yet as good as they could be. The doctor presented her with the options, gave her the price of $9,000.00, and told her the recovery would be four weeks.

While she had no qualms about the money, the four weeks of painful recovery sounded downright intimidating. Also, she would have to wear extremely tight stockings on her legs for several months to help her recover from the liposuction. With summer approaching this sounded like a miserable "side-effect." She asked a lot of questions about the recovery time. With her workouts she already looked great, and she wasn't sure the surgery was worth a month of her life.

The doctor finished answering her questions, started out the door, turned around, and looked back at her. Then before closing the door, he told her, "You are much too cute to have legs that rub together." Letting the words hang in the air for a moment, he shut the door and was gone.

As she sat in that examining room, in a blue paper smock with black pen marks all over her body, an irresistible urge for something better welled up inside her. Having legs that rubbed together became completely unacceptable.

After listening to her friend's story about the doctor's visit, my wife wanted to see if her legs rubbed together when she walked. She was positive she was too cute to have legs that rubbed together.

Just like my daughter learning her multiplication tables, there will be many times when you experience physical pain and seemingly intolerable anxiety as you launch your new info-marketing business. Those feelings are the natural by-products of learning something new. You'll often wonder if it's really worth it. And more often than not, it will be too easy to allow the more familiar work you are accustomed to doing keep you from launching your new info-marketing business.

Create a detailed written description of the information marketing business you'd like to create for yourself. Anytime you feel like it's too hard, take a long look at that picture. Keep it at the forefront of your mind. It's the additional income, the lifestyle, and the freedom that will help you through the frustration of learning something new.

When you are faced with a seemingly insurmountable obstacle and the frustration hits, tell yourself, "I must create a new business. My present circumstances are intolerable, and I will develop the skills and techniques I need to accomplish more in the same amount of time. Yes, I'm busy, but I will create the systems and get the help I need."

Remember, you are too cute to have legs that rub together.

Epilogue

The Story of the Cat that Licked Stamps—How Anyone Can Get a Fast Start in Info-Marketing

---

by Dan Kennedy

Chairman Emeritus, Information Marketing Association

I N THIS CHAPTER, I'VE BEEN CHALLENGED BY THE INFORMATION Marketing Association to tie together all of the pieces presented in this book, in the simplest possible way, so even a complete novice can get a fast start and learn as he earns. This is a daunting challenge. After considerable thought, I decided to go back in time and tell you two stories of information businesses I personally started, then extract the "steps" from the stories.

If you happen to already be active in information marketing and doing well, you could skip this chapter without harm. On the other hand, everybody can benefit from a back-to-basics review from time to time.

In both these cases, the opportunities to use websites, e-mail, and broadcast fax did not yet exist. The use of teleconferences, promoted as teleseminars, to sell was barely in its infancy, little understood, technically difficult, and expensive. Had I those tools and the know-how I have now, the information and examples that you've read about in this book, and the resources offered by the IMA, each of these businesses could easily have generated millions of dollars more than they did—although both were very successful.

As a matter of fact, the chief asset I had in one of my very first forays into information marketing was a cat that licked stamps. Not a computer, not a website, not a big budget. At the time, I was quite poor. I was starting from zero. My cat happened to like the taste of the glue on postage stamps and was happy to sit facing me on my coffee table while I watched TV in the evening and labeled and stuffed envelopes. I held out a strip of stamps. The cat licked the entire strip from left to right. I stuck the stamps on the stuffed envelopes, plop, plop, plop, plop. In retrospect, consuming postage stamp glue was probably not all that healthy for the cat—but, heck, they have nine lives, right?

Along the way, somewhat by accident, I identified a very small niche market: about 3,000 people, all in the same business, with profound interest in and limited knowledge about a subject that I happened to be very knowledgeable about. I did my research at a convention attended by about one-quarter of this group. I came home and did just about the simplest thing anyone could do in info-marketing. I created a very simple catalog offering about 30 different "special reports," each on a very specific topic, each of different length and price—as I recall from as low as $5.00 to as much as $50.00. I used a list of these people compiled from the membership directory of the association they belonged to, manually culling a small number I judged unlikely prospects. I mailed about 2,000 of the catalogs at a pace of about 100 a day. As orders came in, I wrote, copied, and sent out the reports. (Today we have a fancy word for that. It's called "publish on demand.")

Three things occurred. One, I made some money. About $15,000.00. Two, I saw which topics were of the greatest interest. Three, I created a "hot list" of about 250 buyers.

Next, I created a newsletter for this niche. More accurately, I created a sales letter for a newsletter, focused on the topics these people had demonstrated the greatest interest in. I chose the newsletter because I didn't have to create, publish, and inventory product. I first mailed my sales letter to the 250 buyers, several times in sequence with additional cover letters. Within a month, I had nearly 80 subscribers at $149.00 a year. Gradually I mailed to the entire universe of 2,000. I kept at it. Within the year I had nearly 1,000 subscribers.

I could go on, but this is sufficient demonstration. Know, though, that with all the ideas in this book about developing a multiproduct, multifaceted, complete information business, even as few as 1,000 subscribers can easily provide an income of $250,000.00 to $1 million a year.

Later, I also identified a niche market for which both ad media and mailing lists were readily available and in which there was profound interest and limited knowledge about a subject I was very knowledgeable about. This list was considerably larger, about 35,000. In this case, I used advertising and direct mail to direct these people into small, free seminars in their own cities. Initially, I tested different seminar titles and promised different content in different cities and, fortunately, quickly hit on the best offer. I kept one speaker busy 20 days a month and me five days a month. Over a period of three years, I put nearly 10,000 of those people through those introductory seminars, there sold them info-product packages, and also built a newsletter business.

I used the seminars as my sales method for a number of reasons, but one was that these particular customers were accustomed to going to such seminars, welcomed the opportunity to do so, and were responsive to free seminars. I also had a speaker eager and happy to travel. Nearly $10 million in business was done in three years in the early 1980s. As I said, had I the resources and knowledge you have at your disposal, it would have been $30 million or more. Still, some of those customers have followed me through the years all the way to Glazer-Kennedy Insider's Circle™ Membership, my five newsletters, telecoaching, coaching, and seminars today.

That first business was launched with a budget of about $300.00, for printing, postage stamps, and cat food. Then it was bootstrapped with its own money. The second business was launched years later, when I was already doing well, with about $10,000.00, and then it, too, funded its own growth. In the first business I had affinity with the market; I was one of them. In the second I had no affinity.

Now let's extract some "steps" from these two stories. In both cases, the first thing I did was identify a particular, specific, relatively small, manageable, affordably and directly reachable target market. Your choice of market is critically important. There are many different criteria to consider, including but not limited to those I listed here. You should also know that few info-marketers can profitably go after an entire market. Instead, you are looking for a hungry, responsive market within a market. As an example, I work with an info-marketer in the dental profession who does very well with dentists age 50 and above, in practice no less than 20 years, nearing retirement. To be successful, he must focus on that segment of the market, not all dentists.

Second, I determined through research and testing what I knew they would be happy to pay to read about and hear about. The less you do based on your own assumptions, opinions, and ideas, the better. The more you can "listen to the market," the better.

Third, I devised info-products promising the benefits they told me they wanted. This is a very important point made throughout this book. It addresses a critical, costly mistake most info-marketers insist on making: building product, content, or a business and then going in search of buyers rather than finding buyers and then building to suit them. Too many people become so emotionally committed to an idea and invest so much time and money in birthing a product that they are blind to economic and market realities, deaf to what the market tells them.

Fourth, in these cases, I started with very simple publish-on-demand info-products. Today the opportunities to do this are even better and more varied. Information sold can be delivered electronically online, via teleseminars or webinars, or if offline, in print-on-demand formats. Vendors that serve info-marketers are accustomed to producing info-products in small quantities or per order and handling the entire fulfillment process for you. One of the many virtues of this type of business is keeping your money out of dormant product inventory and turning it over again and again in advertising and marketing.

Fifth, I used different sales methods for the different markets, but with all of them I communicated directly.

Sixth, I turned a one-time buyer into a customer of continuing value. In the two examples I used here, our approach was primitive and simplistic by today's standards. Today's info-marketers thoroughly understand that the asset is the customer and that a customer's value increases through membership, continuity, and ascension to different levels of services and pricing in long-term and ongoing relationships. In one of my most popular info-products, The Renegade Millionaire System (**RenegadeMillionaire.com**), I teach a business principle particularly appropriate to info-marketing: Most business owners get customers to make sales, but we make sales to get customers.

And there you have it. To review:

1. Identify a viable market.
2. Determine what the market will buy.
3. Develop info-products to match what they want.

4. Start with simple products.

5. Select direct marketing methods appropriate for the market.

6. Turn a "one-time buyer" into a customer of continuing value.

As you've seen in this book and will appreciate more by rereading the book several times and accessing the other IMA resources, today's info-marketing businesses are much more complex creatures than the two I've described here. Today they also tend to start in more sophisticated ways. With what we know now, it's quite common for someone to go from "start" to $1 million or more in revenue in 12 months or less and to have continuity, multiple levels of continuity, and multiple products and services in place or at least planned from the beginning. Still, the first three fundamentals I've listed above govern even the most sophisticated of these businesses. And even today, you could start with nothing more than those three steps and a cat to lick the stamps.

Want to see the current, evolved version of Dan's info-marketing business? Visit www.IMAKennedy.com, and for a complete insider's look, accept his free-gift invitation. Today's Glazer-Kennedy Insider's Circle™ is a dynamic association of tens of thousands of marketing-oriented entrepreneurs, business owners, self-employed professionals, and sales professionals from all corners of the globe. Members benefit from webinars, teleseminars, guaranteed resources, newsletters, two major conferences per year, and local Chapters meeting regularly in many cities.

You can also be introduced to Dan's popular books at www. NoBSBooks.com. These include his popular No B.S. book series, featuring *No B.S. Sales Success in The New Economy* and *No B.S. Wealth Attraction in The New Economy*.

Glossary of Information Marketing Terms

HERE ARE COMMON TERMS YOU WILL HEAR WITHIN THE information marketing business.

Affiliate. An affiliate relationship is one in which there is an agreement between two people to sell a particular product. One individual has customers he wants to market the product to, and another one has the product or service he wants to offer to customers. Typically, the individual who has the product will create an affiliate program. Many of these are executed online, and most of the popular shopping cart software programs today have this feature built in. The affiliate completes an application. Upon approval of the affiliate relationship, the affiliate is assigned a unique website address and given access to the affiliate toolbox that has e-mails, websites, ads, and other things the affiliate can use to help sell the program. Then the affiliate uses the link, uses those sales techniques to help sell the product, and an affiliate commission is paid on those products. Commissions vary substantially by the different products and services sold. Very often the terms are negotiable for individuals who are able to sell a lot of affiliate programs, but for most folks, you normally have to earn a higher commission rate by performing well for a particular affiliate.

Affinity. This is a measure of your relationship to a market. If you have been a member of a market for a number of years, perhaps having established a career there, then you would have a high affinity with that particular market. If you are new to a market (for example, if you are going to sell to Harley Davidson owners and you have never owned a Harley Davidson and you do not know anyone who owns a Harley Davidson), then you would have very little affinity with that market.

Alexa.com. This is a website that allows you to gather information about competitors and about websites within a particular market. It provides a lot of information about the site, including how much traffic it is receiving from the internet. It's useful to see how much traffic websites in your industry are receiving.

Back end. This is the most profitable part of an information marketing business and what distinguishes info-marketers from all other types of information publishers. Info-marketers are able to sell coaching, consulting, seminars, automatic implementation products, and newsletters, and offer other people's products to their customers as additional revenue opportunities.

Churn. This term refers to the number of new members joining a market at a given time. For instance, the real estate agent industry is a market where there is a lot of churn. Many individuals are joining that market with the hopes of making lots of money as a real estate agent. In contrast, the funeral director industry has very little churn. Most of the entrants in that market have been family-owned businesses for many years, or they are large corporations buying the family-owned businesses. There are not a lot of new companies jumping into the funeral director business that were not in it 12 months ago. The real estate agent industry has lots of churn, and there are lots of new customers to sell to. The funeral director industry has little churn. The customers in it today are pretty much the same ones who will be in it 12 months from now.

Claims. These are the benefits you are telling potential customers they will receive from using your product. Income claims refer to the amount of income you state others have received from using your product.

Coaching. This is an arrangement where you provide advice and counsel to customers to help them implement their own problem solutions. You may have already provided them the information they need, but through a coaching program you are able to give them specific information for their particular problems as well as specific case examples to help them solve the problems. This is generally distinguished from consulting. Consulting is actually doing it for them, whereas coaching is helping them to get it done for themselves.

Continuity. This is a program where on an established interval, usually monthly, customers are charged a set fee for a given level of product and service. Most programs are on a monthly continuity. This entire concept was pioneered and made popular by the Book-of-the-Month program, where customers trusted a publisher to send them a book every month related to their interests. This created an ongoing continuity relationship between these customers and the publisher. Info-marketers have used continuity to completely revolutionize their businesses and add many more subscribers versus using the annual subscription model. (See *Forced continuity*.)

E-book. This is a book in a digital file that communicates information to your prospects and can be delivered electronically over the internet. Rather than printing a product, weighing it, putting postage on it, and mailing it, you are able to instantly deliver an e-book and put your product in the customer's hand immediately.

Endorsed mailing. This is a mailing where an individual is given a letter of endorsement, usually a brief letter that is added to the front of his sales message, that gives credibility and recognition to the offer and sales message that it would not have gotten if it had to stand on its own.

Forced continuity. This is an arrangement where the customers are provided a free trial period of a program and then at the end of the free trial, they are automatically added to the continuity program. It does not require customers to act in order to opt into the monthly continuity. Customers can always opt out if they choose to; however, they do not have to act to opt in. (See *Continuity*.)

Front end. This is marketing your products and services to new customers. This is the first step of your info-business. After you are able to obtain customers through your front end, you can develop the back end of your business by selling additional products and services to the customers who have already made a purchase from you.

Group coaching. This is a model where, instead of the coach interacting with one student at a time, the coach interacts with many students at one time. In general, a coach is providing advice and counsel, examples, and encouragement to students and is not performing actual services for the students. In the group coaching environment, there are many students interacting at the same time with one or more coaches.

Guarantee. This is your assurance to your customers that your product is everything you say it is. You promise to stand behind your product and offer their money back if your customers are not satisfied with it.

Guarantee, conditional. This is a guarantee where you force the customers to go through certain hoops in order to receive their money back. They may have to implement certain features within your product to demonstrate they have tried some things before you will give them a refund.

Guarantee, unconditional. This is a guarantee where the customers can simply ask for the refund, and they are given the refund without any conditions whatsoever.

Herd. A term Dan Kennedy coined to refer to an info-marketer's customer base. Expanding on the herd analysis, Dan teaches info-marketers to build a fence around their herd to protect them against poachers and to prevent customers from escaping.

Joint venture. This is where two or more individuals get together to create and market a product to a particular industry. In many cases, one of the joint venture partners has a list of customers, and the other joint venture partner has a product or will develop a product or service for those customers. The partners work together to sell the product and then split the proceeds.

Kit. This is a collection of materials you are delivering all at one time to your customers.

Lead generation. This is the process of identifying individuals within a market who are interested in more information about the product or service you are offering.

Market. This is a collection of customers who have something in common and, most importantly, have a common problem you can solve as an info-marketer.

Mastermind meeting. The idea of the "mastermind alliance" and "masterminding" grew from Andrew Carnegie, Henry Ford, Harvey Firestone, and Thomas Edison as reported in books like the popular bestseller *Think and Grow Rich* by

Napoleon Hill. One of the factors successful people share is a group of people they can work with to help solve problems. By working together to solve each other's problems, each of them benefits. Many information marketers have been able to duplicate the benefit of mastermind meetings through their coaching programs.

Monthly CD. This is an audio program or other program offered through podcast and other means that individuals subscribe to. They can be provided by one person as a monologue, or they can be in a conversation or interview format between an expert and a host.

Multipay. This is an arrangement where the info-marketer helps customers afford the product by putting it on a payment program. It can be two-pay, three-pay, five-pay, etc., but this helps lower the initial price of the product and decreases the risk that customers may perceive from the sale. For example, if a customer looks at an offer that is $250.00 a month for four months, it may be more acceptable to him than paying $1,000.00 all at once, even though he could probably self-finance that $1,000.00 through a credit card. It feels like $250.00 is all he is risking, so he is more apt to participate in a multipay program than in an all-upfront sale.

Newsletter. This is a publication that is published, usually monthly, by an information marketer to communicate with customers and provide ongoing help and information and to reinforce what the info-marketer has taught them in the past.

Niche. This is a group of individuals with a like interest or a similar demographic. Normally these niches are defined as business oriented—the customers could be plumbers, restaurant owners, chiropractors, doctors, or accountants, for example.

Offers. This is what you are agreeing to provide your customers for a fee. Most teachers within the info-marketing world will tell you your offer is the most important part of your marketing campaign. You should create your offer before you create a product or anything else. You should create a compelling offer, a collection of resources, tools, techniques, manuals, CDs, videos, coaching: whatever you want to package in your offer. You should decide what your offer is going to be first, and then you can go about the job of creating the product and offering it to the marketplace.

One-step sale. This is a process where you go straight from introducing yourself to the customer to asking for the sale within one marketing piece. This is contrasted to lead generation marketing, where you first generate a lead through a lead generation ad and then create a sales sequence to sell to that lead. Through one-step sales, you are trying to sell at the point of first contact.

Online marketing. This is a method where you use the internet to communicate with a large population of people using automated software to handle the lead capture, marketing, and sales process as well as, many times, the product delivery.

Order form. This is also called a response device or an application. This is a piece of paper, the document or the web form, the customer uses to make a transaction. This is where the customer fills in his name, address, and credit card information. The order form is mailed, faxed, or completed online or on the telephone. If completing a telephone order, the person taking the order usually has an order form to fill out for the customer.

Prerecorded message. This is a message, usually through a toll-free number, that you offer within your lead generation ad to encourage your customer to leave his name and contact information so you can deliver the rest of your sales message to him.

Product launch. A series of communications consisting of one or more of the following: emails, special reports, or videos, that build anticipation for a soon-to-be-released product. Often, the product is available only for a limited time, further increasing the customer's desire to make an immediate purchase decision.

Reachability. This is a term referring to a niche that describes the amount of ease with which you can put your marketing message in front of your prospective customers. If a niche already has several magazines, others already marketing there, or its own cable television channel, then that market is highly reachable. If there are no magazines specific to that niche, then its reachability is low.

Response device. See *Order form*.

Risk reversal. This is a marketing term for a guarantee with which you ease a customer's fear of making a purchase by taking on all of the risk of the sale. As the customer evaluates whether or not he wants to buy your product, he is deciding whether or not he can trust you. By offering a refund of the purchase price and to pay for return shipping if the customer returns the product, you are taking on all of the risk of the sale. This will help your customer buy from you with confidence.

S&D. This is a term coined by Bill Glazer that means "steal and distribute." Rather than reinventing new ways of doing business or new marketing programs for a particular niche, you should be adapting programs that have proven themselves successful in other areas and implementing them within your own market.

Self-liquidating leads. This is where your lead generation ad charges the potential customer a fee to receive the rest of the marketing sequence. For example, the ad will have an offer, invite people to respond, and charge them $9.95 to get the rest of the marketing sequence. This type of lead has two benefits: 1) it provides income from the lead generation process that helps pay for more lead generation ads; and 2) it increases the quality of the lead because even though it is a nominal fee, only the most motivated individuals will be willing to go through the work necessary to respond. When you use a free lead generation system and all people have to do is pick up the phone, you are going to dramatically increase the number of leads you get and the number of opportunities you have to sell to individuals, but you are also going to increase the marketing cost.

Squeeze page. This is a web form that captures a name and address from a prospect before you allow the prospect to see the rest of the sales message.

SRDS. This is the acronym for the Standard Rate and Data Service. This is a manual that has details about every list commercially available for sale. From the SRDS manual, you will be able to learn about markets based on the types of lists available for them and evaluate how easy it will be for you to reach this market through direct mail.

Subculture. This is a way of evaluating a potential market. Whereas niches are based on professional designations such as doctors and plumbers, subcultures are based on hobbies and interests of particular individuals. Golfers, fishermen, hobbyists, Star Trekkies, bird lovers, fish lovers—all of these are subcultures you can market to.

Subniche. These are specialties within a particular niche. For example, a plumber could be a commercial plumber who only works in 30-story buildings, or he could be a residential plumber. There are many subniches for doctors: dermatologist, surgeon, gynecologist, anesthesiologist—all of these are subspecialties or subniches within the niche of medicine.

Tele-coaching. This is a process of delivering coaching services over the telephone rather than in person or by mail.

Telemarketing. This is a process of delivering a sales message over the telephone.

Teleseminar. This is a seminar delivered over the telephone. Most teleseminars offered by information marketers are free and designed to provide a sales presentation. The sales presentation can be for a tele-coaching program as a back-end product, and many info-marketers also use teleseminars to convert sales on the front end. So not only will they offer printed sales letters and CDs, but they will also invite their leads to call into a teleseminar to hear a sales presentation.

Tollbooth position. Once you have developed a list of customers, there will be other individuals who want to sell products and services to your list. Because you have a relationship with your list, you are in a position to charge others for access to your customer list, either through an affiliate program, JV opportunity, endorsed mailing, or some other agreement.

Try-before-you-buy. This is often called a "puppy dog close" because it was borrowed from the pet stores that allow you to take a cute and cuddly puppy home for the evening. Once you have taken a puppy home, gotten used to him, shown the puppy to your neighbors and friends, and taken him for a walk, the likelihood of you bringing that dog back to the store is extremely low. An info-marketer very often may offer a try-before-you-buy where the customer is able to complete an order form, fax it in, receive the product, examine it for 30, 60, or 90 days, and then the charge goes through automatically if the customer has not returned the product.

Webinar. A presentation given over the internet that allows your participants to watch your computer screen while hearing you talk through their computer speakers or over the phone. Most presentations include slide presentations created within PowerPoint or Keynote. Some info-marketers prefer webinars because they can have visual aids during their presentations.

Wordtracker.com. This is a website that allows you to find out exactly how many people are searching for particular key words and phrases. When you are trying to determine how to position your product within a market, you can examine the types of key words and phrases individuals are searching for on the internet. That will give you a hint of what you should be offering them.

Index

A

acquiring customers. *See* generating customers

advertising. *See also* marketing
joint ventures and, 143–145
for lead generation, 63–64, 102, 156, 266
in magazines, 64–65
online banner ads, 156
on radio, 262–263
Unfair Advantage system, 172–173

Altadonna, Ben, 15

association industry, 5–6

audio products, 69

authoring, 270–271

automatic implementation products, 71–74

B

backend marketing and fulfillment, 306

banner advertising, 156

belief systems, 328

Berg, Howard, 16

Berkeley, Susan, 148–150

Berns, Fred, 168–169, 175–179

Blazer, Bill, 172–173

books, writing, 270–271

Brown, Ali, 16

business owners, 54–55

business scope, 5

C

Celebrity Black Book, The, 18

certifications, 5

coaching, 115–119, 126
for generating customers, 271–273
group coaching, 29, 85–86
overview, 32
seminars and, 226–229, 249–251

There's a Big Difference Between Creating a Top-Selling Information Product and Creating an Information Marketing Business . . .

Too many people confuse social media, internet marketing campaigns, or information product creation with business building. They chase the next online marketing secret, raise their prices, or try a new joint venture tactic but miss out on what it takes to build a business that lasts. It takes a specific set of skills to create a long-term, sustainable business.

The Information Marketing Business Pyramid™ gives you examples, step-by-step resources, and worksheets to help you get your information marketing business launched. But that's only the beginning. It also guides you through the process of turning your new venture into a long-term wealth generator for you and your family. It even reveals how to build an info-business even if you don't know how to create information products or have no idea what type of information product you should create.

Visit InfoMarketingPyramid.com for free videos, a 24-page outline of how the Information Marketing Business Pyramid™ works, and an opportunity to receive additional free resources. This site is available only for a limited time at InfoMarketingPyramid.com. Grab your Information Marketing Business Pyramid™ today.